I0586414

Arthur Lillie

The Popular Life of Buddha

Arthur Lillie

The Popular Life of Buddha

ISBN/EAN: 9783337246389

Printed in Europe, USA, Canada, Australia, Japan

Cover: Foto ©Lupo / pixelio.de

More available books at **www.hansebooks.com**

OF

BUDDHA,

*CONTAINING AN ANSWER TO THE "HIBBERT
LECTURES" OF* 1881.

BY

ARTHUR LILLIE,

MEMBER OF THE ROYAL ASIATIC SOCIETY.

WITH FIVE ILLUSTRATIONS.

LONDON:

KEGAN PAUL, TRENCH & CO., 1, PATERNOSTER SQUARE.

1883.

INTRODUCTION.

BUDDHA was a religious reformer who died 470 years before the Christian era.

The following are some of the results due to the sojourn of this one man upon earth :—

1. The most formidable priestly tyranny that the world had ever seen, crumbled away before his attack, and the followers of Buddha were paramount in India for a thousand years.

2. The institution of caste was assailed and overturned.

3. Polygamy was for the first time pronounced immoral, and slavery condemned.

4. Woman, from being considered a chattel and a beast of burden, was for the first time considered man's equal, and allowed to develop her spiritual life.

5. All bloodshed, whether with the knife of the

INTRODUCTION.

BUDDHA was a religious reformer who died 470 years before the Christian era.

The following are some of the results due to the sojourn of this one man upon earth :—

1. The most formidable priestly tyranny that the world had ever seen, crumbled away before his attack, and the followers of Buddha were paramount in India for a thousand years.

2. The institution of caste was assailed and over-turned.

3. Polygamy was for the first time pronounced immoral, and slavery condemned.

4. Woman, from being considered a chattel and a beast of burden, was for the first time considered man's equal, and allowed to develop her spiritual life.

5. All bloodshed, whether with the knife of the

priest or the sword of the conqueror, was rigidly forbidden.

6. Also, for the first time in the religious history of mankind, the awakening of the spiritual life of the individual was substituted for religion by body corporate. It is also certain that Buddha was the first to proclaim that duty was to be sought in the eternal principles of morality and justice, and not in animal sacrifices and local formalities invented by the fancy of priests.

7. The principle of religious propagandism was for the first time introduced with its two great instruments, the missionary and the preacher.

8. By these, India, China, Bactria, and Japan, were proselytized; and the Buddhist missionaries overran Persia and Egypt. This success was effected by moral means alone, for Buddhism is the one religion virgin of coercion. It is reckoned that one-third of humanity is still in its fold.

That such results should have been achieved is one of the greatest marvels of history; and when an inquirer consults some of the best-known writers to try and get an explanation of this unusual missionary success, the marvel increases. We see Buddhist holy men exhibiting a self-denial worthy of the early Christians, to gain an "immortality"[1] which is said

---

[1] Amrita, non-death.

to mean death. We see prayers and sacrifices to a non-god, and gorgeous temples scooped patiently out of rocky mountains in his honour. Statues of this non-god are scattered broadcast over half the globe, and the tolerant patience and activity of his missionaries is unique in the history of religions. This is the bewildering Buddhism of popular treatises ; and the activity of one special writer has contributed largely to foster these ideas.

Dr. Rhys Davids is a very hard-working Pâli scholar. I consider that students of Buddhism are much indebted to him for his translations. But he is a confused and untrained thinker. In treatises, in lectures, in encyclopædias, in magazines, and in the weekly press, he is constantly putting forth an aspect of Buddhism which it will be the special object of this work to assail. Stated concisely, his position is this :—

1. Buddha preached flat atheism.[1]

2. He taught, "in a complete and categorical manner," that man has no "soul nor anything of any sort that exists in any manner after death." [2]

3. He despised mysticism, and disbelieved in anything outside of the world of matter.[3]

---

[1] " Buddhism," p. 207.

[2] Ibid., p. 99. See also "Hibbert Lectures," p. 109.

[3] "Buddhism takes as its ultimate fact, the existence of the material world." (" Buddhism, p. 87.)

4. This Buddhism is to be found in its original purity solely in the sacred books of Ceylon, a literature which, if translated into English, would be four times as long as our Bible.[1] These sacred books, according to the Cingalese chronicles, were made canonical three months after Buddha's death, and "re-affirmed" at a convocation summoned by King Aśoka, B.C. 250.

5. In the north of India, about the commencement of the Christian era, an innovating Buddhism arose which proclaimed a belief in God. It was called the Buddhism of the "Great Vehicle," in contradistinction to the original Buddhism of the "Little Vehicle," which denied God and a future life entirely.[2] Ceylon has never known anything of this innovating faith.

As opposed to this, I shall show :—

1. That according to the express declaration of Hwen Thsang, the celebrated Chinese pilgrim who visited India at a time when the controversy between the disciples of the Great and Little Vehicles was furiously raging, the Buddhism of Ceylon was the Buddhism of the Great Vehicle.

2. According to the same authority, the disciples of the Little Vehicle called sarcastically the innovating Great Vehicle "Śunya pushpa" ("The Carriage that

[1] "Buddhism," p. 20.
[2] Ibid., p. 244 ; also pp. 200, 218.

drives to the Great Nowhere "). They said that this agnostic Buddhism did not come from Buddha. And Hwen Thsang confesses that it was due chiefly to Vasubandhu and Asangha, who, about the date of the Christian era, received it in visions from Maitreya, the Coming Buddha. Dr. Rhys Davids has plainly shuffled the two Buddhisms together.

3. I shall show also that King Aśoka, far from "re-affirming" the colossal library of Cingalese books, knew nothing at all about them. On the Bairât Rock he has given a totally different list of seven short tractates that his monks were *then* to begin to learn by heart. These and his profession of faith were to be recited at his stûpa temples, and nothing else.

"Confess and believe in God!" was the motto of Aśoka.[1] "Confess and disbelieve in God!" seems the motto of Cingalese Buddhism.

4. The Buddhists call their religion Prajñâ Pâramitâ, which means literally the "Wisdom of the Other Bank."

At an early date the Âryas of India believed in a world of ghosts. This world had for chief one Yama, the Indian Adam. Once he was the first-born of the living, then he became the first-born of the dead. His kingdom, Yamâlaya, was girt by a mighty river,

---

[1] Dhauli inscription.

the Vaitaranî. This stream the ghosts of good men traversed, not in Charon's boat, but by holding on to the tail of the sacred cow, as the Hindoos, aided by cattle, traverse rivers to this day. The domains of Yama were erected by the celestial architect, Viśwa Karma; and at first they were lovely rather than hateful. In the Mahâbhârata it is announced that fear of enemies is not known by the good, nor hunger, nor scarcity, nor sorrow, nor bodily pain. Mountains of excellent food are piled up for the virtuous. These negative advantages would strike the poor Ârya struggling on earth with hunger, sickness, and the dread of being offered up to Rudra by a successful enemy. Palaces and jewelled wives were promised also. The terrible red-hot iron female who embraced the lustful man, and the grotesque swollen belly that was to be the future of the glutton, were after ideas. The earlier Yama lived in a palace. The later Yama had a terrible mace, red eyes and garments, and extra-sized teeth. He kept a recording angel, "He who paints in secret." "Pits filled with devouring worms and insects and fire" were prepared for the evil-doing Hindû.

This places us in a better position to settle whether Buddhism, or the "Wisdom of the Other Bank," was occupied with this world alone or with the other. In point of fact, Buddhism, like the philosophy of the

Vedas and the Vedantic school, has always been a pure idealism. Let us turn to the treatise named Prajñâ Pâramitâ (the "Wisdom of the Other Bank") to see what Buddha said on the subject. In speaking to his senior disciple, Śâriputra, he said that ignorant men "represent to themselves all things of which in truth not one has any existence;" and a little further on, he explained that the appearances of the phenomenal world were "as if a clever magician, or the pupil of a clever magician, caused a vast concourse of men to appear at a cross-road where four great thoroughfares meet, and having caused them to appear, caused them again to vanish."[1]

I think it is very patent from the "Hibbert Lectures," that the perversions of Dr. Rhys Davids are due to his sympathies with Comtism; but I contend that the study of an ancient religion is not philosophy, but pure history.

I think that signs of a juster appreciation of the great reformer are already patent. Mr. Edwin Arnold has a "firm conviction that a third of mankind would never have been brought to believe in blank abstractions or in Nothingness as the issue and Crown of Being."[2]

The Rev. Professor Beal, too, has uttered a protest

---

[1] Oldenberg, "Buddha," p. 239.
[2] "Light of Asia," preface, p. xv.

against the "lectures and articles" of Dr. Rhys Davids, which against all evidence announce that Buddhism "teaches atheism, annihilation, and the non-existence of soul." [1]

[1] "Romantic Life," introduction, p. x.

CONTENTS

ILLUSTRATIONS.

THE
POPULAR LIFE OF BUDDHA.

CHAPTER I.

BIRTH OF BUDDHA.

AN ancient history of ancient deeds is rendered unintelligible to moderns less by what it states than what it omits. Details and explanations of contemporary customs that were familiar to the writer and his readers have been obliterated by time. I propose to write the story of Buddha, and add amplifications here and there when it is possible to illustrate ancient manners from other sources.

When the legendary life of Buddha opens he is disclosed in the heaven Tuśita. Early Buddhism divided the universe into the Domain of Appetite (Kâmaloka) and the Domain of Spirit (Brahmaloka). Above the earth were six heavens, devoted to those who, according to the theory of the metempsychosis,

B

were destined, after temporary sojourns in the sky, to be reborn on earth.   Tuśita was the highest of these six heavens ; and above it were the heavens of the Buddhas, in many compartments.   Buddha, before reaching Tuśita, had already been on earth as a king, a young Brahmin, a she-bear, an antelope, a king of the serpents, and so on.[1]

What is a Buddha ?   There are two answers to this question.

The first answer is that the Buddha was simply the ascetic who had conquered his lower nature. Buddha himself called them Brâhmaṇas :—

" The man who wears dirty raiments, who is emaciated and covered with veins, who lives alone in the forest and meditates, him I call indeed a Brâhmaṇa."

" Him I call indeed a Brâhmaṇa who is free from anger, dutiful, virtuous, without appetite, who is subdued and has received his last body." [2]

" The man who, after cutting the strap [enmity], the thong [attachment], and the rope [scepticism], with all that pertains to it, has destroyed all obstacles [ignorance]—the Buddha, him I call the Brâhmaṇa."

" Whosoever being innocent endures reproach,

---

[1] The Comtism of Dr. Rhys Davids has been compelled to sweep away Tuśita and the metempsychosis altogether.

[2] Fausböll, Sutta Nipâta, p. 28 ; ibid., vv. 395, 400.

blows, and bonds, the man who is strong in his en-
durance, and has for his army this strength, him I
call a Brâhmaṇa." [1]

But confusion has arisen because a Buddha is
sometimes taken to mean an incarnation of the
Supreme, like Kṛishṇa or Râma. Even the Brahmins admit that Buddha was an avatâra of Vishṇu.

The Lalita Vistara, or Buddha's legendary life, is,
I think, the most mystical allegory in any language.
It blurts out what the other Indian legends hinted
only darkly, the secrets of the higher Indian initiation. This I shall make plain as I proceed. When
the narrative opens, Buddha is described as lecturing
the hosts of heaven. Search is made on earth for
a family worthy to receive him. Many prominent
families are rejected from various causes. In a city
called Kapilavastu, in North Oude, the modern
Nagar Khâs, was an Âryan king called Śuddhodana.
He was married to Queen Mâyâ, a lady as good and
beautiful "as a heavenly spirit." Her hair was glossy
as the body of a black bee ; her voice was as musical
as the bird kokila. To the touch she was as soft as
the cloth of Kâchalindi. "She was so pure," says the
Lalita Vistara, on which I chiefly base my narrative,
"that it was impossible for God, man, or Asura, to
view her with carnal desire."

[1] Sutta Nipâta, p. 113.

Under what form does a Buddha descend to earth for the last time? This question was put in heaven, and answered by a spirit named Ugratejas, an ancient Rishi: "In the ancient holy books, the Brâhmaṇas and Mantras, and in the Rig-Veda, it is explained how a coming Buddha is to reach his mother's womb. What is that form? He must select the body of the most beautiful of elephants, armed with six defences [the war elephant was protected by armour, and had swords on his tusks, scythes on his ears, an iron ball on his tail, etc.[1]], and covered with a spangled netting of gold. His head must be proud and red. He must be open jawed. He must be majestic in appearance."

When I first read this passage I thought it puerile extravagance. I must now confess that the ancient Rishi Ugratejas knew much more about the Rig-Veda than I did. The ancient Brahmins, though they acknowledged nothing but pure spirit, the ineffable Brahma, allowed the vulgar to worship God's attributes personified. They believed, with modern geologists, that each race of men has only a certain duration on earth, which is put an end to sometimes by a fiery and sometimes a watery catastrophe. Thus a popular aspect of God was as the Vicegerent of the universe during a Day of Brahma,

[1] Beal, "The Dhammapada," p. 143.

or the life of a race. By a fiction, this Vicegerent
was then supposed to die, but to leave behind him
the "Egg of Death."[1] By the titles the "Egg of
Death," the "Golden Germ," the new Vicegerent
commenced his reign. His symbol was the elephant, according to the "Satapatha Brâhmaṇa."[2]
This is why Buddha came down to his mother's
womb as an elephant. Before quitting Tuśita, the
abode of unemancipated spirits, he handed over
his diadem to Maitreya, the future Buddha. The
second school of Buddhism, the "Carriage that drives
to the Great Nowhere," got by-and-by to commit the
inconceivable folly of worshipping this unemancipated
being, this denizen of the Domain of Appetite. Of
this more anon.

And now, what was the avowed object of Buddha's
avatâra? Was it to teach atheism? Let us listen
to what Buddha himself said of his mission before he
left the Tuśita heaven.

"He acquainted the gods with his intention re-
specting his descent into Jambudwîpa [India]. They,
knowing that there were at that time many atheistical teachers, endeavoured to divert him from his
purpose, but in vain. He assured them that he would
overcome them all, that his doctrine would be established and flourish in Jambudwîpa. And he recom-

Mârtaṇḍa.   [2] Satapatha Brâhmaṇa, iii. 1, 33.

mended to the gods, that whoever among them might wish to taste of the food of immortality, he should be incarnated among men, in this same division of the earth." This is given to us by Csoma Korösi, from a life of Buddha in the Dulvâ,[1] or collection of the Scriptures of Tibet. It is from Tibet, also, that we have the Lalita Vistara which I am making the basis of this popular life.

So in spring, when the constellation Viśâkhâ appears, the future Buddha—having donned the body of a young white elephant of six defences, with a head shining like a ruby, with tusks of yellow gold, an elephant perfect in his organs and limbs—entered the right side of Queen Mâyâ. In the Rock Edicts of King Aśoka, the earliest authentic record of Buddhism, Buddha is called "the White Elephant, whose name is the Bringer of Happiness to the Whole World."

In a vision of extasia Queen Mâyâ was made conscious of the mighty honour that had come to her. In the morning she repaired to the Aśoka wood near the palace, and told the king what had happened. Cunning Brahmins, well versed in astrology, and also in the Ṛig-Veda, were summoned to the palace, and asked to interpret the apparition.

"This dream bodes no misfortune," they answered. "On the contrary, great joy will be yours, O queen.

---

[1] "Asiatic Researches," vol. xx. p. 286.

You will bring forth a son who will be a universal ruler [Chakravartin]. If he should abandon earthly desires, and quit his kingdom and palace to become a religious teacher out of love for the world, he will become the Buddha, and give joy and immortality[1] to all flesh."

Another portent is related in the Lalita Vistara :—

"The night on which the future Buddha entered his mother's womb, on that same night a huge white lotus, springing from the waters and parting the earth for sixty-eight millions of yoganas [a yogana is the day's march of an army, seven miles], rose up into the middle of the world of Brahma. This lotus only the Guide of men and Brahma are able to perceive. All that there is of life and creative essence in the three thousand great thousand worlds [the Kosmos] is collected in the dewdrops of this mighty lotus. This essence, drained off in a cup of lapis lazuli, was given to the future Buddha to drink."

The lotus is a symbol of Mâyâ, the universal mother, and the creative essence is the Golden Germ of the Ṛig-Veda.

During the time that the future Buddha was in his mother's womb, her body was transparent, so that she

---

[1] Amṛita, Pâli amata, means "non-death." How Dr. Rhys Davids has transformed it into "death" may be seen in the "Hibbert Lectures," pp. 109 and 137.

could see him plainly. The good queen, "having taken the five bases of study, practised the ten virtues." Her mind was virginal; and in the city of Kapilavastu, all men, women, boys, or girls, who were troubled with evil spirits (Bhûtas), when they were brought into the presence of Queen Mâyâ were exorcised, and recovered the use of their faculties. Also all who were sick with ulcers, cancer, consumption, leprosy, throat disease, etc., as soon as Queen Mâyâ placed her right hand upon their heads, were cured, and returned home. And if the queen took up a handful of the holy kuśa-grass, that, too, proved an infallible remedy.

Dr. Rhys Davids points out the interesting fact that certain mediæval frescoes represent Christ as visible when in His mother's womb.[1] The Rev. Spence Hardy has some remarks well worth attention, on the analogy between the Buddhist narrative and the "doctrine of the perpetual virginity of the mother of our Lord."[2] The Rev. E. Eitel draws attention to two other points of similarity—the pre-existence of Buddha in heaven, and the salutation by angels.[3] This was one of the hymns sung by the Gandharvas, or Indian cherubs, to the king, immediately after the miraculous conception: "The Spirits of the Pure

---

[1] "Birth Stories," p. 65.   [2] "Manual," p. 145.
[3] "Three Lectures on Buddhism," p. 5.

Abode, flying in the air, showed half of their forms, and hymned King Śuddhodana thus :—

> " ' Guerdoned with righteousness and gentle pity,
> Adored on earth and in the shining sky,
> The Coming Buddha quits the glorious spheres,
> And hies to earth to gentle Mâyâ's womb.' " [1]

Seydel[2] has a chapter headed " Conception by the Holy Ghost." He cites several passages of the Buddhist legends, amongst others the following : " Thus, O monks, Buddha was born, and the right side of his mother was not pierced, was not wounded. It remained as before." [3]

Amongst the "thirty-two signs" that indicate the mother of a Buddha, the fifth is that, like Mary the mother of Jesus, she should be " on a journey" at the time of her expected labour. It so happened that Queen Mâyâ fulfilled this as well as every other requirement ; for when her time had nearly come, her father, King Suprabuddha Grihapati, sent the following message to King Śuddhodana, at Kapila-vastu: "As I am informed that my daughter Mâyâ, your Majesty's queen, is now with child, and already far advanced in pregnancy, and as I fear that when the child is born my daughter will be short-lived, I have

---

[1] Lalita Vistara, Foucaux, p. 62.

[2] " Evangelium von Jesu in seinen verhältnissen zu Buddha-sage," p. 110.

Foucaux, p. 97.

thought it right to ask you to permit my daughter to come back to me. I have prepared a palace in the Lumbini Garden for her reception."

And so, on a canopy sparkling with gems, upreared upon the back of a beautiful white elephant, Queen Mâyâ commenced her journey, accompanied by guards and music. Courtiers, soldiers and servants, elephants, horses and chariots, joined in the procession. And in the air, invisible, were countless spirits, headed by the mighty Indra himself, the governor of the three thousand great thousand worlds. Sixty thousand of the beautiful cloud-maidens[1] sang soft chants. In this manner the Lumbini Garden was reached.

Exquisite as were the trees of this garden, and the flowers and rich scents, there was one especial tree, the palâśa (scarlet butea), that eclipsed all its neighbours. Its boughs were spreading, its leaves were soft, its buds were green; and the pearl, mani, glistened in the morning upon its branches. Beneath this tree was grass, like the shining green of the peacock's neck, and soft as the cloth of Kâchalindi. Lured to this gentle shade, the queen advanced, when, lo! a marvel was visible. Suddenly the branches of this tree bent down to overshadow her, "as the luminous bow of heaven," says the narrative, "bends across the sky." At this moment the infant Buddha came forth from

---

[1] Apsarases.

a gap in his mother's right side.   In one version of
the Gospel of the Infancy, in the library of Berne,[1] a
palm-tree bends down in the same way to Mary.

At once the infant made four paces, one towards
each of the cardinal points.   After each pace a lotus
sprung up and supported him.   The infant Buddha on
the cosmical lotus is a favourite object of Buddhist

Fig. 1.

art.   The infant Hermes on the lotus is still found on
many Gnostic talismans.   In the Catacombs the infant
Christ figures also on a lotus or lily (Fig. 1).

When a Buddha is born into the world other

[1] Given, with the other Apocryphal Gospels, by Voltaire, Œuvres,
vol. xl.

marvels take place. The earth rocks, soft rain falls
from heaven, and scented winds blow gently on mankind. Instruments of music play without the contact
of mortal fingers. A light composed of one hundred
thousand varied tints illumines the three thousand
great thousand worlds. All flesh is filled with peace
and joy. The sick are healed, the deaf are cured, the
blind see, the poor are relieved, the prisoners are
released, the hungry fed, the naked clothed. Flowers,
scents, and even garments fall down from the skies.
A shudder of strange ecstasy is in each individual.

Also, in the hell Avîchi, says the Lalita Vistara,
all torments cease. The Buddhists of China have
a legend that every thousand years Buddha, as a
beautiful young man, descends into hell, and com-
passionately empties that region of expiation.

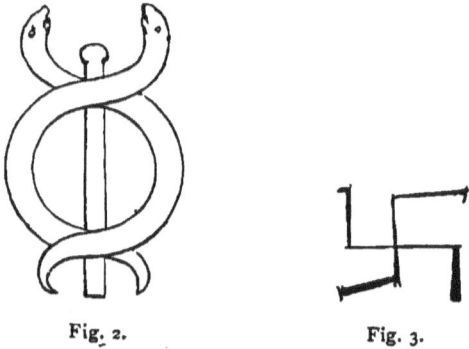

Fig. 2.   Fig. 3.

Whilst the new-born babe was standing upon a
large white lotus, two paradisiacal serpents, Nanda
and Upananda, appeared in the sky, and rained down

a spout of water to baptise the young infant. The most holy symbol of Buddhism is the Triratna, formed by two serpents twined round a rod (Fig. 2). The Swastika, or Indian cross (Fig. 3), had the same origin. Of this, more hereafter.

In the First Gospel of the Infancy it is recorded that when Jesus was in His cradle He said to His mother, " Mary, I am Jesus the Son of God, that Word which thou didst bring forth according to the declaration of the angel Gabriel to thee, and My Father hath sent Me for the salvation of the world."[1]

In the Buddhist Scripture it is stated that Buddha, on seeing the light, said—

" I am in my last birth. None is my equal. I have come to conquer death, sickness, and old age. I have come to subdue the spirit of evil, and give peace and joy to the souls tormented in hell."

Now, at this time, upon the rugged steeps of the Himâlaya mountains, was a holy dreamer named Asita. This man, by the usual practices of the Indian ascetic, had obtained the divine vision. He was able to detect the denizens of the ghost world in his ecstasies, and to guess secrets unknown to mortals. Looking abroad from his rude cave over Jambudwîpa, the "Land of the Rose Apple," as the Indians prettily call the peninsula of Hindostan, he was able,

---

[1] Chap. i. 3.

from certain indications in the spirit world, to detect that an avatâra of the Supreme God was about to take place. Suddenly his "divine eye" lighted on the city of Kapilavastu, and he perceived a young infant shining with an unusual spiritual lustre. The Gospel of the Infancy records that "the old man Simeon saw the child Jesus glistening like a column of bright light." [1]

Colebrooke tells us that the Treatise of Magic (Yoga Śâstra) of Patanjali attributes eight supernatural faculties to the adept or proficient in Yoga. One of these is the power of levitation, or "rising like a sunbeam to the solar orb." [2] It so happened that this power was possessed by the Rishi Asita, for, "after the manner of the King of the Swans, he rose aloft into the sky, and proceeded to the great city of Kapilavastu." [3] Soon a message was brought to King Śuddhodana, that a stranger was at the gate. Admitted, the stranger marched up to the king, but remained erect and unabashed. King Śuddhodana perceiving instinctively that he was in the presence of some one very different from the silken courtiers around, offered him the Arghya, the gift that it is customary to present to a holy prophet. This Arghya consists of water, milk, kuśa-grass, curds, clarified

---

[1] Chap. vii.   [2] "Essays," vol. i. p. 250.
[3] Foucaux, p. 104.

butter, rice, barley, and white mustard. He also offered him water to wash his feet with, and a seat.

"Holy sir, I don't remember to have seen you before. What is your command?"

"King," said the Rishi, "to you a child has been born. I have come to see it."

"The child sleeps," said the king.

"It will wake presently," said the Rishi.

News came that the infant, in point of fact, had woke up.

Carried into the presence of Buddha, the holy man took the little child in his arms. He remained pensive for some moments, and then, to the astonishment of the king, he burst into a flood of tears.

"What means this, O Rishi, that you sigh and sob?" said the monarch, alarmed. "Do you see any malefic influence around?"

"I weep, O king," said the Rishi, "because I am old and stricken in years, and shall not see all the glory that is about to come to pass. The God Almighty Buddha [Buddha Bhagavat] only visits the world after many kalpas. This bright boy will be Buddha. For the salvation of the world he will teach the divine law. He will succour the old, the sick, the dying; dry tears, still pangs, comfort broken hearts. He will release those who are bound in the meshes of natural corruption. He will quicken the spiritual vision of those whose eyes are darkened by the thick darkness of ignorance. Hundreds of thousands of millions of beings will be carried by him to the 'other bank.' He will proclaim the mysteries of the students of Brahma [Brahmacharins]. He will bring immortality to light [les conduira à l'immortalité].[1] And this salvation I shall not see; this is why I weep."

Thirty-two "greater signs" and eighty "minor signs" proclaim a Buddha. These were detailed by the holy man. They are, for the most part, symbolical; and describe the conventional statue of Buddha in a temple, rather than the actual body of Buddha when living on earth. Thus the sole of his foot and the palm of his hand must be even, the toes and fingers united by a membrane. On each sole the mystic chakra figures—the wheel of a thousand spokes. This on some statues is represented by the Swastika, which is also set down as one of the "signs." The Śrîvatsa, Kṛishṇa's special emblem, is

, another "sign," which is an important fact. The Buddha's hairs all go one way (with the sun). His voice is loud as that of the great Brahma, for it symbolizes heaven's thunder. His tongue is very long, for it symbolizes the lightning. His eye is

[1] Foucaux, p. 107.

white, like the lotus. His body is like the Lion of the zodiac. His trunk is firm as stambha, the trunk of the Indian fig-tree. His leg is the leg at once of the antelope and the shrivelled Indian ascetic. His cry is the cry of the Elephant of the zodiac. On his brow is a tuft of hair like that of Brahmâ.[1] The Lalita Vistara says that when Buddha was under the bo-tree he had "fingers like copper."[2] The thirty-two signs plainly refer to the statue in the temple.

[1] For signs, see Foucaux, p. 107 et seq.　　　[2] Ibid., p. 261.

C

CHAPTER II.

THE INFANT BUDDHA.

GOD, imaged as Vicegerent, was worshipped by the Brahmins under the special aspects of the year. "The year is Prajâpati," says the Aitareya Brâhmaṇa. God, imaged as the Universal Mother, was also symbolized by the year. Buddha was born seven days before the commencement of the new year—the 1st of March,—and in seven days his mother died. All mothers of Buddhas die seven days after bearing their divine son, say the Buddhists. The fact that the life of a Buddha follows the fleeting aspects of nature during a yearly cycle, will throw much light on the symbolical portion of the narrative. Queen Mâyâ was anxious to be in a beautiful garden with flowers and budding trees at the date of her parturition, because the spring festival took place in the open air. Three incidents in the early life of Buddha also allude to this festival.

The first is an actual detailed account of the spring or ploughing festival. The second and third are called by the Rev. S. Beal, respectively, the "presentation of gifts" and the "presentation at the temple."

Certain elders came and gave counsel to the king, saying, "It is meet, O king, that the infant should be now presented at the temple of the gods."

"It is proper that this should be done," said Śuddhodana. "Let the streets and bazaars be splendidly adorned. Beat the drums, ring the bells. Let the lame, the deaf, the blind, the unsightly be removed from the line of procession, and everything else of evil augury. Assemble the neighbouring kings, the nobles, the merchants, the householders in gala dress. Let the Brahmins decorate the temples of the gods."

The king's orders were promptly obeyed. In due time, accompanied by the loud blare of Indian instruments—the conch shell, the flute, the tambourine, the "drum of joy"—the young infant went in "great and pompous royal ceremony" to the temple. Elephants in crowds, and horses and chariots, citizens and soldiers, joined in the procession. Parasols were reared aloft, streamers waved, banners were unfurled. Villagers and nobles, the poor and the rich, pressed forward to the show. The streets and the squares were carpeted with flowers, and vases of sweet scent were lavishly flung about. Also, in harmony with the crude ideas of early art that a perfectly smooth plain was the highest ideal of beauty, rough places were made smooth and tortuous paths straightened. Rude designs of these flags and drums, and "long horns and flageolets,"[1] are given in the earliest sculptures. The men have kummerbunds, and bare legs and chests; the women are clothed chiefly in heavy arm and leg bangles. We can see the procession of good King Śuddhodana in modern India.

The car of the young Buddha was borne respectfully along by a procession of gods. Beautiful apsarases sounded seraphic notes; flowers fell from heaven.

When the procession reached the temple, the images of the gods—Indra, Brahmâ, Nârâyana, Kouvera the god of wealth, Skanda, and the Four Mahârâjas—stood up in their places and saluted the feet of the young infant, and worshipped him as the transcendental Deity revealed on earth. A hymn which they sang on the occasion plainly shows this :—

" Tall Meru, King of Mountains, bows not down
To puny grain of mustard seed. The sea,
The yeasty palace of the Serpent King,
Ne'er stoops to greet the footprint of a cow :
Shall Sun or Moon salute a glistening worm?
Or shall our Prince bend knee to gods of stone?
Who worships pride, the man or god debased,
Is like the worm, the seed, the cow-foot puddle ;

---

[1] See Cunningham, " Bhilsa Topes," p. 30, also plate xiii.

> But like the sun, the sea, and Meru Mount,
> Is Swayaṁbhû, the self-existent God ;
> And all who do him homage shall obtain
> Heaven and Nirvritti."

Nirvritti and Nirvâṇa have the same meaning, namely, matter at rest. The Brahmins feigned that heaven was matter kept eternally at rest by the great Śesha (God, imaged as a serpent), who enfolded it in his coils. Pravritti was matter not "fixed" nor eternal. It was the seen universe, which was periodically destroyed and restored by the "breath" of the Spirit. Nirvâṇa is that which cannot be blown or breathed upon at all. This is the interpretation of the first of all Sanscrit authorities, Pâṇini.[1] Professor Monier Williams still translates Nirvâṇa, "blown out like a candle," "complete annihilation ; " but, thanks to Max Müller, Oldenberg, and Rhys Davids, this idea is exploded. Of course this heaven of the Buddhists is in the mind as well as in the eternal skies. I quite agree with Dr. Rhys Davids, who in a letter in the *Spectator*, February 25, 1882, pointed out that Nirvâṇa with the Buddhists merely meant "the peace of God, which passeth human understanding." But a casuist might here ask, How can an "atheist" make it the one object of his life to seek the peace of a God which it is his main tenet to deny? Also, if the "atheist"

---

[1] Goldstücker's "Pâṇini," p. 227.

has no "soul," where is he to put the peace of God when he finds it?

When the gods had finished their hymn the statues became animate, and the temple shone with all the glory of the heavenly host.

A passage from the First Gospel of the Infancy may be cited here. When Mary and Joseph fled to Egypt, they reached a city where a mighty idol was worshipped. This idol made the following revelation to its priests: "In this city has arrived an unknown God, who is the true God, and none other but He is worthy of worship, because He is the Son of God." [1] The idol then tumbled off its pedestal, and was broken to fragments. These coincidences are curious. The Gospel of the Infancy was a favourite Gospel of the Gnostics. It was also found in the hands of the Malabar Christians.

A short time after this, a Brahmin named Purohita respectfully suggested to the king that the young Buddha should receive the customary "gifts." So at sunrise he was carried in the arms of his aunt, Mahâ Prajâpatî Gautamî, to the beautiful Vimalaviyûha, the Stainless Garden. There, for seven days and nights, he was decked with rings and bracelets and diadems, with strings of pearls, with rich silks and golden tissues; and young girls in thousands gazed at him in

[1] Chap. x.

rapture. In China, God depicted as an Infant is as popular as Bala Kṛishṇa in India, or the Virgin and Child in Italy. But on this occasion, in the Stainless Garden, those who believed in the efficacy of trinkets and tawdry finery received a rebuke. Suddenly a majestic spirit made half of its divine form visible, and sang in the clouds :—

> "Cast off this tawdry show !
> The streams of earth wash down their shining gold ;
> Men gather it for their bedizenments,
> But in that far-off river, on whose banks
> The sweet rose-apple [1] clusters o'er the pool,
> There is an ore that mocks all earthly sheen—
> The gold of blameless deeds."

The third incident was the ploughing festival, the great Spring festival of India. This attracted countless crowds to see the labourers contest for the prize. The king ploughed with a plough ornamented with gold. The nobles ploughed with ploughs ornamented with silver. All who have been in Rome will remember St. Anthony's Day, and the Pope blessing the cattle. The Pongal, the Spring festival, still takes place in modern India. Cows, decorated with flowers and cakes and tinsel, are driven in for a solemn ceremonial. If the cakes drop off during the transit, the poor may scramble for them.

Near the fields where all this was going on, was a

---

[1] Jambu.

wood in which grew a fine specimen of the holy rose-apple (jambu). To this wood the infant prince, vexed at seeing the poor oxen sweat and bleed, chanced to stray. Seeing the rose-apple, he sat under its shade, crossing his legs, and adopting the attitude of a Buddha in his mystic trance. Whilst he was meditating, five holy Rishis, or prophets, came past the wood, flying through the air by means of their magical powers. But suddenly these powers ceased, and they were forced to alight. They gazed with astonishment on the young boy.

"Who is this?" they asked. "Is it Vaiśravaṇa, or Rudra, or the God of Love, or Krishṇa?" The goddess of that holy grove answered that it was the son of King Śuddhodana who had arrested their flight.

The Rishis then began to repeat the following gâthâs.

The first Rishi said :—

> "In a world devoured by the fire of sin
> This lake hath appeared ;
> In him is the Law
> Which brings happiness to all flesh ! "

The second Rishi said :—

> "In the darkness of the world
> A light has appeared,
> To lighten all who are in ignorance ! "

The third Ṛishi said :—

> " Upon the tossing ocean
> A bark has approached
> To save us from the perils of the deep ! "

The fourth Ṛishi said :—

> " To all who are bound in the chains of corruption,
> This great Saviour has come :
> In him is the Law
> That will deliver all ! "

The fifth Ṛishi said :—

> " In a world vexed by sickness and old age
> A great Physician has appeared,
> To provide a Law
> To put an end to both."

Soon the king appeared searching for his son, when, lo ! this marvel was visible. The shadows of all the other trees had turned, but the jambu-tree still screened the young boy with its shade.

The Ṛishis having saluted the feet of Buddha, flew off through the air.

The Lalita Vistara professes to " reveal " the secrets of the Buddhas. It professes to show a mortal how to obtain mastery over his bad passions, how to gain calmness, purity, the " divine vision," supernatural powers, the mystic " lion throne," the mystic " carpet of the Zodiacal King," the mystic " carpet of Indra," the mystic " carpet of Brahma," etc.[1]

[1] See p. 7 ; also pp. 401 et seq.

To quite understand this passage, it must be pointed out that Brahminism had—

1. A hierarchy of gods in heaven.

2. A hierarchy of priests, who represented these gods on earth.

3. A hierarchy of upright monoliths in the open-air temples, that represented the same gods.

4. These gods also symbolized the gradation of spiritual states, the "condition of Yaksha, or demon," the "condition of Indra, or conqueror," etc., passed through by the mystic before he reached the "carpet of the Supreme Brahma." And the rites of the Brahmins had also a mystic side. They exhibited the same passage from the lower to the higher life. In the rudest enclosure of monoliths a veil parted that portion of the open-air temple which represented heaven, from that which represented the seen world. The main rite was a dramatic exhibition of the birth of the Śiśur Jâtah (new-born child). "The clarified butter is the milk of the woman," says the Aitareya Brâhmaṇa; "the husked rice grains belong to the male."[1] This eternal marriage of matter and spirit, Aditî the Mother and Varuṇa the Father, was the one meaning of almost every rite. Exoterically was produced the amṛita, or immortal food. Esoterically was produced the mystic "man,"

[1] Vol. ii. p. 5.

the prophet, the Voice of Brahma. The officiating priests masqueraded as Prajâpati, Indra, Brahmâ, etc., and the leading one was supposed to engender a spiritual duplicate of himself, who was able to visit heaven and obtain wealth and cattle for the worshippers.

Dr. Neale's "Liturgies of the Greek Church"[1] show that similar ideas existed in the Eastern Church. The Bishop coming down from his throne in the cathedral represents the condescension of God the Son in coming down from heaven. The stole means putting on mortal flesh. The deacons standing round typify apostles and also holy angels. The priest in the great entrance is supposed to be Christ coming in, borne by angels. The solemn hymn, chanted forth by angel voices, "Lift up your heads, O ye gates, for the King of Glory to come in!" preludes his entrance into the Holy of Holies, or heaven. The incense rising near the altar means the advent of the Holy Spirit. The grand procession with lamps and holy vessels, "readers, deacons, and priests," represents the last advent. The fans that the priests held in their hands in the early Church, like modern Buddhists, represent angels' wings. In a word, a complete service represented the birth, life, passion, and triumph of the mystic Christos.

[1] Preface.

Now, I feel certain that the Lalita Vistara also gives a veiled account of the temple rites, as well as the initiation of the mystic. In those days the year began on the first of March, immediately after Aditî, as the black Durgâ, had been consigned to the flames; hence, according to Wilson, the yule-log. Professor Haug tells us that even in modern India, when the greatest sacrifice is performed, a stem of a banian-tree has to be set up. In early Buddhism the tree was the rude temple; and the amrita, or Bread of Life, was produced by the mystic marriage of rice and scented water.

This sheds light on the Śiśur Jâtah, or new-born infant, sitting cross-legged under a tree, being wor-shipped by saints and shaded miraculously. It throws light on the gold bangles and silks presented to the little idol. We see a meaning in the statues becoming animate, and in the priests, dressed up as gods, carrying the little child in a pompous procession, and bowing humbly to him. We see a meaning in thë detailed account of the costly festival, the bell-ringing, the music, the flowers, and scents. Also in all Brahmin and Buddhist worship the dust or mud is studiously levelled to make a smooth mandala, or mystic ring;[1] even when an old native officer is making a rude altar before taking his dinner in camp. In the earliest sculptures we

[1] Beal, " Catena," p. 399.

see the symbols of the Siśur Jâtah, the wheel of Dharma, the footprints, etc., being worshipped under a tree. We see, sometimes, on the rude altar a globular object, almost as big as a foot-ball, being also worshipped. To this day, in Brahminism a large globular rice pudding is the chief offering of the Bloodless Sacrifice. In Ceylon the epoch of Buddha is called the Epoch when the Rice Milk came into the World. The amṛita, or food of immortality, was imaged by this, as it was the chief sustenance of dreaming mystics. Dr. Rhys Davids, comparing the rites of Northern Buddhism and those of the Roman Catholics, says that each creed " lays peculiar stress upon the mystic sacrament in which the priest reverently swallows a material thing and by so doing believes himself to become partaker, in some mysterious way, of a part of the Divine Being, who during the ceremony has become incorporated therein." [1]

The First Gospel of the Infancy announces that Christ was born in a cave, and that the shepherds who tended their flocks near it sang hymns to Him.

"The cavern resembled a splendid temple, where Kings, mortal and heavenly, celebrated the glory and praised God for the birth of the Lord Jesus Christ." [2]

Seydel, in a chapter headed " Gold and frankincense

[1] " Hibbert Lecture," p. 193.   [2] Chap. iv.

and myrrh," draws attention to the similarity of the gift presentations in the Indian and Christian narratives.

In the Dulvâ it is more than once announced that " myrrh, garlands, incense, etc.," were sacrificed to Buddha.[1] Gold pieces are placed on the Buddhist altar by the Chinese, and the consecrated elements remain on the altar in a lacquered tabernacle.[2]

A little Brahmin was " initiated," girt with the holy thread, etc., at eight, and put under the tuition of a holy man. Buddha's like Râma's guru was named Viśvâmitra, which is another point of connection with the Brahmin avatâras. But the youthful Buddha soon showed that his lore was far greater than that of his teacher. When Viśvâmitra proposed to teach him the alphabet, the young prince went off :—

" In sounding ' A,' pronounce it as in the sound of the word ' anitya.'

" In sounding ' I,' pronounce it as in the word ' indriya.'

" In sounding ' U,' pronounce it as in the word ' upagupta.' "

And so on through the whole Sanscrit alphabet.

In the First Infancy, chap. xx., it is recorded that when taken to the schoolmaster, Zacchæus—

[1] " Asiatic Researches," vol. xx. p. 312.
[2] Langles, " Rituel des Mantchoos Tartares."

"The Lord Jesus explained to him the meaning of the letters Aleph and Beth.

"8. Also, which were the straight figures of the letters, which were the oblique, and what letters had double figures ; which had points and which had none ; why one letter went before another ; and many other things He began to tell him and explain, of which the master himself had never heard, nor read in any book.

"9. The Lord Jesus further said to the master, Take notice how I say to thee. Then He began clearly and distinctly to say Aleph, Beth, Gimel, Daleth, and so on to the end of the alphabet.

"10. At this the master was so surprised, that he said, I believe this boy was born before Noah."

In the Lalita Vistara there are two separate accounts of Buddha showing his marvellous knowledge. His great display is when he competes for his wife. He then exhibits his familiarity with all lore, sacred and profane, "astronomy," the "syllogism," medicine, mystic rites.

The disputation with the doctors is considerably amplified in the twenty-first chapter of the First Gospel of the Infancy :—

"5. Then a certain principal Rabbi asked Him, Hast Thou read books ?

"6. Jesus answered that He had read both books and the things which were contained in books.

"7. And He explained to them the books of the law and precepts and statutes, and the mysteries which are contained in the books of the prophets—things which the mind of no creature could reach.

"8. Then said that Rabbi, I never yet have seen or heard of such knowledge! What do you think that boy will be?

"9. Then a certain astronomer who was present asked the Lord Jesus whether He had studied astronomy.

"10. The Lord Jesus replied, and told him the number of the spheres and heavenly bodies, as also their triangular, square, and sextile aspects, their progressive and retrograde motions, their size and several prognostications, and other things which the reason of man had never discovered.

"11. There was also among them a philosopher, well skilled in physic and natural philosophy, who asked the Lord Jesus whether He had studied physic.

"12. He replied, and explained to him physics and metaphysics.

"13. Also those things which were above and below the power of nature.

"14. The powers also of the body, its humours and their effects.

"15. Also the number of its bones, veins, arteries, and nerves.

" 16. The several constitutions of body, hot and dry, cold and moist, and the tendencies of them.

" 17. How the soul operated on the body.

" 18. What its various sensations and faculties were.

" 19. The faculty of speaking, anger, desire.

" 20. And, lastly, the manner of its composition and dissolution, and other things which the understanding of no creature had ever reached.

" 21. Then that philosopher worshipped the Lord Jesus, and said, O Lord Jesus, from henceforth I will be Thy disciple and servant."

Viśvâmitra in like manner worshipped Buddha by falling at his feet.

D

CHAPTER III.

MARRIAGE OF BUDDHA.

I THINK that the good King Śuddhodana is a little open to the grave allegations brought against him by Mr. Edwin Arnold in his graceful poem, "The Light of Asia." The soothsayers had pronounced that the infant would be one of two things—a mighty earthly conqueror or a hermit. This prophecy plainly gave the king much concern. An earthly emperor, surrounded by elephants and horsemen, and spearmen and bowmen, was a tangible object—tangible as his rich palaces and towers and shining emeralds; but the advantages of the pious hermit were very unsubstantial indeed—

> "Gaining, who knows what good, when all is lost
> Worth keeping."[1]

So by-and-by it came into the mind of the king that he would consult more soothsayers, to see if more definite knowledge about the young man's future

[1] "The Light of Asia," p. 25.

could be obtained. A number of pious hermits, gifted with the divine wisdom, were in consequence got together. They pronounced the following :—

"The young boy will, without doubt, be either a king of kings or a great Buddha. If he is destined to be a great Buddha, four Presaging Tokens will make his mission plain. He will see—

" 1. An old man.

" 2. A sick man.

" 3. A corpse.

" 4. A holy recluse.

" If he fails to see these four presaging tokens of an avatâra, he will be simply a Chakravartin." [1]

The Chakravartin was the King of the Chakra (Zodiac). M. Senart has shown that the Buddha and the Chakravartin were in reality the same, and that the word implied a spiritual ruler or judge. The Chakravartin has received the consecration (abhisheka) of Indra. He holds, also, the sun-god's chakra, or disc. But although the Vedic Indra hurls this disc at his enemies, the Ṛig-Veda specially tells us that he "does no harm to man." The Buddhist Chakravartin conquers likewise the kingdoms of the world, but "not with arms and with violence."

Dr. Rhys Davids draws a parallel between this Anointed One, this "Bread of Life," this "Word of

---

[1] Spence Hardy's "Manual," p. 154.

God made Flesh," and the Christian Messiah. "The Cakkavatti Buddha," he says, giving the Cingalese spelling of the word, "was to early Buddhists what the Messiah Logos was to early Christians."[1] If this is the case, what about Cingalese Buddhism "taking for its ultimate" a material world alone? And how can an atheist believe in a Word of God made Flesh?

The flattery of a court by-and-by called the earthly king "Indra." The King of the Zodiac has seven treasures :—

1. An elephant (Capricorn).
2. A horse (Aries).
3. A jewel (Libra).
4. A wife (Virgo).
5. A Brahmin guide of the Household (Aquarius).
6. A general (Sagittarius).
7. The missile called the chakra (Pisces).

King Śuddhodana was very much comforted by the last prediction of the soothsayers. He thought in his heart, It will be an easy thing to keep these four presaging tokens from the young prince. So he gave orders that three magnificent palaces should at once be built—the Palace of Spring, the Palace of Summer, the Palace of Winter. These palaces, as we learn from the Lalita Vistara, were the most beautiful palaces ever conceived on earth. Indeed,

---

[1] "Hibbert Lectures," p. 147.

OLD BUDDHIST ZODIAC. [Page 36.

they were quite able to cope in splendour with
Vaijayanta, the immortal palace of Indra himself.
Costly pavilions were built out in all directions, with
ornamented porticoes and furbished doors.   Turrets
and pinnacles soared into the sky.   Dainty little
windows gave light to the rich apartments.   Galleries,
balustrades, and delicate trellis-work were abundant
everywhere.   A thousand bells tinkled on each roof.
We seem to have the lacquered Chinese edifices of
the pattern which architects believe to have flourished
in early India.   The gardens of these fine palaces
rivalled the chess-board in the rectangular exactitude
of their parterres and trellis-work bowers.   Cool lakes
nursed on their calm bosoms storks and cranes, wild
geese and tame swans ; ducks, also, as parti-coloured
as the white, red, and blue lotuses amongst which
they swam.   Bending to these lakes were bowery
trees—the champak, the acacia serisha, and the beautiful aśoka-tree with its orange-scarlet flowers.   Above
rustled the mimosa, the fan-palm, and the feathery
pippala, Buddha's tree.   The air was heavy with the
strong scent of the tuberose and the Arabian jasmine.
One such garden has since appeared in India, I cannot
help thinking.   It was constructed by another Chakravartin—the " Company Bahadur," as the natives called
him.   It was called the Botanical Garden, and its
smooth green slopes were washed by the river

Hooghly. Stately Indiamen sailed past to the great city of Calcutta hard by, and frail Indian craft with ragged sails. Pleasure-seekers, the poor and the rich, sought the shade of its unrivalled trees—the plantain, the palm, the camphor cinnamon, the Indian fig. One of the latter shaded about a quarter of a mile of the garden. I have seen this rare garden, but no one will see it again. In a terrific typhoon the swollen river swept it completely away. Another typhoon disposed of the great Chakravartin, the East India Company.

It must be mentioned that strong ramparts were prepared round the palaces of Kapilavastu, to keep out all old men, sick men, and recluses, and, I must add, to keep in the prince.

And a more potent safeguard still was designed. When the prince was old enough to marry, all the young girls of the kingdom were marshalled before him. To each he gave a rich bangle, or a brooch set in diamonds, or some expensive gewgaw. But the spies who had been set to watch him, remarked that he gazed upon them all with listless eye. When the rich collection of jewels was quite exhausted, a maiden of exquisite beauty entered the apartment. Buddha gazed at her spell-bound, and felt confused because he had no gift to offer to her. The young girl without any false modesty went to him, and said abruptly—

" Young man, what offence have I given thee, that thou shouldst contemn me thus ? "

" I do not contemn thee, young girl," said the prince, " but in truth thou hast come in rather late ! " And he sent for some other jewels of great value, which he presented to the young girl.

" Is it proper, young man," she said, with a slight blush, "that I should receive such costly gifts from thee ? "

" The ornaments are mine," he said, " therefore take them away ! "

The young girl answered simply, " Not having any trinkets I could not deck myself, but now I will bear me bravely." The spies, cunning in furtive glances and blushes, reported everything to the king.

The name of the young girl was Gopâ. M. Foucaux conceives that the name is identical with the " milkmaid," beloved by Krishṇa.[1]

The king was delighted that his son had fallen in love. He at once sent the Brahmin Purohita to Śâkya Daṇḍapâṇi, the young girl's father, to demand her hand in marriage for his son. Daṇḍapâṇi's reply to the king was this :—

" The noble young man has lived all his life in the sloth and luxury of a palace, and my family never gives a daughter excepting to a man of courage and

[1] Page 135.

strength, one who can wrestle and ply the bow, and wield the two-handed sword."

This answer made the king sad. Many other haughty Śâkya families had previously said, " Our daughters refuse to come near a young milksop."

When the king confided the source of his sadness to his son, the latter said, with a smile—

" If this is the cause of thy grief, O father, let me try conclusions with these valiant young Śâkyas."

"Canst thou wrestle ? Canst thou shoot with the bow ? "

" Summon these young heroes, and we will see."

Immense importance was attached by the Âryas to the festival of the Summer Solstice. The Greeks had their Olympia, when the whole population met together to witness the wrestling, the bow-shooting, the chariot races. The victor in these was carried home in a pompous procession. In ancient India a woman, famous for her beauty, was made the chief prize, and the marriage was called Swayaṁvara (marriage by athletic competition). By this institution the manhood and courage of the State were powerfully stimulated. It must be borne in mind that a skilful use of the bow, the club, and the war-chariot meant independence to the community. On the other hand, an unskilful use subjected the whole tribe to be

captured and detained as prisoners of war. They
might be sacrificed to Rudra at the autumn festival.
Or if they were lucky enough to escape this, they were
certain to be stripped naked, man, woman, and child,
and be slaves for the rest of their lives. As details of
the memorable Swayamvara where the beautiful Gopâ
was the prize are rather meagre, perhaps I may be
permitted to supply some from the epics.

A vast plain was selected on these occasions, and
levelled and swept. Round this pavilions and lacquered
palaces of the Chinese pattern were hastily erected.
Their dainty spires and columns and roofs stood out
against the blue sky, " like the snowy pinnacles of
the mountain range Kailasa," says the Mahâbhârata.
Carpets and sofas and thrones were spread in these
for the kings and competing heroes. In front of each
pavilion were heavy awnings on glittering poles. The
powerful perfumes of India, the aloes, and the balm,
could be scented from afar. The priests poured clarified butter into the holy fire. Mummers and dancers
and singers performed miracle plays, not differing much
from the modern pantomime ; religious disputants
chopped logic. Each guest was expected to be lavish
of his gifts. This made the poor man as merry as
the rich one.

Devadatta, a rival of Buddha, slaughters an elephant,
and places it in the pathway of Buddha when he was

proceeding to this memorable Swayañvara. Buddha, with unexpected strength, removes it to a distance, to prevent it from infecting the neighbourhood. The elephantine cloud, says M. Senart, and the lightning were much to Indian myth-makers.

A competition for a high-born princess includes learning, as well as the athleticism. Buddha, as I have already mentioned, first eclipses his neighbours in the former. Then come swimming, jumping, running, and none have a chance against him. Then comes the important issue of wrestling. This in India has been cultivated and honoured from time immemorial. Buddha first vanquishes Nanda and Ânanda. Ânanda is the brother of the unfriendly Devadatta, who next comes forward to avenge him :—

" Then the young Sâkya Devadatta, puffed with the pride of race and the insolence of strength, came forth to the contest. He circled round with much rapidity and skill, and watching his opportunity he sprang upon the prince."

But Buddha is merciful as well as strong. He causes the conceited young man to execute a somersault in the air, and then catches him before he can be hurt. Afterwards, all the young heroes in a body attack the prince, but with the same ill fortune.

But the Âryas, like their descendants, the Anglo-Saxons of Crecy, were unrivalled bowmen. Archery was the real test of a hero in the old epics. Preparations now take place for that crucial issue.

Ânanda sets up a drum of iron. Devadatta sets up another at double the distance. Sundarananda sets up a third drum at a distance of six krosas. Daṇḍapâni sets up a drum at a greater distance still. By Daṇḍapâni's drum are seven tall palm-trees, and beyond this a figure of a wild beast in iron.

Ânanda lets fly a shaft. It pierces the drum which he had set up. Beyond that distance he cannot shoot. Devadatta pierces his drum. Sundarananda pierces the drum set up at six krosas. Daṇḍapâni smites his drum. But beyond his selected distance each archer is powerless.

And now it is the turn of Buddha to shoot, but no bow is strong enough to bear the strength of his arm. One after another they break in the stringing. At last it is recollected that, in one of the shrines, there is the bow of his grandfather, Siṁhahanu (Lion Jaw), a weapon so mighty that no warrior can even lift it. Attendants are set off to fetch it. The strongest Śâkyas attempt to string it, but all in vain.

Then the prince himself takes up the bow of the mighty Lion Jaw. With ease he strings it, and the sound of its stringing re-echoes through the wide city of Kapilavastu. Amid immense excitement he adjusts an arrow and prepares to shoot. His shaft transfixes the first drum, the second drum, the third drum, the fourth drum, and then, tearing swiftly through the seven trees and the wild beast of iron, buries itself like the lightning in the ground.

Other competitions take place. The prince shows his superiority in riding the horse, riding the elephant with an iron goad ; in poetry, painting, music, dancing, and even jocularity ; in the " art of the fist," and in " kicking." He also shines in his knowledge of occult mysteries,[1] in "prophecy," in the explanation of dreams, in "magic," in "joining his hands in prayer." [2]

After this manner Buddha won the beautiful Gopâ. She is called Yasodhara in the Southern narrative.

Let us imagine the imposing nuptials. A prince in modern India and a prince residing in the ancient city of Kapilavastu would go through much the same ceremonies, for they are all rigidly laid down in the Yajurveda. The young prince would have to pay a formal visit to Dandapâni, his father-in-law, who would have to slaughter a cow in his honour. A little kusa-grass cushion and some holy water would be presented to the guest, and the rice of plenty in a conch shell. He would also be expected to eat up a mess composed chiefly of honey. Meanwhile the

---

[1] Yoga.   [2] Foucaux, p. 179 et seq.

bride would be bathed by her women, and the following mantra recited :—

> "Love, I know thy name !
> Bring the bridegroom happily !
> For thee was framed the inebriating draught !
> Fire, thy best origin is here,
> Through devotion wert thou created.
> May this oblation be efficacious."

The bride and bridegroom may now be introduced. They join hands, and the hands are actually bound together with a nuptial knot of kuśa-grass ; and the guests would, perhaps, sing out, as in the pretty drama of " Nala and Damayantî " :—

> "He hath eaten the honey,
> And now will taste the honey of the bride's lip.
> The bridegroom's hand exults in the slaughter of his foes.
> The bride's hand has filched the bloom of the lotus.
> Happy day ! "

Then the bride's father gives to the bridegroom a piece of gold, and by-and-by the mantles of bride and bridegroom are pinned together ; the many guests, in their diamonds and silks and muslins, being regaled all through the long ceremonies with much music and hymns and prayers. Let us write down a few of the latter :—

" May the assembled gods unite our hearts.

" May the Creator unite us.

" May the God of Love unite us.

" Death, follow a different path from that by which we proceed !

" May Indra, lord of beings, protect us."

The bride and bridegroom then cast rice in the fire to Agni.   The bridegroom then points to the pole-star in the sky, supposed by the ancients to support the Kosmos.   He says—

" Heaven is fixed.   Earth is fixed.   These mountains are fixed.   May this woman be stable in her husband's family ! "

He says also—

" I need prosperity.   Thou art Lakshmî.   I am the sky, thou the earth."   Varuṇa as the sky, and Aditî as the earth, have been husband and wife in India from the earliest days.

The crucial ceremony consists in seven mystic steps made by the bride.   At the seventh step the marriage is considered completed.

With pretty Gopâ, eighty-four thousand other wives entered the Palace of Summer.   Eighty-four thousand with the Buddhists vaguely means a large number.   Eighty-four thousand is also the number of the stars.   It has been debated whether the wives were merely attendants.   Gopâ was the chief lady.

By-and-by there was a scandal in the palace.   The officials reported to the king that Gopâ refused to veil her face like the other ladies.   She replied thus :—

> "Bright is the pearl upon the standard's crest ;
> The Kalibiṇka softly croons of love
> When poised on giddy wing or bowered in leaves.
> In rags good deeds shine forth ; and robes of silk
> Make crime more flaunting than it was before.
> The steps of righteousness are like the steps,
> The honoured steps of tanks by ancient fanes.
> True wives are like the moon, who veils her face
> Or races through the welkin unabashed ;
> The mighty Ṛishi,[1] versed in secret thoughts,
> Sees that my heart is pure."

When the king heard this answer, he was very pleased with his daughter-in-law, and gave her two white dresses covered with jewels.

"My daughter and my son," he said, "are like cream mingled with milk."

[1] Brahma.

CHAPTER IV.

THE FOUR PRESAGING TOKENS.

PERHAPS, at this time, the good King Śuddhodana was more happy than even the prince in the ecstasy of his honeymoon. He had found for that prince the most beautiful wife in the world. He had built him palaces that were the talk of the whole of Hindostan. No Indian mahârâja before had had such beautiful palaces, such lovely wives and handmaidens, such dancing girls, singers, jewels, luxuries. In his bowers of camphor cinnamon, amid the enchanting perfumes of the tuberose and the santal-tree, his life must surely be one long bliss, a dream that has no awakening.

But suddenly this exultation was dashed with a note of woe. He dreamt that he saw his son in the russet cowl of the beggar-hermit. Awaking in a fright, he called an eunuch.

"Is my son in the palace?" he asked abruptly.

"He is, O king."

The dream frightened the king very much, and he

ordered five hundred guards to be placed at every corner of the walls of the Palace of Summer. And the soothsayers having announced that a Buddha, if he escapes at all, always escapes by the Gate of Benediction, folding doors of immense size were here erected. The sound of their swing on their hinges resounded to a distance of half a yogana (three and a half miles). Five hundred men were required to stir either gate. These precautions completely quieted the king's mind, until one day he received a terrible piece of news. His son had seen the first of the four presaging tokens. He had seen an Old Man.

This is how the matter came about. The king had prepared a garden even more beautiful than the garden of the Palace of Summer. A soothsayer had told him that if he could succeed in showing the prince this garden, the prince would be content to remain in it with his wives for ever. No task seemed easier than this, so it was arranged that on a certain day the prince should be driven thither in his chariot. But, of course, immense precautions had to be taken to keep all old men and sick men and corpses from his sight. Quite an army of soldiers was told off for this duty, and the city was decked with flags. The path of the prince was strewn with flowers and scents, and adorned with vases of the rich kadalî plant.

E

Above were costly hangings and garlands, and pagodas of bells.

But, lo and behold ! as the prince was driving along, plump under the wheels of his chariot, and before the very noses of the silken nobles and the warriors with javelins and shields, he saw an unusual sight. This was an old man, very decrepit and very broken. The veins and nerves of his body were swollen and prominent ; his teeth chattered ; he was wrinkled, bald, and his few remaining hairs were of dazzling whiteness ; he was bent very nearly double, and tottered feebly along, supported by a stick.

" What is this, O coachman ? " said the prince. " A man with his blood all dried up, and his muscles glued to his body ! His head is white ; his teeth knock together ; he is scarcely able to move along, even with the aid of that stick ! "

" Prince," said the coachman, " this is Old Age. This man's senses are dulled ; suffering has destroyed his spirit ; he is contemned by his neighbours. Unable to help himself, he has been abandoned in this forest."

" Is this a peculiarity of his family ? " demanded the prince, " or is it the law of the world ? Tell me quickly."

" Prince," said the coachman, " it is neither a law of his family, nor a law of the kingdom. In every being youth is conquered by age. Your own father and mother and all your relations will end in old age. There is no other issue to humanity."

" Then youth is blind and ignorant," said the prince, " and sees not the future. If this body is to be the abode of old age, what have I to do with pleasure and its intoxications ? Turn round the chariot, and drive me back to the palace ! "

Consternation was in the minds of all the courtiers at this untoward occurrence ; but the odd circumstance of all was that no one was ever able to bring to condign punishment the miserable author of the mischief. The old man could never be found.

King Śuddhodana was at first quite beside himself with tribulation. Soldiers were summoned from the distant provinces, and a cordon of detachments thrown out to a distance of four miles in each direction, to keep the other presaging tokens from the prince.[1] By-and-by the king became a little more quieted. A ridiculous accident had interfered with his plans : " If my son could see the Garden of Happiness he never would become a hermit." The king determined that another attempt should be made. But this time the precautions were doubled.

On the first occasion the prince left the Palace of Summer by the eastern gate. The second expedition was through the southern gate.

[1] Spence Hardy, " Manual of Buddhism," p. 155 et seq.

But another untoward event occurred. As the prince was driving along in his chariot, suddenly he saw close to him a man emaciated, ill, loathsome, burning with fever. Companionless, uncared for, he tottered along, breathing with extreme difficulty.

"Coachman," said the prince, "what is this man, livid and loathsome in body, whose senses are dulled, and whose limbs are withered? His stomach is oppressing him; he is covered with filth. Scarcely can he draw the breath of life!"

"Prince," said the coachman, "this is Sickness. This poor man is attacked with a grievous malady. Strength and comfort have shunned him. He is friendless, hopeless, without a country, without an asylum. The fear of death is before his eyes."

"If the health of man," said Buddha, "is but the sport of a dream, and the fear of coming evils can put on so loathsome a shape, how can the wise man, who has seen what life really means, indulge in its vain delights? Turn back, coachman, and drive me to the palace!"

The angry king, when he heard what had occurred, gave orders that the sick man should be seized and punished, but although a price was placed on his head, and he was searched for far and wide, he could never be caught. A clue to this is furnished by a passage in

the Lalita Vistara.   The sick man was in reality one
of the Spirits of the Pure Abode, masquerading in
sores and spasms.   These Spirits of the Pure Abode
are also called the Buddhas of the Past, in many
passages, as I shall shortly show.

Dr. Rhys Davids, in his translation of the Life of
Buddha, calls them vaguely " angels," " fairies," etc. ;
but the whole question of early Buddhism is really
bound up in the matter.   In the Southern Scriptures
it is explained that the Spirits of the Pure Abode
dwell in the heaven of Brahma.[1]   I may mention too,
that in a valuable inscription, copied from an old
column in the island of Ceylon, by Dr. Rhys Davids
himself, it is announced that in the reign of the king
who erected it, the Buddha devatâs " talked with
men "[2] in the great temple.   Here we have plainly the
Buddhas of the past, of the Lalita Vistara.   The
disciples of the " Carriage which drives to the Great
Nowhere " have senselessly interlarded this book with
certain " Bodhisatwas of the Ten Regions," which,
figuring side by side with the " Buddhas of the Ten
Regions," confess the cheat.   When the " Great
Vehicle " movement dethroned the Buddhas of the
past, it substituted Bodhisatwas (mortals who have
reached the last stage of the metempsychosis), and

[1] Turnour, Journ. Beng. As. Soc., vol. vii. p. 798.
[2] Journ. As. Soc., vol. vii. p. 364.

transferred the old saint-worship, the sacrifices, processions, relic expositions, etc., to them.

For another valuable fact we are indebted to the Southern Scriptures. They announce that the answers of the charioteer were given under inspiration from the unseen world.[1] On the surface this is plausible, for we shall see that the speeches of the charioteer were not always pitched in so high a key.

And it would almost seem as if some influence, malefic or otherwise, was stirring the good King Śuddhodana. Unmoved by failure, he urged the prince to a third effort. The chariot this time was to set out by the western gate. Greater precautions than ever were adopted. The chain of guards was posted at least twelve miles off from the Palace of Summer. But the Buddhas of the Ten Horizons again arrested the prince. His chariot was suddenly crossed by a phantom funeral procession. A phantom corpse, smeared with the orthodox mud, and spread with a sheet, was carried on a bier. Phantom women wailed, and phantom musicians played on the drum and the Indian flute. No doubt also, phantom Brahmins chanted hymns to Jâtavedas, to bear away the immortal part of the dead man to the home of the Pitris.

"What is this?" said the prince. "Why do these women beat their breasts and tear their hair? Why

[1] Spence Hardy, "Manual," p. 157.

do these good folks cover their heads with the dust of the ground. And that strange form upon its litter, wherefore is it so rigid?"

"Prince," said the charioteer, "this is Death! Yon form, pale and stiffened, can never again walk and move. Its owner has gone to the unknown caverns of Yama. His father, his mother, his child, his wife cry out to him, but he cannot hear."

Buddha was sad.

"Woe be to youth, which is the sport of age! Woe be to health, which is the sport of many maladies! Woe be to life, which is as a breath! Woe be to the idle pleasures which debauch humanity! But for the 'five aggregations' there would be no age, sickness, nor death. Go back to the city. I must compass the deliverance."

A fourth time the prince was urged by his father to visit the Garden of Happiness. The chain of guards this time was sixteen miles away. The exit was by the northern gate. But suddenly a calm man of gentle mien, wearing an ochre-red cowl, was seen in the roadway.

"Who is this," said the prince, "rapt, gentle, peaceful in mien? He looks as if his mind were far away elsewhere. He carries a bowl in his hand."

"Prince, this is the New Life," said the charioteer. "That man is of those whose thoughts are fixed on the eternal Brahma [Brahmacharin]. He seeks the divine voice. He seeks the divine vision. He carries the alms-bowl of the holy beggar [bhikshu]. His mind is calm, because the gross lures of the lower life can vex it no more."

"Such a life I covet," said the prince. "The lusts of man are like the sea-water—they mock man's thirst instead of quenching it. I will seek the divine vision, and give immortality to man!"

In the Lalita Vistara the remedy for age, sickness, and death is immortality.[1] In Dr. Rhys Davids's "Buddhism" the remedy for death is death. If the apologue was composed outside of Bedlam, it is plain that the Lalita Vistara gives us the correct version. If a prick with a dagger is the amṛita, why go through all the tortures of yoga to gain it?

King Śuddhodana was beside himself. He placed five hundred corseleted Śâkyas at every gate of the Palace of Summer. Chains of sentries were round the walls, which were raised and strengthened. A phalanx of loving wives, armed with javelins, was posted round the prince's bed to "narrowly watch" him. The king ordered also all the allurements of sense to be constantly presented to the prince.

"Let the women of the zenana cease not for an instant their concerts and mirth and sports. Let

---

[1] " Un fruit de vie, de bien être, et d'immortalité " (Foucaux, p. 185).

them shine in silks and sparkle in diamonds and emeralds."

Mahâ Prajâpatî, the aunt who since Queen Mâyâ's death has acted as foster-mother, has charge of these pretty young women, and she incites them to encircle the prince in a "cage of gold."

The allegory is in reality a great battle between two camps—the denizens of the Kâmaloka, or the Domains of Appetite, and the denizens of the Brahmalòka, the Domains of pure Spirit. The latter are unseen, but not unfelt.

For one day, when the prince reclined on a silken couch listening to the sweet crooning of four or five brown-skinned, large-eyed Indian girls, his eyes suddenly assumed a dazed and absorbed look, and the rich hangings and garlands and intricate trellis-work of the golden apartment were still present, but dim to his mind. And music and voices, more sweet than he had ever listened to, seemed faintly to reach him. I will write down some of the verses he heard, as they contain the mystic inner teaching of Buddhism.

" Mighty prop of humanity
  March in the pathway of the Rishis of old,
  Go forth from this city !
  Upon this desolate earth,
  When thou hast acquired the priceless knowledge of the Jinas,
  When thou hast become a perfect Buddha,
  Give to all flesh the baptism (river) of the Kingdom of Righteousness.

Thou who once didst sacrifice thy feet, thy hands, thy precious body,
    and all thy riches for the world,
Thou whose life is pure, save flesh from its miseries !
In the presence of reviling be patient, O conqueror of self !
Lord of those who possess two feet, go forth on thy mission !
Conquer the evil one and his army."

Thus run some more of these gâthâs :—

" Light of the world ! [lamp du monde—Foucaux],
    In former kalpas this vow was made by thee :
'For the worlds that are a prey to death and sickness I will be a
    refuge !'
Lion of men, master of those that walk on two feet, the time for thy
    mission has come !
Under the sacred Bo-tree acquire immortal dignity, and give Amrita
    (immortality) to all !
When thou wert a king (in a former existence), and a subject inso-
    lently said to thee : ' These lands and cities, give them to me ! '
Thou wert rejoiced and not troubled.
Once when thou wert a virtuous Rishi, and a cruel king in anger
    hacked off thy limbs, in thy death agony milk flowed from thy
    feet and thy hands.
When thou didst dwell on a mountain as the Rishi Syama, a king
    having transfixed thee with poisoned arrows, didst thou not
    forgive this king ?
When thou wert the king of antelopes, didst thou not save thine
    enemy the hunter from a torrent ?
When thou wert an elephant and a hunter pierced thee, thou forgavest
    him, and didst reward him with thy beautiful tusks !
Once when thou wert a she-bear thou didst save a man from a torrent
    swollen with snow. Thou didst feed him on roots and fruit
    until he grew strong ;
And when he went away and brought back men to kill thee, thou
    forgavest him !
Once when thou wert the white horse,[1]

---

[1] Yearly the sun-god as the zodiacal horse (Aries) was supposed by
the Vedic Âryans to die to save all flesh. Hence the horse-sacrifice.

In pity for the suffering of man,
Thou didst fly across heaven to the region of the evil demons,
To secure the happiness of mankind.
Persecutions without end,
Revilings and many prisons,
Death and murder,
These hast thou suffered with love and patience,
Forgiving thine executioners.
Kingless, men seek thee for a king !
Stablish them in the way of Brahma and of the ten virtues,
That when they pass away from amongst their fellow-men, they may
   all go to the abode of Brahma.
In times past, having seen men fallen into evil ways, and vexed by
   age, sickness, and many griefs, thou didst make them understand
   which was the straight way from this world of destruction !
Conqueror of the darkness, thou hast done priceless service to the
   worlds !
To creatures of all sorts thou madest many offerings.
Thou gavest thy wife, thy son, thy daughter, thy body, thy kingdom,
   thy life !
Strong king ! thou didst prefer the glory of blameless deeds.
Thou who art Kṛishṇa, Nimindara, Nimi, Brahmadatta, Dharma-
   chinti, etc., having pondered upon the aim of life, thou hast
   abandoned to mortals things difficult to abandon.
Ṛishi of kings, of body like the moon-god (Chandra), thy march
   is over the horizon and the dust.
King of Kaśi (Benares), thou proclaimest the peace of heaven.
Long hast thou seen that the life of men is like the sands of the
   Ganges.
In pursuit of the spiritual knowledge (Bodhi), O first of the pure !
   thou hast made innumerable offerings to the Buddhas :
To Amoghadarsi, the flowers of the Sâla-tree ;
To Vairochana, a gentle thought ;
To Chandana, a torch of kuśa-grass ;
To Remi thou didst fling a handful of gold-dust !
Didst thou not encourage Dharmeśvara, when he was teaching the
   law, by saying, ' Well !'
Upon beholding Sarmantadarsi thou didst cry, ' Adoration ! Adora-
   tion !'

Thou gavest the garb of the Muni to Nâgadatta !
To Sâkya Muni [1] thou gavest a handful of suvarṇas (pieces of gold)."

"By these gâthâs the prince is exhorted," says the narrative. And whilst the Jinas sing, beautiful women, with flowers and perfumes, and jewels and rich dresses, try to incite him to mortal love. Again the music of the immortals breaks through their songs :—

" Guide of the world ! think quickly of thy resolve to appear in it ;
  Make no delay !
  In the old times a precious treasure, gold, silver, and ornaments,
      were abandoned by thee.
  To Bhaichadyarâja thou didst offer a precious parasol ;
  Thou gavest thy kingdom to Tâgaraśikhin ;
  To Mahâpradîpa thou didst offer thine own self;
  To Dîpañkara a blue lotus ;
  Remember the Buddhas of the past, their teachings and thy sacrifices.
  Contemn not poor mortals without a guide.
  When thou didst see Dîpañkara thou didst acquire the Great Patience
      and the five transcendental sacrifices !
  Then, after innumerable kalpas, in all parts of the world, having
      taken delight in making offerings inconceivably precious to all
      these Buddhas,
  The kalpas have rolled away,
  The Buddhas have gone to Nirvâṇa,
  And all their bodies, that once belonged to thee, and even their
      names—Where are they ?
  It is the work of the Law of Righteousness to put an end to the
      aggregations of matter.
  That which has been created is not durable.
  Earthly empire, earthly desire, earthly riches are as a dream.
  In the terminable kalpas of the world, like a fire that burns with
      a fearful light, sickness, age, and death draw near with their
      tremors.

---

[1] Much of this is plainly esoteric Buddhism. The inspirer of prophets, and not the prophet himself, is addressed.

The Law of Righteousness alone can put an end to substance. What
    is composite is not durable.
Look at the unhappy creatures of earth ;
Go forth into the world ! ''

But the king was on the other side.

It is recorded that he offered to resign his royal umbrella in favour of his son. His urgent entreaty that the prince should abandon all thoughts of a religious life was answered thus :—

"Sire, I desire four gifts. Grant me these, and I will remain in the Palace of Summer."

"What are they ?" said King Śuddhodana.

"Grant that age may never seize me. Grant that I may retain the bright hues of youth. Grant that sickness may have no power over me. Grant that my life may be without end." [1]

This gives us the very essence of the apologue, and seems to make Dr. Rhys Davids's interpretation quite puerile. Even the devil himself seems to have seen the matter more shrewdly. Mâra, the tempter, describes the story in a sentence :—

"This is a son of King Śuddhodana, who has left his kingdom to obtain deathless life [amṛita]." [2]

[1] Lalita Vistara, p. 192.   [2] Ibid., p. 287.

CHAPTER V.

THE GREAT RENUNCIATION.

ABOUT this time Gopâ had a strange dream. She beheld the visible world with its mountains upheaved and its forests overturned. The sun was darkened, the moon fell from heaven. Her own diadem had fallen off her head, and all her beautiful pearl necklaces and gold chains were broken. Her poor hands and feet were cut off; and the diadem and ornaments of her husband were also scattered in confusion upon the bed where they were both lying. In the darkness of night lurid flames came forth from the city, and the gilded bars that had been recently put up to detain the prince were snapped. Afar the great ocean was boiling with a huge turmoil, and Mount Meru shook to its very foundations.

She consulted her husband about this dream, and he gave her the rather obvious interpretation that this dismemberment of her mortal body, and this passing away of the visible universe and its splendours, was of good, and not bad augury. She was becoming detached from the seen, the organic ; her inner vision was opening. She had seen the splendid handle of Buddha's parasol broken. This meant that in a short time he was to become the "unique parasol of the world."

But to bring about this result more quickly, the Spirits of the Pure Abode have conceived a new project. The beautiful women of the zenana are the main seductions of Mâra, the tempter, whom philologists prove to be closely connected with Kâma, the god of love. The Spirits of the Pure Abode determine that the prince shall see these women in a new light. By a subtle influence they induce him to visit the apartments of the women at the moment that they, the Jinas, have put all these women into a sound sleep.

Everything is in disorder—the clothes of the women, their hair, their trinkets. Some are lolling ungracefully on couches, some have hideous faces, some cough, some laugh sillily in their dreams, some rave. Also deformities and blemishes that female art had been careful to conceal are now made prominent by the superior magic of the spirits. This one has a discoloured neck, this one an ill-formed leg, this one a clumsy fat arm. Smiles have become grins, and fascinations a naked hideousness. Sprawling on couches in ungainly attitudes, all lie amidst their tawdry finery, their silent tambourines and lutes.

"Of a verity I am in a graveyard!" said the prince, in great disgust.

And now comes an incident in his life which is of the highest importance. He has determined to leave the palace altogether. "Then Buddha uncrossed his legs, and turning his eyes towards the eastern horizon, he put aside the precious trellis-work and repaired to the roof of the palace. Then joining the ten fingers of his hands, he thought of all the Buddhas and rendered homage to all the Buddhas, and, looking across the skies, he saw the Master of all the gods, he of the ten hundred eyes [Daśaśata Ṇayana]." Plainly he prayed to Indra. The Romantic Life also retains this incident, but it omits Indra, and makes Buddha pray only to all the Buddhas.

At the moment that Buddha joined his hands in homage towards the eastern horizon, the star Pushya, which had presided at his birth, was rising. The prince on seeing it said to Chandaka—

"The benediction that is on me has attained its perfection this very night. Give me at once the king of horses covered with jewels!"

"Guide of men!" said the poor charioteer, "thou knowest the hour and the commands of the king. The great gates are shut!"

But the troops of spirits that were in the air had brought about another marvel. Chandaka looked, and, to his astonishment, the huge portals, that required so many hundred men to stir them, were wide open. Then heavenly songs fell upon his ear :—

"O Chandaka ! thwart not the Guide of men !
Millions of spirits are singing,
Drums sound, and śankha-shells,
And many instruments of music ;
And yet the city slumbers,
Around thee is a brightness not of earth !"

Thus exhorted, Chandaka saddles Kaṇṭaka, and when the prince has mounted on his back, earth rocks and the light around is perfectly dazzling. The *genius loci* in saddened tones addresses the unrivalled horseman as he passes through the Gate of Benediction :—

"Oh, thou who hast the face of a lotus,
Without thee this city is desolate !
The prophecy of the Rishis has been made false ;
They said that thou shouldst be a Chakrabâla.
Great Tree of all the Virtues !
If thou departest thy house will wither,
Thy race become extinct !"

And then, accompanied by millions of gods and apsarases flinging flowers, Buddha enters upon his divine mission.

A terrible scene took place in the palaces of Kapilavastu when it was discovered that the prince

F

had fled. The king was beside himself, and Mahâ Prajâpatî Gautamî threw herself on the ground in her despair. The wives beat their breasts and sobbed ; and called out, some, " Where is our brother ? " and others, " Where is our husband ? " for every one adored the prince.

And when Chandaka with the good horse Kantaka returned the next morning and narrated the flight, a very tender scene took place. Poor Gopâ, who since the catastrophe had been more dead than alive, suddenly recovered a little energy and seized the horse's neck with her shining arms, and remembering the happy hours of the past, she wept and uttered the following :—

> " Two human beings loved one another ;
> He was my joy.
> His face was like the moon, spotless ;
> His form was peerless ;
> His limbs without a blemish.
> He was born of a race pure and without peers ;
> He was strong as Nârâyana, conqueror of many foes.
> More compassionate than gods,
> He was born in the Lumbini garden, amid the murmuring of
>   bees ;
> His lips were red as the fruit Bimba,
> His teeth were like milk, his skin like gold,
> His legs were like the antelope Ena,
> His thigh like the trunk of the elephant.
> Here are his jewels, but where is he ?
> Pearls without him are like the rubble of a demolished palace.
> Alone on my bed, where he was sleeping by my side, I found
>   myself.   He had abandoned me !

Kaṇṭaka, good horse, whither didst thou take him?
Chandaka, pitiless, wherefore didst thou not awake me?
Chandaka, fathers and mothers are honoured by all,
Why then should a wife be abandoned?
Henceforth I feel I cannot eat nor drink ;
My hair shall grow vile and matted ;
An unblest thing is the forcible parting of a man and a woman
    who love.
Tree of knowledge ! Guide of men !
Well didst thou say :
In the realms of Change,
In the dominions of Death,
Are no friends ! "

Buddha, on leaving the palace, made perhaps the most noteworthy journey ever made by mortal. Every step almost has since been marked by costly marble carvings and shrines and statues under canopy-mounds, which successive generations of pilgrims have smothered in flowers.

To follow in the footsteps of the great Tathâgata was the mystic meaning of these pilgrimages. I think that what is called the Charan symbol, the impress of two of Buddha's feet on an altar, was due, in the first instance, to the pilgrimage idea. In the early carvings we frequently see the worship of these footprints. The symbol is also a well-known one in the lives of Râma, Kṛishṇa, etc., and the footprints of Jesus were an important feature in the pilgrimages in Palestine.

Kapilavastu, according to General Cunningham, is Nagar Khâs, and the first ride of Buddha was forty-two miles in the direction of Vaiśâlî. In the morning he reached the Anoma (modern Aumi) River below Sangrâmpura. At this point the god Indra, disguised as a hunter,[1] induced him to take off his emeralds and silks and put on a hermit's dress. The prince cut off his flowing locks with his own sword. He sent back the charioteer and the good horse Kantaka. Each of these incidents was afterwards commemorated by a chaitya at the spot. They meant, of course, that Buddha's guru, personifying Indra, had made Buddha go through the customary initiation, the tonsure, vows of poverty, etc.

Leaving the Anoma, which is a branch of the modern Raptee, the prince made his first real halt at Vaiśâlî (the modern Besârh), a spot about twenty miles north of Patna. Here he found a number of yogis undergoing their initiation in yoga-vidya, or white magic, in a forest.

The Chinese story gives an interesting picture of these Brahmins. Some were clad in deerskins ; some in hempen vesture ; some in the rags off corpses. They fed on fruits and herbs and the sprouting shoots of certain trees. Flowing streams quenched their thirst. They kept cows and calves for their milk, and also for sacrificial purposes. Some practised the more cruel initiations of the Tapas. Some sat between five

---

[1] " Twelve Acts of Śâkya."

fires. Some faced the sun through his daily journey.
Some kept their arms above their heads till they
withered. Some sat in cemeteries. An unsavoury
initiation with cow-dung is not omitted in the nar-
ration. In the cool shade of the wood were many
flowers. As the future Buddha entered it the birds
carolled hymns of joy.[1]

In this wood, Buddha commenced what the Lalita
Vistara calls the " ecstatic meditation on Brahma and
his world." But to obtain yoga, or the mystic union
with Brahma, the novice must become a servant-pupil
of some eminent Adept (Brahmajnâni). At Vaiśâlî was
a holy man, Arâṭa Kalama, and Buddha said to him,
" By thee, O Arâṭa Kalama, must I be initiated into
the condition of a Seeker of Brahma [Brahmacharin]."[2]

Buddha was by-and-by dissatisfied with his teacher,
and he crossed the Ganges and went to the neighbouring kingdom of Magadha. Running diagonally
across this kingdom was a range of hills, abounding
in natural caves and mountain ingles and secluded
wastes. From Râjâgriha, the capital, these stretch
in a south-westerly direction as far as Buddha Gayâ.
These hills and caves were by-and-by profusely
sprinkled over with shrines and chaityas, to encase
legends which affirmed that Buddha sat cross-legged
in this cave and preached on such a hill. Near Râjâ-

---

[1] " Romantic History," p. 153 et seq.   [2] Page 227.

griha alone "the number of natural caves," says Fa
Hian, the Chinese pilgrim, "is several hundred."[1] The
kingdom is now called Bihar, from vihâra, a monastery. An Indian would sound " vihâra " " Bihar."

And in truth, this range of hills was admirably
adapted to be the cradle of a mighty creed. Protected
by its rich tropical growth of bush and palmyra palms,
the mystic could gather together a band of choice
disciples, and train them without molestation. The
many natural caves would protect them in winter. In
summer the huge banian-tree, the sturdy teak, the
mimosa, and the pippala would screen them from the
sun, and allow them to dream on without any other
disturbance than the screaming green parrots or the
humming bees. Or the ascetic could climb up some
of the higher steeps. These hills were visited by
Hwen Thsang, the intelligent Chinese. This is his
description of the hill of the Teacher's Foot (Guru-
pada). It is, I understand, a little overcharged.

" At this point are seen tall peaks abruptly scarped,
valleys and caves without end. Swift torrents race
by the hill foot, and enormous forests clothe the
valley. Tangles of bush and creeper make shade for
the caverns. Above, shining through the mists, and
touching heaven itself, are three bold peaks." [2]

---

[1] Fa Hian, p. 273.
[2] " Mémoires " (translated by S. Julien), vol. ii. p. 6.

On this steep Kaśyapa obtained Nirvâna. Another high mountain, the Vulture's Peak (Gridhrakûta), was also visited by the pilgrim. It is said to be crowned with the pearl maṇi; and, indeed, the lustre of this imaginary gem seems to have attracted him all the way from China. Buddha himself loved this mountain, and a large statue of him, in the act of preaching, was seen by the Chinaman far up in the mists. The White Lotus of Dharma, the most mystical of the Buddhist Sûtras, was here delivered.[1] This hill is an isolated hill to the south of Râjâgriha. It is of prodigious height, presenting the appearance of a tall tower, round which the vultures fly. "The blue tints of heaven are seen on it, pale tints and dark tints." The pilgrim also visited a cavern where Buddha sat cross-legged and dreamed. The Lalita Vistara announces that he had a teacher called Rudraka, when in this neighbourhood. The "Twelve Acts of Śâkya" tells us that he "visited several hermits living in the hills."

"Be ye a light unto yourselves!" this is the motto of the Higher Buddhism. By-and-by Buddha forsook his various teachers, and trusted alone to his own inspiration. It is impossible to gauge the amount of happiness that this decision has brought to the human race. At Buddha Gayâ, by the tranquil

---

[1] "Mémoires," vol. ii. p. 20.

Nairanjana, Buddha plunged into a tangled thicket—
plunged into solitude.

All who know the green jaṅgals of Bengal and
the rich tropical growth on the low red hills, can
picture the scene. I can imagine the cactus-like
euphorbias, the tangle of climbing ferns and clinging
creepers, the parasite fig, and the convolvulus, that
bespatter with their large flowers the dark trunk of
the great teak-tree, or strangle the *Aśoka Jonesia* with
a network of twigs. Here and there flash out the
bright broad leaves of the plantain; or the white stem
of the tall cocoanut carries skyward its leafy crown.
Bamboos shoot up aloft a flight of green rockets.
Here is the mimosa and the champak. To the left is
a forest growing from one stem, for the great Indian
fig has the faculty of sending down innumerable roots
from many great branches, which grow and grow
until acre after acre is screened by its dark green
leaves. Here is the crooked stem of the pandanus,
forked like a candelabrum, each bough carrying a
bunch of leaves twisted into a screw, whilst the
base of the trunk rests as if on stilts on a number
of air roots. Flowers of every conceivable tint are
plundered by butterflies of every conceivable hue.
Green jays scream, and other birds, blue, red, and
orange, quiver on the boughs. Snakes and lizards
sparkle in the grass. The little yellow and green

squirrels are untiring. And I can imagine, for I have seen such when campaigning in a neighbouring district, the miraculous coruscation of fireflies round the bushes that fringe the river, in the hush of a warm evening in the rains, when the amazing blaze of cadmium and vermilion that makes a Bengal sunset a thing apart has toned down to a cold russet. In that jañgal Buddha sat cross-legged under the pippala (*Ficus religiosa*), which has become the most celebrated tree in the world.

As the traveller approaches Buddha Gayâ he sees a mighty red tower erect amid the ruins of the palaces and temples around. As in the day of Hwen Thsang, the Chinese pilgrim, this tall tower stands sentry over the famous tree. Pilgrims in hundreds of thousands still visit it yearly, the Brahmins quite as zealously as in old days the Buddhists. Shrines and holy tanks feed quite an army of priests. The devotee leaves his globular rice pudding at each. A king once spent £10,000 in his offerings.

The poor tree now is choked up by bricks and mortar and the rubble of old sculptures, but it still lives on. The ruins of Aśoka's palace are near ; and the ruins of the large Buddhist tope are to the south of the palace. A hill to the south-east is the Prâgbodhi, where, according to General Cunningham, Buddha first meditated, but was driven away by the spirits of evil.

A few of the details of this Buddhist mystical initiation may be appropriate here. The novice must select an able teacher. He must be shaved, washed, cleaned. Of particular importance is the choice of the place of initiation. It must be without distinctions, free from the terrors of wild beasts and haunted by the spirits of the past Buddhas.

The place must be well swept and otherwise cleaned; and fresh earth must be thrown upon it in order to make its surface even and smooth. A magical circle of the five sacred colours must be drawn in order to overcome evil spirits, who will do all they can to mar the efforts of the devotee. Within the circle an altar is erected, upon which various vessels are ranged, filled with grain and perfumed water. The ceremonies consist in the reciting of incantations and the presentation of food offerings to the good spirits. The incantations must be recited slowly, without raising or lowering the voice. They must be repeated something like a hundred thousand times a day. A rosary with 108 beads helps the counting. A Vajra (toy thunderbolt) all this time must be held tightly in the hand. The spirit prayed to is Vajrapâni, the holder of Indra's thunderbolt. Sweet dreams and sweet supernatural scents prelude the advent of the supernatural powers. In the rite called Dubed the novice has to fix his gaze on water in a vessel tricked out with knots of the five sacred colours. The modern mesmerist gains power over a sensitive in a somewhat similar manner. Vajra means " diamond " as well as " thunderbolt," and this second idea has been worked into the first. The head of the thunderbolt is shaped like a diamond. It is stated in one passage of the Lalita Vistara, that Buddha indulged " in that ecstatic meditation whose essence is the diamond." [1] The Buddhists call the spirit body the " diamond body." [2]

The Lalita Vistara, as we have seen, professes to reveal all the mysteries of the Indian occult teaching. It professes to carry a mortal through the eight mystic grades, to the eighth and the highest : " the mystic state of Brahma ; this is the highest of the eight mystic states." [3] The more I study the work the more I feel convinced that of all books in the world it is the book that has preserved to us the ancient Indian mysteries under the thinnest disguise. Buddha's life is the career of Prajâpati—the passage of the human soul from embryo to pure spirit.

It must be mentioned that this penance of Buddha was not carried on without good-natured molestations from the other world. The good King Śuddhodana

[1] See p. 206.

[2] For details of initiation see Subâhu Pariprichcha, Schlagintweit, " Buddhism in Tibet," p. 242.

[3] See p. 404.

sent several messengers to urge him to return. The king pointed out that the celebrated King Râma had been able to obtain salvation, and yet had been able to discharge the duties of an earthly king. "Therefore return, O my son. I willingly resign to you the kingdom. You shall be anointed as king!"[1] These constant allusions to Râma show certainly that that epic cannot, as Professor Monier Williams suggests, be due to the inspiration of the Christian Gospels.

It is recorded that another king, King Bimbisâra, visited the young ascetic, and also offered him an earthly throne if he would forsake the ascetic life.

The reply of Buddha is, I think, instructive: "I have given up a powerful kingdom, putting aside earthly ambitions. To obtain calm, I have become a yogi. Arrived at the springtide of youth, when vigour and grace and beauty are its portion, I desired troops of women and much wealth. And in the middle of my kingdom I gratified all my appetites."[2]

Romance has thrown a halo round Queen Gopâ, called in the South Yaśodhara; but I think this passage shows that the conflict inside the Palace of Summer really typifies a man's struggle with his bad passions, imaged as women. But as Buddha was

---

[1] "Romantic History," p. 163.   [2] Lalita Vistara, p. 230.

also an aspect of God Almighty, and as such the husband of Aditî, the lives of Yaśodhara and Buddha reach a lofty ideal in all Buddhist writings. This is the account of Buddha's parting with her, in Spence Hardy's Cingalese biography :—

"Whilst the charioteer was absent in the stables the prince, in order that he might see his son, went to the apartment of Yaśodhara ; and on opening the door he saw the princess upon a couch surrounded by flowers, but she was asleep embracing the infant, which was also asleep and laid upon her bosom. The prince perceived that in order to take up his son he must remove the mother's arm, which would probably cause her to wake. And as he knew that if she awoke she would probably speak to him, which might change his resolution, he remained on the threshold, holding the door-post with his hand, but not proceeding any further." [1]

For six years Buddha sat cross-legged, seeking to obtain the visions of the Higher Buddhism and the magical faculties which by all old mystics were considered a guarantee that the visions were genuine. He stopped his respiration, says the narrative, and got to eat only one grain of the jujube-tree per diem.

These practices began by-and-by to reduce the prince to a mere mass of dried skin and bone. The

[1] "Manual," p. 162.

villagers thought he was dying. In the Chinese version it is recorded that he fasted forty-seven days and nights without taking an atom of food. When he was in this strait an important person came upon the scene, Mâra the tempter. Two of his temptations are the same as those of Christ. Mâra offers to make Buddha a Chakravartin, or king of all the kings of the earth. He also urges him to save his life by breaking his long fast and eating food.

"Sweet creature," said the tempter in dulcet tones, "you are at the hour of death. Sacrifice food, and eat a portion of it to save your life."

The reply of Buddha is a fine one.

"Death, demon, is the inevitable end of life. Why should I dream of avoiding death? Who falls in battle is noble. Who is conquered is as good as dead. Demon, soon I shall triumph over thee. Lust is thy first army, ennui thy second, hunger and thirst are thy third. Passions and idleness, and fear and rage and hypocrisy, are amongst thy troops,—backbitings, flatteries, false renown. These are thy inky allies, soldiers of a chief whose doom is near."

In our picture of Buddha in the "wilderness" of Uravilva, trying to solve the mighty riddles of the universe, we get a piece of pure history. But the Lalita Vistara is not a life of Śâkya Muni alone, but the higher life of humanity as interpreted by ancient

mysticism. It is also, as I have explained, the life of
the Buddha as presented in the ritual of the Buddhist
temple. This last circumstance must be borne in
mind in approaching a very important incident which
is recorded in all the narratives. This is the presentation to Buddha of what Dr. Rhys Davids calls
the Bread of Life. In Buddhism it takes the form of
rice milk, and is called amṛita (immortality).

"I have entered the bed," said the Initiates of
Eleusis. This bed was the tomb, the cave of Yama,
the fleshly covering of the soul. To obtain the
"whole-birth," as the Buddhists call it, the lower
nature, the old Adam, must die. This is why Buddha
was taken by the villagers of Uravilva for a corpse
escaped from the adjacent cemetery.[1]

"Like Yama, the God of Death, let us seek the
happiness of deep meditation in the world of
Brahma!"[2] The Brahmin mystic carried Yama's
mace with a skull on it.[3]

Here is also a forcible passage from Dr. Rhys
Davids's version :—

"I lay me down in the cemetery, making a pillow of dead bones.
The village children mocked and praised : to all I was indifferent."[4]

This accounts for a contradiction in the narrative.
At first Buddha is made to sit cross-legged in a

[1] Page 250.   [2] Page 204.   [3] Page 240.
[4] "Birth Stories," p. 57.

wilderness ; afterwards it is announced that his initiation took place in a graveyard. The early Buddhists
were called Smâsânîka (dwelling among the tombs).

The real meaning is this. Human life is the
graveyard of the mystics. "Of a verity I am in
a graveyard," said Buddha amid the surfeiting
pleasures of his zenana.   It must be remembered, too,
that the temple was actually a cemetery, and its main
rite the birth of the Śiśur Jâtaḥ, the holy child, in
the divine portion of it beyond the mystic rails.   In
early days, when sculpture had got no further in its
representation of a human being than a rude log or
rough piece of rock, food was selected as the most
appropriate emblem of this divine spiritual wisdom,
this food of the soul.

This will explain what follows.   When Buddha
was emaciated and almost dead with his terrible
fastings, a mystic woman, named Sujâtâ, appeared
upon the scene. She took the milk of a thousand
cows ; and skimming the cream seven times, she
boiled it with rice. It was placed in a golden pot, and,
lo and behold, prodigies—the outline of the Indian
cross (Swastika) and Krishṇa's St. Andrew's cross
(Śrîvatsa)—appeared on the surface. Sujâtâ with her
slave appeared before the failing devotee, and the
latter, ashamed of his nakedness in the presence of
the young girls, dug up the shroud of a slave recently

buried.   Buddha accepted the offering.   When he
had eaten the rice milk his body assumed a beauty
never known before.   From that time he was called
"the comely śramaṇa" (ascetic).   The gold pot was
thrown into the river; it floated up the stream against
the current.   A serpent king got possession of it.

The name of Sujâtâ ("of happy birth") is a very
thin disguise for the happy birth of the new Adam.
She is, of course, Dharma or Prajñâ, divine wisdom
personified as a woman.   That there may be no
mistake about this, a second episode in the Lalita
Vistara brings down Queen Mâyâ from heaven to
persuade her son to eat food.

It is said that Buddha after his long fast had his
skin loose as a camel, that his ribs pierced through
his poor skin and gave him the aspect of a crab.
How could this poor emaciated, fainting being be
called the handsome śramaṇa ?

In the Aitareya Brâhmaṇa it is announced that the
mystic marriage of the rice and milk each day in
the temple rites was designed to produce a "sacrificial
man," a spiritual double of the officiating priest, who
was able to visit the heaven of Indra, and obtain
cattle, propitious rain, and so on, for the worshippers.
This was the exoteric explanation ; but the esoteric
one is, I think, revealed in a Cingalese book, the
Sâmañña Phala Sutta.   Buddha details at consider-

G

able length the practices of the ascetic, and then
enlarges upon their exact object. Man has a body
composed of the four elements. It is the fruit of the
union of his father and mother. It is nourished on
rice and gruel, and may be truncated, crushed, destroyed. In this transitory body his intelligence is
enchained. The ascetic finding himself thus confined,
directs his mind to the creation of a freer integument.
He represents to himself in thought another body
created from this material body—a body with a form,
members, and organs. This body, in relation to the
material body, is like the sword and the scabbard, or
a serpent issuing from a basket in which it is confined. The ascetic, then, purified and perfected, commences to practise supernatural faculties. He finds
himself able to pass through material obstacles, walls,
ramparts, etc.; he is able to throw his phantasmal
appearance into many places at once; he is able to
walk upon the surface of water without immersing
himself; he can fly through the air like a falcon
furnished with large wings; he can leave this world
and reach even the heaven of Brahma himself.

Another faculty is now conquered by his force of
will, as the fashioner of ivory shapes the tusk of the
elephant according to his fancy. He acquires the
power of hearing the sounds of the unseen world as
distinctly as those of the phenomenal world—more

distinctly, in point of fact. Also by the power of
Manas he is able to read the most secret thoughts
of others, and to tell their characters. He is able to
say, "There is a mind that is governed by passion.
There is a mind that is enfranchised. This man has
noble ends in view. This man has no ends in view."
As a child sees his earrings reflected in the water,
and says, "Those are my earrings," so the purified
ascetic recognizes the truth. Then comes to him the
faculty of "divine vision," and he sees all that men
do on earth and after they die, and when they are
again reborn. Then he detects the secrets of the
universe, and why men are unhappy, and how they
may cease to be so.

The Lotus tells us that "at the moment of
death thousands of Buddhas show their faces to the
virtuous man." [1] This clairvoyance of Buddhism
seems very like the "discerning of spirits" recorded
by St. Paul. Professor Beal shows that the aureole,
adopted afterwards for saints in the Christian religion,
proceeded from an idea of the Buddhists that the
ascetic after practising *tapas* was supposed to be
furnished with an actual coruscation on his head. In
all Buddhist writings the double of Buddha, the
"glorified body," to use St. Paul's words, is described
as being exquisitely beautiful. I think the words,

[1] Lotus, p. 279.

" the handsome śramaṇa," must allude to this phantasmal appearance, and not to the visible body shrivelled and marred by long fastings.

Another important question is raised by the incident of Sujâtâ and her immortal food. The similarity of the religious rites of the Buddhists and Roman Catholics, processions, hymns, relic-worship, etc., have been often dwelt on. Dr. Rhys Davids himself has brought this prominently forward. But it must be remembered that Ceylon, with its non-God, has got these rites as well as Tibet and China. She has her Chakravartin, which Dr. Rhys Davids considers the same as the Christian Messiah. She has her "bread of life."[1] She has a "mystic sacrament in which the priest reverently swallows a material thing, and by so doing believes himself to become partaker, in some mysterious way, of a part of the Divine Being."[2] She has processions to the non-God, oblations to the non-God, hymns to the non-God, prayers asking the non-God to forgive sins. Once a year the non-God used to make a pompous journey from Anurâdhapura to a convent in the hills ; and all Ceylon threw itself in the dust before him. These are the paradoxes that send the casual student of Buddhism perfectly frantic. Under the hypothesis that the non-God was once deemed a God, these paradoxes may

---

[1] "Hibbert Lectures," p. 147.   [2] Ibid., p. 193.

be explained ; but Dr. Rhys Davids forbids any such explanation. It has been urged that the Buddhist rites were taken from the Christian rites, and Dr. Rhys Davids has given a qualified support to this view.[1] But this, in the case of Ceylon, only makes the puzzle still more excruciating. Who were the preternaturally acute missionaries who could persuade a nation to adopt fastings, penances, sacrifices, lenten retirements, all that is burdensome in religion without its promises and without its hopes ?

To reach the abode of Yama the Indian had to cross the Vaitaranî, the River of Death. This river became with Buddhists the Nairanjana, which ran past Buddha's tree. To cross this river and reach the "other bank," the heaven of the mind, was the object of the Buddhist baptism. Buddha plunges into the water. Before plunging in, he exclaims—

"I vow from this moment to deliver the world from the thraldom of death and the wicked one! I will procure salvation for all men, and conduct them to the 'other shore.' " But his strength has been so reduced by the penance of six years that he cannot reach it. When, lo! a spirit of the tree stretches forth a hand and assists him. In the Burmese version the tree itself bends down its branches as at the birth of the prince.

[1] "Buddhism," p. 207.

In the Lalita Vistara, Mâra opposes in person, and makes the bank grow higher as the prince tries to get out. There is a certain significance in an incident likewise of the Burmese version. On emerging, Buddha dons for the first time the holy yellow dress of the Muni.

The advantage of the Lalita Vistara, in my view, is that is a jumble of many schools of Buddhism piled the one on the top of the other. Each school has added its quantum and left the earlier matter still on its pages. In it Buddha bathes in the mystic Jordan of India, the Nairanjana. But a second narrative describes the gods and cherubs and nymphs of the sky coming down with vases and garlands and fans and umbrellas to perform the mystic abhisheka (baptism).[1] The great dome of heaven, glittering with many stars, is described as having become one vast chaitya,[2] or Buddhist temple. Vases of water of exquisite perfume are poured over the body of Buddha, and all that trickles down is seized eagerly by some of the spirits, for has it not touched his diamond body? In the Gospel of the Infancy many miracles are done with water that has bathed the infant Jesus. I will here give the rite of Buddhist baptism (abhisheka) when a novice is about to become a monk. It consists of many washings, borrowed plainly by the early Buddhists

---

[1] Page 351.   [2] Page 349.

from the Brahmins, and brings to mind the frequent use of water attributed to the Hemero baptists or disciples of John. It may be mentioned that in some Buddhist countries, Nepâl for instance, the various monkish vows are now taken only for form sake. This makes the letter, retained after the spirit has departed, all the more valuable.

The neophyte having made an offer of scents and unguents (betel-nut, paun, etc.) to his spiritual guide (guru), the latter, after certain formalities, draws four circles in the form of a cross in honour of the Tri-ratna (trinity) on the ground, and the neophyte, seated in a prescribed position, recites the following text: "I salute Buddha-nath, Dharma, and Sañgha, and entreat them to bestow upon me the Parivrajyâ Vrata." It is plain here that the prayer is addressed to the transcendental triad. The first and second day of the ceremonial are consumed in prayers and formalities carried on by the guide and his pupil alone ; on the second day another mystic cross is drawn upon the ground, called the " Swastika âsan." A pot containing water and other mystic ingredients, a gold lotus, and certain confections and charms, figures conspicuously in these early rites, and is at last poured on the neophyte's head. This is the baptism.

The abbot, or head of the vihâra, now appears

upon the scene, and sprinkles four seers of rice and milk upon the head of the aspirant. This ceremony is repeated three times. The next day a barber makes a clean shave of the neophyte's head, leaving only the forelock. Previous to this, the latter has pledged himself to forsake intoxicating liquors, women, evil thoughts, pride; and promised not to injure any living creature. More washings take place, including a fresh baptism by four ecclesiastics of rank. It must be mentioned that a Buddhist baptism is preceded by a confession of sins and much catechising. The catechumen's name is changed after the baptism. He promises to devote his future life to the divine triad. The monks of rank then invoke a blessing on his head: "May you be as happy as he who dwells in the hearts of all, who is the Universal Soul, the Lord of all, the Buddha called Ratna Saṁbhava!"

The change is called the "whole birth;" and at one moment a light is kindled. The early Christians after initiation were called the "Illuminati." A solemn address is made to the triad individually— Buddha, whom "gods and men alike worship," who is apart from the world, "the quintessence of all good;" Dharma, who is the Prajñâ Pâramitâ, the mother, the guide to perfect wisdom and peace; and Sangha, the son. A mitre like the Mithraic cap is put on at one portion of the ceremonial. The ceremonies for

Buddha's new birth of water and the spirit must sound hollow indeed, now that nothing but form remains; but this form to an inquirer into early Buddhism has a special value.

In Tibet this baptism also exists. In Japan that excellent authority Mr. Pfoundes tells me that he has frequently seen neophytes being baptized, or sprinkled with water mixed with aromatic simples. Mr. Oung Gyce tells me that baptism is unknown in Southern Buddhism, although in Burmah they sometimes initiate the novice at the bank of a river, without sprinkling. This last seems a trace of it as having once existed, and so do the mighty tanks excavated in Ceylon. Wung Puh informs us that at Vaiśâlî, Buddha resided under a tree (the music-tree), and there delivered a Sûtra entitled " The baptism that rescues from life and death and confers salvation."[1]

There is also a second description of Buddha advancing to the tree of knowledge; and an abundance of mystic writing on the "way" that leads to it. This "way" was as favourite an expression with Buddha as with Christ. A vendor of kuśa-grass, named Swastika, gives him a wisp of that holy herbage. He makes a little seat of matting with it, and squats down under the holy pippala cross-legged. Dr. Rhys Davids

---

[1] Journ. As. Soc., vol. xx. p. 172.

states, erroneously, that the tree of knowledge of Buddha was the banian-tree, and this he does when translating a Life of Buddha which says distinctly that it was the aśwattha [1] (Pâli, assattha).

When Buddha was seated under the tree of knowledge, says the Lalita Vistara, the vast parasol of the Kosmos became visible, and the lapis-lazuli rim of the fields of the Buddhas.

Then through the air resounded heavenly voices singing this gâthâ :—

"Mine of Diamonds! Sacred Flag! Joy of the Three Worlds! O Good Report! Righteous Law-giver! Precious Triad! It is for him that this offering is made !"

The story delays a long time whilst Buddha sits under this tree upon the throne of knowledge. The serpent Muśalinda encircles him and covers his head, as seen in many sculptures, with its quintuple hood. The spirits from the lapis-lazuli fields of the Buddhas are constantly around him, chanting songs of triumph :—

> "He hath o'erthrown the flag of Pride,
> He hath obtained the Triple Knowledge !
> The aggregations of the seen world
> Give place to the aggregations of the unseen world !
> The King of Physicians,
> With his heavenly Amṛita,

---

[1] "Birth Stories," p. 14.

Will dull all human pain,
And lead all flesh to Nirvâna.
Having entered the City of Omniscience
And become one with all the Buddhas,
He is now indivisible!"

But the legions of the Wicked One have also been around him ; and now they have planned a terrible ordeal. His third great temptation is to be with women.

At once the pretty crew come round Buddha, and they show him the thirty-two sorceries of woman.

"What are the thirty-two sorceries of woman ?" These are forthwith detailed by the pious chronicler.

Some pressed forwards veiling half the face. Some showed the tiny pearly "garland" of their teeth. Some "yawned," and in the action threw aloft arms conspicuous for very graceful dimples at the elbow. Some showed lips red as the fruit bimba. This one smiling, showed a very lustrous pair of eyes half closed. The fine muslin of this one exposed a portion of her bosom. The next beauty, proud of her waist, had gathered up her transparent tissues of fine silk so that the golden girdle could be seen. One sorceress made her ankle bangles jingle. Some show on their breasts beautiful flowers, and some on their arms and heads jays and patraguptas. Some throw sidelong glances at Buddha. Some make their golden waist-girdles glitter by imperceptible movement. Some walk and laugh with their companions, as if they had forgotten all about the holy man, and then had suddenly remembered him. Some giggle, and then blush with pretty shame. Some are rather loud in their joy. Some dance. Some sing. Some expose arms perfumed with priceless essences. Some show the fine lines of the cheek adorned with a sparkling little earring. Some, proud of unusual beauty, completely veil the head and face, and only allow Buddha the hastiest little peep. Some seem very young girls. Some seem wives who have not yet been mothers. The beauty of some is of a more mature and matronly type. One suddenly marches boldly up to him and throws fresh flowers at his feet, and then looks inquiringly into his face to see if she can guess his thought—that face calm as the lotus, sturdy as an elephant, immovable as Mount Meru.

The pretty demons then begin to dance, and sing gâthâs as pretty as themselves :—

> " Beautiful spring is the soft season of the year ;
> The trees are peopled with Kokilas and peacocks,
> Swans sing upon the waters.
> Nature is glad in the springtide,
> Men and women rejoice.
> Thy lustrous body, O Prince, is peerless,
> Endowed with the thirty-two signs.
> Around thee are daughters of gods ;
> They shine with a lustre not of earth ;
> Their march is like the swan, soft and proud ;

They are thy slaves!
A man once found a priceless treasure,
He threw it away!
That man was a madman;
Be not like him, O Prince!"

Buddha gazes at them calm and unabashed. He then replies to the demon crew in the following gâthâs :—

"Appetites gather together many miseries,
Lust is insatiable ;
It is like the thirst of a man that has drunk sea-water,
It grows and grows!
Your bodies are beautiful,
But the water-bubble is tinged with many exquisite colours ;
You are illusions, sickly dreams!
This truth I have been bitterly taught.
The human body is like the fruit of a malady,
Impure, filled with fetid humours ;
It is a mechanism of pains,
A mechanism of blood and vapour and filthy issues.
He who has women for slaves himself is not free.
My soul is awakened ;
Human joys and woes to me are one ;
The heart of the Victorious One (Jina)
Is calm as the vault of heaven !"

In strophe and antistrophe this poetic operetta runs on. It is now the turn of the demons :—

"Austerities are for the aged,
The self-tortures of the Muni for those whose span of life is
drawing to a close.
Prince! thou art young,
Disease and age have not yet approached thee,
Thy body is peerless ;
Thou mayst be king,
The lord of the kings of the earth!"

The man with the calm of the white lotus answers :—

"I will be king
  Away in the sun's pure realms,
  My subjects my disciples,
  And the myriad sons of those who are not my disciples.
  In the presence of the pleasures of the Kingdom of Righteousness
  Pleasures of the senses are dull.
  I march along the pathway that leads to the city exempt from fear."

The chorus of demons reply in less confident tones :—

" Proud lord and pure of heart,
  Thou hast conquered the world,
  Thou hast conquered Mâra,
  Quarrels, hatred, corruption, and the shedding of blood :
  But in the bright skies,
  Indra, the king, and all the gods
  Do not contemn our smiles ;
  Indra is girt with beautiful apsarases,
  But none so fair as we !
  Cast off that sour grimace of the Muni ;
  Thy face is like the lotus,
  Let it light up in smiles !
  Bees hum in the noontide,
  Kokilas sing and the trees are rich with leaves,
  The grass is green and velvety,
  The wood is haunted by the Buddhas [lit. first of men].
  Repay our love ;   .
  Wherefore have we offended thee ? "

Buddha replies :—

" The bees hum because they hunger and thirst,
  Flowers and leaves are due to the domination of the seasons,
  The most beautiful body
  Is the home of a family of worms

In the cities of the gods,
In the cities of the asuras,
In the cities of man,
Are the miseries of unrest.
I go to the city where fears are not,
And will give supreme happiness to creatures with souls, and
creatures without souls."

The words of Buddha filled the beautiful spirits with shame and penitence. That one so holy should gaze so calmly at wicked spirits filled them with astonishment. Without passion and without pursing the eyebrow he had so gently reproved them. These penitent Magdalens kissed his feet with very shame, and went away filled with a novel joy.

They thus addressed Mâra :—

"Father, he speaks gently to all, and surveys us as calmly as he
surveys the mighty mysteries of the heavens !
He believes that the sin of unchastity has very far-reaching effects ;
He is like Mount Meru, unassailable !
Father, it was no conflict, no quarrel between us ;
He was kind and gentle.
All beings that have a soul, and all beings that have no soul, the
tree spirits, the mountain spirits, the gods, the Yakshas, and
Garudas, fall down before him.
Father, change sides in the conflict ;
His mercy is immeasurable !
Those that are against him he overthrows them not,
He uproots not those who will not turn from evil ;
His patience is for all,
And he will not do anything to cause pain to any sentient thing !"

When the demons had left Buddha, it is recorded that bright spirits came and comforted him.

But the Wicked One has by no means given up the

battle. He debates with his companions in the realms of darkness. Again he accosts Buddha :—

"I am the lord of desire, I am the master of this entire world. Gods and men and beasts have all fallen into my power. Thou art in my domain. I charge thee, leave that tree and speak to me!"

"If thou art the lord of appetite," replies Buddha, "thou art not the prince of light. I am the lord of the kingdom of righteousness. Forsake the way of evil."

"Ascetic," said the Wicked One, "what you seek is not easy to attain. Bhrigu and Angiras by many austerities sought emancipation and failed to find it."

The introduction of the names of two of the seven Rishis of the Vedas is to be noticed.

The Wicked One draws a sword from its scabbard, and thunders out in a menacing voice, "Rise up as I order. Obey me, or like a green reed thou shalt be cut in pieces."

At the same time the spirits of darkness hurl mountains and flames and mighty trees at Buddha. Globes of fire dart through the air, and huge masses of iron, and terrible javelins tipped with a deadly poison. From the four corners of heaven the turmoil rages, and huge monsters are summoned from the vast abyss beneath the earth.

With majestic calmness, Buddha views all these

demon hostilities as a sickly dream, as illusion. By the aid of his guardians of the unseen world, the bolts launched against him are turned into beautiful flowers.

In the most solemn manner, Buddha then calls to Brahma Prajâpati, lord of creatures, and to his heavenly host, to "all the Buddhas that live at the ten horizons." He smites the ground, and earth reverberates like a huge vessel of brass. His prayer is, "Disperse this inky crew!"

Immediately the horses and chariots and elephants of the demon army are tumbled into the mud and the mighty warriors dispersed. They fly like birds before a blazing forest. The Wicked One himself is haggard, immensely aged, depressed, overcome. A spirit of the immortal tree takes compassion upon him, and restores him with consecrated water.

"Because I refused to listen to the wise words of my daughters, and opposed this pure being, misery has been my lot, and fear and humiliation. Cursings and contempt have come upon me by mine own seeking."

The Tibetan version is the only one that records this baptism and conversion of the Wicked One.

I must notice here a variorum reading from Mr, Turnour's Cingalese biography, the Maduratthavilâsinî. Brahma is also introduced into the conflict, but he flies away in abject terror with his umbrella of dominion in his hand, and throws it down on the

H

confines of the Chakravâla.[1] But this low comedy
business of Brahma with his umbrella really lets in a
great deal of light. The umbrella is the emblem of
God and the permanent heavens, and the symbol of
supreme dominion. The paragraph is plainly a later
addition, for two paragraphs further on occurs this
passage :—

"The great mortal, as if he were Mahâ Brahma
himself, alone retained his station."

I think it will scarcely be contended that the picture
we get in the Lalita Vistara of Buddha, with copper
feet, seated on a jewelled throne with the serpent
Muśalinda, and its five hoods acting as what is
called a snake-canopy (ahi kshetra) over him, is a
piece of pure history. It belongs to that part of the
narrative which, I contend, is an idealized description
of Buddha's life as read by the ritual of the temple.
But as such it is most valuable, as it gives an antiquity to the modern Buddhist rites, and also to the
hymns that the worshippers, disguised as Devas, chant
to him. It must be remembered that the Southern
narratives, as well as the Northern ones, have the lion
throne, the serpent Muśalinda, and the various details
that can only refer to Buddha's life as read by temple
rites. Dr. Rhys Davids's version also mentions the
hymns, but does not give them. As it is, as I shall

---

[1] Pâli Buddhistical Annals, Journal Beng. As. Soc., vol. vii. p. 812.

show, confessedly an abridgment of other narratives, this evidence is important. The sacramental nature of the rice and milk after it had been offered to Buddha, was as plainly the early teaching as well as the latest. Sujâtâ's slave, in Dr. Rhys Davids's version, sees a golden Buddha under a tree, and takes him for the tree deva. Before Sujâtâ makes her offering, a mighty bell like the usual temple-bell sounds through the Kosmos.

This struggle of Buddha with Mâra and his daughters has been thought by some to be only a veiled account of the dramatized conflict which constituted the ancient "lesser mysteries." These gnomes and pantomime divinities have reached our day, and M. Foucaux points out that even on the sculptures of the old Gothic cathedrals their presence is to be noticed. The refused crown was said to be a prominent rite in initiations at the Bloodless Altar of Mithras. Also in the days of Wieshaupt and the Illuminati of Germany a striking scene was enacted. The novice, who had been brought in blindfolded, was shown an altar on which was a sceptre and crown, some gold pieces, and some valuable jewels. Above was a picture of the "Founder of Illuminism"—an Ecce Homo that was solemnly unveiled.

"Here are the attributes of virtue," cried the Grand Master; "here are the attributes of tyranny. Choose!"

It was explained to the aspirant that the masked
brothers around were quite competent to push his
career for him in court or camp. It was explained
also to him that the aim of the society, "the Family
of the Human Race," was very far-reaching, and
exacted extremes of devotion and self-denial.   It
was directed against all despotism and class privileges,
secular and religious.[1]   By many writers, hostile and
friendly, the French Revolution has been traced to
this curious and powerful German movement. The
late Duke of Sussex, a profound student of Freemasonry, is said to have declared that, if its real
secrets were known, every throne in Europe would
totter.

But before ideas are represented in pantomimes
and miracle-plays, they exist in matter-of-fact experience.   Buddha in the wilderness of Uravilva
could scarcely have had a dramatic troupe around
him.   And these visions of the fasting ecstatic are
singularly alike in all ages.   St. Anthony, a rich man,
was induced by an inner voice to abandon all his
wealth and go off to the desert in Egypt.   The
"devil" urged him to take up a life of wealth once
more.   He retired to an "old sepulchre," and for
years lived on a little bread and salt, and drank
nothing but water.   Phantom women tempted him

---

[1] Victor Huriot, "Mystères des Sociétés Secrètes."

like Buddha. The legions of hell assailed him, and a voice from heaven comforted him when the victory was won.

He gives these curious instructions about the "discerning of spirits" in the visions of the mystic :—

"The sight of good angels provokes no disturbance in the mind ; the sight of bad angels throws the soul into a painful disquiet."[1]

The solitaries of the early Christian movement held language, as Dr. Rhys Davids shows, very like the language of Buddhism, and he cites the following from St. Jerome :—

"O desert blooming with the flowers of Christ ! O solitude in which are found those stones of which the City of the Great King is built in the Apocalypse ! O loneliness delighting in intercourse with God ! What do you, brother, in secular life ?—you, who are greater than the world ? How long shall the shadows of roofs oppress you ? How long shall the prison-house of smoky cities enclose you ? Believe me, I know not how much more light I gaze on. It is well, having cast off the burthen of the body, to fly off to the pure effulgence of the sky.

"Do you fear poverty ? Christ called the poor blessed. Do you dread labour ? No athlete is crowned without sweat. Do you think of diet ?

---

[1] Migne, "Dictionnaire d'Ascètes," *sub voce* "S. Antoine."

Faith fears not hunger. Do you fear to lay your
body, wasted with fasting, on the naked ground?
The Lord will lie down with you. Do you shrink
from the undressed hair of a neglected head? Your
head is Christ. Are you fearful of the boundless
extent of the solitude? You mentally walk in paradise. As often as you ascend thither in contemplation
you will not be in solitude." [1]

We have now come to a point in the reformer's life
in which it is necessary to give a sketch of the creed
he professed to reform.

[1] "Hibbert Lectures," p. 169.

CHAPTER VI.

THE HIGHER BRAHMINISM.

IT is recorded in the Atharva Veda that Śaunaka, a wealthy householder, having interrogated the great Rishi Angiras, was informed by him that there were two sorts of knowledge, the "superior knowledge" and the "inferior knowledge."

The superior knowledge was handed jealously down in certain "mystery" treatises called Upanishads. This is the interpretation of the title given by Pânini. Śankara calls these Upanishads, "knowledge of Brahma," the great Spirit of the Universe.[1] They were also called Tree Mysteries (Âraṇyakas), because they were whispered to initiates in a forest. "Know Brahma alone," was the motto of this secret wisdom summed up in a word, says Rajah Rammohun Roy, citing the Muṇḍaka Upanishad of the Atharva Veda.

The initiation into the higher wisdom was called

---

[1] Rajah Rammohun Roy, "Translation of the Veds," p. 27.

Yoga (Union). The novice had to commence his initiation as a servant-pupil of a Yogi.

After a preliminary fast, an auspicious day must be chosen. The novice must bathe, and then present himself to his teacher. He must bring with him an offering of betel-nut, white raiment, and the humble money of the Indian poor. He must take in his hands a small copper dish with some water in it, and place upon it a plantain, some flowers, some sesamum, some kuśa-grass, and some rice. In these words he must then demand a mystic incantation :—

"For the removal of all my sins, and to obtain happiness after death, I take the incantation from my guru."[1]

As with Roman Catholics, a patron saint is then selected for the novice. The guru then presents a burnt offering to the deva whose name has been selected. He then whispers thrice in the right ear of the novice the incantation (Vîja mantra). It is a monosyllable, with the initial consonant of the name of the god, and a final "a" or "oo." Thus Krishna would be "Kra" or "Kroo." The novice then presents a fee to the guru.

The phenomena of obsession, trance, catalepsy, extasia, had much to do with all early religious rites. This is specially patent in the rites of the Indian

[1] I take these details from Ward's "Hindoos," ii. 253.

novice. From this moment the novice would have to consider his guru an incarnation of the patron deity. He would have to treat him like an idol on its shrine, to worship his feet, and to present to him the sweet-meats and cloths and flowers and fruits that are presented to Krishna. When he washes the guru's feet he must drink the water, for has it not touched the sacred feet of Krishna himself?

In all this we have relics of the old ancestor worship, which was the early Âryan faith. Anthropologists are showing us that with savage races the dead are more feared than the living. A holy man dies, or a chief, and the house that he lived in whilst on earth is made his home when he has left the earth. In wintry Bactria the cave and the chamber of a rude tumulus were the first poor shelters that the savage man devised against the frost and snow. Houses in Central Asia preserve this form to this day, and when a peasant wishes to shelter a cow for the night he makes a hasty chamber with boughs or stones, and erects a tumulus over it with earth or dust. Within the memory of people still alive, a similar tumulus has been used as a dwelling in the Isle of Skye and the Lewis. This rude tumulus, under the name of chattra (the Kosmos under the symbol of umbrella), became the great temple of India.

The phenomena of obsession explain, I think, the

development. A Rishi, or prophet potent in magic, dwelling in a rude cave or tumulus, dies. He is buried in the cave or the tumulus. Another Rishi, practising yoga at the dead man's grave, becomes obsessed by the departed saint, and exhibits the usual phenomena of fortune-telling, clairvoyance, magnetic healing. Little by little the grave becomes a holy place, and the bones of the saint priceless treasures. The fame of the dead Rishi spreads and spreads until he becomes a Râma or Krishna. Three thousand years ago Zarathustra accused the Indian Âryas, the "worshippers of Daevas," of summoning spirits in a cemetery (dakhma),[1] and after a lapse of three thousand years the dead Krishna or Râma is still believed to obsess the holy anchorite.

The novice is being instructed in yoga. This word signifies "union." It has got to mean magic, extasia, the knowledge of the mysteries of the kingdom of heaven. In the old religions magic and mystic studies were inseparable. The adept is called Brahmajnâni (he who knows Brahma).[2]

Mr. Ward gives the magical training of the Yoga-yug from the Pâtanjala Darśana and the Goraksha Samgîti. The novice must squat down cross-legged, in the conventional attitude of the images of Buddha.

---

[1] Avesta. Farg. vii. 137–139.
[2] Wilson, "Vishnu Purâna," p. 652, note.

He must then learn to stop his breathing. To assist him in this, a piece of cloth, fifteen cubits long and four fingers in breadth, must be forced into the throat and kept there as long as possible. After sips of water the process must be repeated. He must sit under a tree, near a natural linga stone, not a carved one. He must sit on the holy kuśa-grass, or the skin of a tiger or deer. His back, neck, and head must be exactly erect. He must remain motionless, keeping his eyes fixed on his nose. The act of yoga consists of several parts. The novice must with his fingers and thumbs and feet prevent the air from issuing through his eyes, ears, nostrils, mouth, or other avenue. This he must practise until by degrees he is able to exist without inspiration or respiration. He who is thus far perfected will be able to subdue his passions, and to disrelish all the pleasures of the senses. He must bear in mind that life is a dream, and that all earthly things are in essence vain. He must try to gain the state of samâdhi, or mystic trance, by the reflection that God is all in all. As Krishna tells Arjuna, he must be like the tortoise, able to restrain his members. To him, as to that lethargic animal, " pleasure and pain, gold, iron and stones," must be as one.[1]

" Know holy wisdom to be the same with yoga,"

[1] For these details, see Ward, vol. ii.

says Yâjnyavalkya. " That which is termed yoga is the union of the living with the Supreme Soul.[1]   To attain this happy result the five states of yama must be mastered.

Wilson's description of these, taken chiefly from the Vishṇu Purâṇa, gives us practically the same process described by Ward.   The suspension of the act of breathing is assisted by pinching the nostrils, and not by using a cloth.   Silent mantras (incantations) must be used.   The mystical syllable A. U. M., the invocation to the earlier Indian triad, is considered the most efficacious of these.[2]   The novice must fix his mind first of all on the visible form of his guardian deity.   He must try and conjure up an avatâra of the Supreme God imaged as a man, the Brahmâ as distinguished from Brahma, or pure Spirit. He must conceive him as the sun, the moon, the shining stars, the mountains, the rivers, the trees ; clothe him, in fact, in the visible Kosmos.   He must conceive him as the great legion of gods, and of the one-footed, two-footed, many-footed conscious or un-conscious creatures.   The universal world is pervaded by God.

When the mind of the novice is sufficiently clarified from the grosser deposits, he may begin to meditate

[1] Wilson, " Vishṇu Purâṇa," p. 652, note.
[2] See Colebrooke, i. 251.

on the formless Brahma. The Supreme, for the
ignorant, clothes himself from time to time with the
bodies of mortals. These avatâras are concessions to
mortal weaknesses. But it must be patent to the
higher wisdom that the universal spirit can never be
actually confined in a limited envelope. It is the
formless, omnipresent, all-pervading Brahma that the
adept, or Brahmajnâni, must study. That god, seated
in the heart, burns out sin as fire blazing in the wind
consumes dry grass.

The process of the Samâdhi, or dreamy entrance-
ment, is a little whimsical. At first the vulgar eidolon
of the god must be always in the mind of the novice,
" whether he be going or standing, or be engaged in
any other voluntary act." Hari, "with smooth cheeks
and a broad, brilliant forehead," must be in his
imagination ; Hari, with four arms and with splendid
earrings ; Hari, with a painted neck and the Srîvatsa,
or St. Andrew's cross, on his breast ; Hari, with a
" belly falling in graceful folds ; " Hari, with mystic
shell, mace, quoit, and bow. But by-and-by the
mystic dreamer will be visited by less anthropomorphic conceptions. He will meditate on the mystic
symbols alone—the shell, the chakra, etc., until at
length his enfranchised mind will be able to conceive
the Supreme Spirit quite detached from matter.

The invaluable missionary Ward gives an account

of a hermitage such as our novice might have dwelt
in, on the holy island of Sâgara, at the mouth of the
Ganges. The Englishman went there in the year
1806. Two followers of Râma were practising yoga
in the jaṅgal. Near them were two huts stoutly built,
as Sâgara swarms with tigers. A rope was round
the waist of each, supporting an apron of the bark of
the plaintain-tree. Each squatted on an antelope's
skin, and wore his hair in a " large bunch at the top
of his head." One of these, interrogated by the
missionary, announced that he was full of joy and
calm. If he had food it was well ; if not, he contented
himself with the name of Râma. Some good water
from a rude well near was given to the guest. He
offered the Brahmajnâni a rupee. The latter asked
very pertinently what he was to do with it. Close by
was a shrine of Kapila. This philosopher has long
ago been promoted to the rank of one of the seven
great Ṛishis, or prophets, of India. His festival is
at the end of the year, as he is the guardian spirit of
the Ganges. It is on a scale of great magnificence.
Pilgrims from all parts of India hurry to it in flocks.
Gaṅgâ losing itself in the mighty ocean, is plainly a
proper symbol of the soul being merged into the
eternal Brahma. The pilgrims bathe in the sea, and
many are drowned. The legend is that the solar
horse, when loosened by King Sâgara, wandered to the

mystic cavern of the unseen world. Sixty thousand
sons of the king starting off in pursuit, found it in
those shadowy regions. Seeing also the Rishi Kapila
performing yoga near it, they accused him of stealing
it. The lambent flame from his head immediately
reduced them all to ashes. Eventually the holy Rishi
was pacified, and the holy Ganges was given as a boon
to man. Washing over the bones of the sixty
thousand sons of Sâgara, that stream transported
them to heaven. Since that day millions of Hindoos
have died on its banks, for the boon given to the sons
of Sâgara has been promised also to them. As the
steamship from England glides by the cocoa-palms
and noble teak-trees, and the rich tangle of creepers
and ferns and parasite figs that choke with luxuriant
greenness the rich island of Sâgara, the passengers
are sure to meet some of these poor pilgrims gnawed
by vultures, floating away to the dim unknown.
Sâgara is also the title of the Bay of Bengal.

Mr. Ward adds interesting details regarding the
little hermitage at the island of Sâgara. The adepts
are constantly killed by tigers ; indeed, the number
of pilgrims, recluses, etc., that thus perish annually
is stated to be enormous. Twitted with tempting
Providence, the Brahmajnâni replied that Providence
had given the tiger the instinct to prey upon the flesh
of man. One recluse had held his left arm above his

head for three years. It was perfectly stiff, and the
finger-nails were as long as the claws of a bird of
prey. As early as the Mahâbhârata, holy men swung
supported by hooks in their backs, pierced their
tongues and sides, danced on fire, threw themselves
on spikes. These practices still continue all over
India.[1] It is a manifest perversion of the mystic
dreaming of God.

Mr. Ward relates that, whilst he was in India, an
Englishman came across what "seemed to be a
human being,"[2] in the thick jungle of the delta of the
Ganges. The Englishman, I think with much inhu-
manity, "beat this lump of animated clay until the
blood came," but the ascetic, for it was an ascetic,
uttered no cry and seemed completely indifferent.
The Englishman, astonished, appealed to his native
servants, who told him the man must be a yogi. The
Englishman carried him home, and fed him for a time,
and then the servants grew weary of him. He was
transferred to the house of a Brahmin, and certain
wild young men played tricks upon him, tempting
him with impure females, etc., but no ill-usage could
ruffle for a moment his dreamy lethargy. The
Brahmin also grew tired of his guest, and started him
off in a boat to Benares. One evening when the
ascetic went on shore a marvel occurred. A shining

[1] Ward, vol. ii. p. 24.   [2] Ibid., p. 378.

Ṛishi suddenly appeared and embraced the poor friendless one. Both disappeared, and left no traces behind them. "This story," says Mr. Ward, "is universally credited among the Hindoos in the neighbourhood of Calcutta."[1]

In hymns of the Ṛig-Veda, said by Max Müller to have been composed at least three thousand years ago, we learn that the Ṛishi Ṛibhu retired to a forest, to perform penance and gain wisdom.[2] Yama, too, the Indian Adam, we are told, "conversed with gods under a leafy tree." Century after century has rolled away, yet still the Indian yogi, clad in his poor bark, squats on his deerskin, and calmly watches the panorama of history pass on before him. He has seen the early cattle-lifters and bowmen of the Five Rivers. He has seen Alexander clad in shining mail, and Nadir Shah smeared all over with diamonds and blood. He has seen the great noses and great cocked hats of great Wellington and great Napier. He has seen Aśoka the tolerant, Râma the loving, and the great Tathâgatha, Buddha himself. Gods and creeds and philosophies he has imagined in his mystic reverie, and scattered them broadcast amongst the nations of the earth. Calmly he squats on the antelope's skin, like John in his raiment of camel's hair.

---

[1] Ward, vol. ii. p. 378. [2] Ṛig-Veda, i. 7, 24.

CHAPTER VII.

THE LOWER BRAHMINISM.

FEW suspect how much in religion grew out of an early and necessarily crude cosmology. The ancients believed, at the date of Homer, that the earth was a vast flat circular plain, bounded by an immeasurable sea. They believed with the Indians that the heavens were a solid umbrella on which the stars were fixed. The sun was seen every morning to rise out of the earth and give light to the world ; it was seen every evening to sink again into the earth : whence it was concluded that for twelve hours it was buried in the bowels of the earth. This gave rise to many myths, as winter was also conceived as one long night. The Egyptian Osiris was buried in a box, the earth, during this rayless period, and then he rose again. Plainly also, if the organs of sense could be trusted, the mighty umbrella to which the stars were nailed revolved. But to this law there was a palpable exception—the pole-star, the α of Draco, and indeed the companion stars of the same constellation. They were fixed, immovable. The remainder of heaven was movable. This immovable portion of the sky became the eternal heaven of theology, and earth's bowels the region of gloom and death and expiation. I must mention that the seven large stars of the Great Bear were also visible all night ; in consequence they became the Seven Rishis, or Great Prophets. Each Rishi had his cohort of followers in his star ; hence the seven heavens. I must now show the influence of the stars on the Indian religion. In Vedic days this consisted in the worship of the Twelve Âdityas, or months. The great goddess Nature, or Aditî, was imaged as the year, and her sons were the twelve gods.

"They [the Brahmins] have always observed the order of the gods as they are to be worshipped in the twelvemonth," says the Rig-Veda.[1]

"The year is Prajâpati [the Divine Man]," says the Aitareya Brahmana.[2]

"Thou dividest thy person in twelve parts," says a hymn of the Mahâbhârata to the divinity, "and thou becomest the Twelve Âdityas."[3]

The "God in twelve persons" is another expression from the same poem.

"These pillars, ranging in rows like swans, have

[1] Rig-Veda, vii. 103.   [2] Haug, vol. ii. p. 6.   [3] Vana Parva, v. 189.

come to us erected by pious Ṛishis to the East. They proceed resplendent on the path of the gods." [1]

The Sanscrit word for an upright unhewn monolith is "stambha." The same word was used later on for the temporary "posts" erected during a horse sacrifice. A monolith is also called "Mahâdeo" (Great God), even in modern times. A controversy arose a few years ago as to whether the Indians knew anything of the zodiac before 500 or 600 A.D. This is too large a subject to enter into here. Suffice to say, that as early as the hymns of the Ṛig-Veda they worshipped the Twelve Âdityas, or twelve months personified. Sir John Lubbock, in his "Prehistoric Times," is inclined to think that the cromlech, or circle of twelve stones representing the months, chiefly distinguished the stone or earliest age of the megalithic monuments. He instances the two inner circles of Abury, the lesser circle of Stennis, and a circle of Stanton Drew, all belonging to the stone age, and consisting of twelve stones.[2] This brings us to the Indian cultus at the date of Buddha.

Of what nature was it? If we accept Lassen's chronology on the subject, the non-Vaishṇava portions of the Mahâbhârata may be accepted as a fair guide here. It will give us a sketch of the creed

---

[1] Translated by Max Müller, from Ṛig-Veda, iii. 8.
[2] Page 117.

that existed in India when the Buddhist movement occurred.

Readers of that epic must be astonished, on first perusing it, to find no mention of temples. Forests with Rishis, or prophets, dwelling in them, and performing the initiation of yoga under trees, are mentioned in almost every episode ; but even in the long descriptions of sumptuous towns, religious edifices seem conspicuous chiefly by their absence. Alongside of the Rishis and their forests, there is, however, the Tîrtha. What is a Tîrtha? Our lexicographers tell us that it is a sacred tank. Colonel Tod, who studied natives all his life amongst natives, calls it a shrine. At any rate, the Tîrtha was of dominant importance in the ancient religion, for we read thus of it : " It is the greatest mystery of the Rishis, excellent son of Bharata. The holy pilgrimage to the Tîrthas is more important than sacrifices to the gods." [1]

In another verse it is stated that five nights' sojourn at the Tîrtha of Jambumârya is equal to the fruit of a horse sacrifice.[2] The horse sacrifice was the most important of Âryan rites. A hundred performances of it raised the sacrificer to the level of Indra, the Supreme.

Assisted by the Mahâbhârata, let us try and make

---

[1] Mahab. Vana Parva, v. 4059.   [2] Ibid., v. 4083.

out what was a Tîrtha. Without doubt pilgrims bathed there : "May the pilgrim bathe, O son of Bharata, in all the Tîrthas." [1]

Illustrious saints resided in Tîrthas, the dead as well as the living. [2] Kapila has his Tîrtha, the Rishi Matanga, [8] the Saint Bhrigu. [4]

"Go where the greatest Rishis Valmîki and Kaśyapa, Kundajathara, the son of Atri, Viśvâmitra, and Gautama, Asita Devala, Mârkandeya and Gâlava, Bharadwâja and the Solitary Vaśishtha, Uddâlaka, Śaunaka, and his son Vyâsa, the greatest of ascetics, Durvâsas, the most virtuous of anchorites, Jâvâli, of the terrible macerations ; go where these, the greatest of saints, rich in penances, are waiting for thee." [5]

To gods, to dead saints, to ancestors, rites were performed in Tîrthas. "The shining hero [Bhishma]," it says in one passage, "feasted the ancestors, the gods. He feasted the Rishis after the manner laid down in the Śâstras." [6] All these passages occur in the book of the Mahâbhârata where King Yudhishthira, the eldest of the five sons of Pâṇḍu, is enjoined to make a round of pilgrimages to the Tîrthas.

We have shown that Tîrthas were places of pilgrimage with tanks. They were also shrines of dead saints. Does this mean that they were stone circles

---

[1] Mahab. Vana Parva, v. 4074.
[2] Vana Parva, v. 8056.
[8] Ibid., v. 8079.
[4] Ibid., v. 8234.
[5] Ibid., vv. 8262 et seq.
[6] Ibid., v. 4035.

and sepulchral mounds like the Stennis stones in Orkney, like Abury, like Stonehenge ?

I think this question must be answered in the affirmative for the following reasons :—

1. The Western Âryas, the Norsemen, Goths, etc., invariably used the stone circles and the sepulchral mound (haug) for worship and also for burial.

2. In many parts of India these circles and mounds are still used by sections of the Hindoos, as an interesting set of papers by Dr. Stevenson in the *A. S. Journal* has shown.

3. These two institutions figure very prominently in Buddhism. And when one religion breaks away from another, it may make many changes, but must be credited with having retained a large number of the institutions of its parent creed. To dispose of the dead is a pressing need. This is scarcely the point at which a religious reformer would begin.

I think also that there are passages in the Mahâbhârata that bear me out :—

" When King Suhotra governed this globe according to the laws of justice, columns of sacrifice and sacred trees were planted about the surface of the earth [jalonnaient la terre—Fauche] in hundreds of thousands. They shone every season with an abundant harvest of men and grains." [1]

[1] Mahab. Adi Parva, v. 3717.

"He offered then, O most virtuous son of Bharata, an hundred solemn sacrifices, bidding gods and Brahmins. There were columns of sacrifice in precious stones and chaityas [sepulchral mounds] of gold." [1]

"The Long-Haired God gave by thousands and millions columns of sacrifice and chaityas of great splendour." [2]

It seems to me that these columns of sacrifice planted about by hundreds of thousands must be our standing stones. Professor Whitney publishes the translation of a Vedic hymn which shows that in the early days the body was buried without cremation :—

> "Forth from about thee thus I build away the ground,
> As I lay down the clod may I receive no harm ;
> This *pillar* may the Fathers here maintain for thee,
> May Yama there provide thee with a dwelling." [3]

The sacred tree considered in the light of a shrine and place of worship is also prominent in the Mahâbhârata. Indeed, the word chaitya, usually applied to a sepulchral mound, is also used to designate the tree. "A tree, in fact, spread with leaves and fruits, if it be solitary in a village, becomes a venerable chaitya, without successors, honoured with the offerings of all." [4] In the narrative of which

---

[1] Mahab. Sabha Parva, v. 69.

[2] Ibid., v. 74.

[3] Rig-Veda, x. 18, cited from Whitney's "Oriental and Linguistic Studies," 1st series, p. 55.

[4] Adi Parva, v. 5913.

I am going to quote a passage, superstitious importance is plainly attached to it; for the heroes,
when they find themselves in an enemy's city, at
once run and demolish the sacred tree, probably to
annul the charms and hostile influences of their
enemy's household gods and patron saints :—

"Then they [Krishna, Bhîma, and Dhananjaya]
rushed upon the splendid chaitya of the inhabitants
of Magadha, and smote it on the crest as they wished
to smite Jarâsandha.

"And with the blows of their great arms they felled
that ancient tree, vast, firmly rooted, with airy top,
respected by all, and ever honoured with incense and
garlands." [1]

The sacred tree was plainly an important accom-
paniment of the Tîrthas, for it figures in the description of those that Yudhishṭhira was advised by the
Brahmins to visit.

"Where, as Brahmins tell, was born that Indian
fig-tree of which the cause is eternal?" This was at
Gayâ.[2]

At Yamounâ too it is announced: "There is the
beautiful and the holy Tîrtha, named the Descent of
the Holy Fig Tree." [3]

From this we see that the pilgrimage, which after-

---

[1] Mahab. Sabha Parva, v. 816, 817.   [2] Vana Parva, v. 8307.
[3] Ibid., v. 8375.

wards became the chief method of extortion of the Brahmin priesthood, was in the first instance only means to an end. A great Ṛishi dies and is buried or cremated. Round his corpse or ashes some upright monoliths are erected; and a huge capstone, by mechanics unknown to moderns, is hoisted on the top of these. Here we have the dolmen, or stone sepulchral chamber; which is as conspicuous on the plains of India as at Karnac in Brittany or by Stennis Loch.

Over this dolmen was piled a mighty hemisphere of earth. Here we get at once the tope or chaitya of the Buddhists and early Brahmins, the Norse haug. The great Maes Howe in Orkney, the great Sanchi tope, the great sepulchral mound at Abury are kith and kin. And having built the palace of the dead Ṛishi or chief, it would of course be necessary to provide in some way for the wants of those that came to visit him and ask him favours. A supply of good water would be a first necessity. Thus large tanks would be prepared, which by-and-by would attain a special sanctity of their own, the dead Ṛishi communicating his power to the actual water. Then holy circles of monoliths would be set up round the chaitya of the Ṛishi. These, with a few big trees, would be required for the early worship. When Rajah Rammohun Roy published his strictures on the lower Brahminism, a Hindoo, a Professor in the Madras College, Senkara Sastri, published a remarkable letter in defence of his creed. He said that the higher wisdom has always been known in India by the term Adwaitam, the negation of dualism, the rejection of more than one first cause. The Supreme Being is pronounced by the old sacred writings to be infinite, eternal, self-intelligent, indivisible, pervading, universal, unalterable and almighty. But as minds of limited capacity cannot conceive such a being, "allegorical representations of his attributes" have been provided for these with the institutions of fastings, mysticism (yoga), the adoration of the divine avatâras, consecrated objects, etc. A similar principle, the learned Brahmin contests, has been adopted in Christianity, which, as he conceives it, has three Persons united yet occasionally distinguished, of whom Christ represents the attribute of mercy, and so on.[1]

This principle must be borne in mind in estimating the lower Brahminism. Its rites consisted in a worship of the great Spirit of the Universe, under her shifting aspects during the year's complete cycle. When the use of iron was unknown, these presentments took the form of vast monoliths, imposing, mystic, colossal. The numbers of these vast sentries

[1] Cited by Rajah Rammohun Roy, p. 131.

that were placed round the maṇḍala, or mystic circle, seems to have varied very much. At times they were regulated by the twenty-seven lunar asterisms and moon worship. At one period they were the twelve Âdityas, and represented the twelve months. It is patent that at one time the four cardinal points had a most important bearing on religious rites and theology. The hymns of the Ṛig-Veda give us the early worship of these vast monoliths, the great stone gods of our ancestors the Âryas. When winter was over, radiant Agni was hymned. He represented spring, the new year. In murky autumn the terrible Rudra, the god of the Indian typhoon, came in for a homage in which fear predominated. And the phenomena of the sun's daily journey found illustration, as well as the phenomena of his yearly journey. Dawn was hymned as pretty Ushas, with her golden hair. The cloud riven by lightning was the demon Vṛitra, smitten with the terrible vajra (thunderbolt) of Indra.

But symbolism is easily misunderstood by the vulgar. These personified attributes quickly changed into a legion of powerful divinities, whom the priest and his sacrifices alone could propitiate. And by-and-by the worship dethroned the god. The lower Brahminism became, not the machinery of worship, but the worship of machinery. The creed became flat atheism. God became useless, the Brahmin powerless, the ceremonial all in all. It was recorded that, by accurate and repeated ceremonial rites, Indra had raised himself to the position of Supreme God. The creation of the world was figured as the fruit of a sacrifice. Râvaṇa, a foul fiend, by putting this machinery in motion was able to defy for a time the whole host of heaven, and could only be dethroned by a quibble, an alleged error in his rites. Over gods and priests and starry systems was an unintelligent Causation, a force of rice-balls and butter, of postures and bleeding bulls, primeval, unswerving, irresistible. No wonder that the spirits in the heaven Tuśita influenced the great Buddha to go down and confront these atheistical teachers.

The nickname given by the Buddhists to the apostles of the lower Brahminism was Tîrthakas, men of tank-worship, shrine-worship. To this day these pilgrimages are the chief vehicle of extortion in India, since they include all other priestly extortions. The rich men and râjas are incited to make these to gain offspring, to gain wealth, to gain restored health, to gain heaven. At that very Gayâ where Buddha first brooded over the evils of the priestly system, pilgrims come in thousands of thousands and are mulcted heavily at this shrine, and that tank, and a dozen other holy spots. Another great source of priestly wealth was the animal sacrifice. No animal could be slaughtered for food except by priests, and at the feast held upon the occasion it was enacted that they were to receive a good share of the carcase. In the Âryan ancestor-worship it was ruled that the food, the gold, the house, the slaves, etc., that it was customary to offer to the dead, should be consigned, not to the flames, but to the Brahmins. The caste system, too, which had helped society in its ruder states, had now become intolerably oppressive. When hunting and fighting and tilling from night to morning could scarcely give the savage food enough to support life, it was a step in a forward direction to intrust the fighting to skilled hands, and set apart a small body of thinkers, some to compose the hymns and ballads of the people, and some to carry down these compositions by learning them by heart, and by chanting them in the simple leafy temples. But at the date of Buddha this system was oppressing the many in the interests of the few, and producing the corruption of stagnation. None but the Brahmin could communicate with heaven, could lead a spiritual life.

In short, in India, as elsewhere, the marriage of politics and religion had made the priest a simple politician. The priesthoods had become vast materialisms, and the rites in honour of the gods had gradually dethroned the gods themselves.

CHAPTER VIII.

BUDDHA'S REFORM.

THE Buddhist movement was the revolt of the higher Brahminism against the lower. It was led by one of the most searching reformers that ever appeared upon the page of history. He conceived that the only remedy lay in awakening the spiritual life of the individual. The bloody sacrifice, caste, the costly tank pilgrimages, must be swept completely away.

This is proved by a very valuable Sûtra, the " Sutta Nipâta," one of the most ancient books of Ceylon.

It records that when the great Muni was at Śrâvasti (Sahet Mahet), certain old Brahmins came to listen to his teaching. They asked him if the Brahmin religion (Brâhmaṇa Dharma) was the same as in ancient days. Buddha replied that, in the olden time, the Brâhmaṇa Dharma was completely different. It was this Dharma that he proposed to restore in its original purity. The points of difference that he detailed were these :—

1. The ancient Brâhmanas were simple ascetics (isayo), who had abandoned the "objects of the five senses."

2. They ate contentedly the food that was placed at their door. They had no cattle, or gold, or corn. The gold and corn of holy dreaming alone was theirs.

3. They never married a woman of another caste, or bought wives. The most rigid continence was theirs.[1]

4. They made sacrifices of rice, butter, etc., and never killed the cows, the best friends of man, the givers of medicines.

5. But the kings of the earth by-and-by grew powerful, and had palaces and chariots and jewelled women.

6. Then the Brâhmanas grew covetous of these beautiful women and this vast wealth, and schemed to gain both. They instituted costly sacrifices, the horse sacrifice (assa-medha), the man sacrifice (purisa-medha), and other rites. Through these they obtained costly offerings—gold, cows, beds, garments, jewelled women, bright carpets, palaces, grain, chariots drawn by fine steeds.

7. "Hundreds of thousands of cows" were

---

[1] Fausböll, Sutta Nipâta, p. 49, ver. 10. It is not clear whether Buddha means that marriage was quite unknown to them. The verses are contradictory.

slaughtered at these sacrifices—"cows that like goats do not hurt any one with their feet or with either of their horns—tender cows, yielding vessels of milk."

"Seizing them by the horns the king caused them to be slain with a weapon."

The true Dharma being lost, the world plunged into sensuality, caste disputes, blood. That lost Dharma it is the mission of Buddha to hold up once more, "as an oil lamp in the dark, that those who have eyes may see." [1]

I now come to another piece of evidence. As I have to fight Dr. Rhys Davids "all along the line," it is a pleasure to be able to give him warm praise. He has translated the Tevigga Sutta ; and this seems to me out and out the most valuable gain to Buddhism since Csoma Korösi unearthed the Lalita Vistara.[2] The Sûtra plainly belongs to the "Little Vehicle," and shows that in the view of its disciples Buddha proclaimed the existence of an intelligent eternal God.

When the great Tathâgata was dwelling at Manasâ-kata in the mango grove, some Brahmins, learned

[1] Sutta Nipâta, p. 52.

[2] Dr. Rhys Davids has also started a Pâli Text Society, which will unearth, no doubt, many other treasures of the Cingalese sacred books. The earlier missionaries did good service, but their selections were naturally chosen with a view to missionary enterprise, and not to an impartial exposition of Buddhism.

K

in the three Vedas, come to consult him on the
question of union with the eternal Brahma. They
ask if they are in the right pathway towards that
union. Buddha replies at great length. He suggests
an ideal case. He supposes that a man has fallen in
love with the "most beautiful woman in the land."
Day and night he dreams of her, but has never seen
her. He does not know whether she is tall or short,
of Brahmin or Śûdra caste, of dark or fair com-
plexion ; he does not even know her name. The
Brahmins are asked if the talk of that man about that
woman be wise or foolish. They confess that it is
"foolish talk." Buddha then applies the same train
of reasoning to them. The Brahmins versed in the
three Vedas are made to confess that they have never
seen Brahma, that they do not know whether he is
tall or short, or anything about him, and that all
their talk about union with him is also foolish talk.
They are mounting a crooked staircase, and do not
know whether it leads to a mansion or a precipice.
They are standing on the bank of a river and calling
to the other bank to come to them.

Now it seems to me that if Buddha were the uncompromising teacher of atheism that Dr. Rhys
Davids pictures him, he has at this point an ad-
mirable opportunity of urging his views. The Brahmins, he would of course contend, knew nothing

about Brahma, for the simple reason that no such being as Brahma exists.

But this is exactly the line that Buddha does not take. His argument is that the Brahmins knew nothing of Brahma, because Brahma is purely spiritual, and they are purely materialistic.

Five "Veils," he shows, hide Brahma from mortal ken. These are—

1. The Veil of Lustful Desire.
2. The Veil of Malice.
3. The Veil of Sloth and Idleness.
4. The Veil of Pride and Self-righteousness.
5. The Veil of Doubt.

Buddha then goes on with his questionings:

" Is Brahma in possession of wives and wealth ? "

" He is not, Gautama ! " answers Vâsettha the Brahmin.

" Is his mind full of anger, or free from anger ? "

" Free from anger, Gautama ! "

" Is his mind full of malice, or free from malice ? "

" Free from malice, Gautama ! "

"Is his mind depraved or pure ? "

" It is pure, Gautama ! "

" Has he self-mastery, or has he not ? "

" He has, Gautama."

The Brahmins are then questioned about themselves.

" Are the Brahmins versed in the three Vedas in possession of wives and wealth, or are they not ? "

" They are, Gautama ! "

" Have they anger in their hearts, or have they not ? "

" They have, Gautama."

" Do they bear malice, or do they not ? "

" They do, Gautama."

" Are they pure in heart, or are they not ? "

" They are not, Gautama."

" Have they self-mastery, or have they not ? "

" They have not, Gautama."

These replies provoke, of course, the very obvious retort that no point of union can be found between such dissimilar entities.   Brahma is free from malice, sinless, self-contained, so, of course, it is only the sinless that can hope to be in harmony with him.

Vâsettha then puts this question : " It has been told me, Gautama, that Śramaṇa Gautama knows the way to the state of union with Brahma ? "

" Brahma I know, Vâsettha ! " says Buddha in reply, "and the world of Brahma, and the path leading to it ! "

The humbled Brahmins learned in the three Vedas then ask Buddha to " show them the way to a state of union with Brahma."

Buddha replies at considerable length, drawing a

sharp contrast between the lower Brahminism and the higher Brahminism, the "householder" and the "houseless one." The householder Brahmins are gross, sensual, avaricious, insincere. They practise for lucre black magic, fortune-telling, cozenage. They gain the ear of kings, breed wars, predict victories, sacrifice life, spoil the poor. As a foil to this he paints the recluse, who has renounced all worldly things and is pure, self-possessed, happy.

To teach this "higher life," a Tathâgata "from time to time is born into the world, blessed and worthy, abounding in wisdom, a guide to erring mortals." He sees the universe face to face, the spirit world of Brahma and that of Mâra the tempter. He makes his knowledge known to others. The houseless one, instructed by him, "lets his mind pervade one quarter of the world with thoughts of pity, sympathy, and equanimity ; and so the second, and so the third, and so the fourth. And thus the whole wide world, above, below, around, and everywhere, does he continue to pervade with heart of pity, sympathy and equanimity, far-reaching, grown great, and beyond measure." [1]

"Verily this, Vâsettha, is the way to a state of union with Brahma," and he proceeds to announce that the Bhikshu, or Buddhist beggar, "who is free from anger, free from malice, pure in mind, master of himself,

[1] "Buddhist Suttas," p. 201.

will, after death, when the body is dissolved, become united with Brahma."[1]   The Brahmins at once see the full force of this teaching.   It is as a conservative in their eyes that Buddha figures, and not an innovator.   He takes the side of the ancient spiritual religion of the country against rapacious innovators.

"Thou hast set up what was thrown down," they say to him. In the Burmese Life he is described more than once as one who has set the overturned chalice once more upon its base.

I own I am a little puzzled at the attitude assumed by Dr. Rhys Davids, in the presence of this Tevigga Sutta.   The Sûtra is one of the original Pâli Sûtras which Dr. Rhys Davids considers the paramount authorities on early Buddhism. One of two inferences seem inevitable. Either the pretensions claimed for these Sûtras or the charge of atheism must be withdrawn. Dr. Rhys Davids will do neither; moreover, he confuses Brahma and Brahmâ. All through the Sûtra he talks of union with Brahmâ; which was what the yogi never sought to obtain. And this is the more astonishing, because in a footnote he lets us see that the Pâli writer used the word Brahma.[2]

Brahmâ is the anthropomorphic god with four heads, who rides on a goose. Brahmâ gets drunk

[1] "Buddhist Suttas," p. 203.   [2] Ibid., p. 168.

and tries to seduce his daughter. Brahmâ had one of his heads knocked off in a fight with Śiva. Brahmâ, Śiva, and Vishṇu are worshipped in the month of Mâgha, and then their earthen images are flung into the river.[1] Brahma, on the other hand, is the formless, pure, pervading, eternal, passionless God.

An extract from the Muṇḍaka Upanishad of the Atharva Veda may here throw a light on Brahma and union with him : " He is great and incomprehensible by the senses, and consequently his nature is beyond human conception. He, though more subtle than vacuum itself, shines in various ways. From those who do not know him he is at a greater distance than the limits of space, and to those who acquire a knowledge of him he is near ; and whilst residing in animate creatures is perceived, although obscurely, by those who apply their thoughts to him. He is not perceptible by vision, nor is he describable by means of speech, neither can he be the object of any of the organs of sense, nor can he be conceived by the help of austerities or religious rites ; but a person whose mind is purified by the light of true knowledge through incessant contemplation perceives him the most pure God. Such is the invisible Supreme Being. He should be seen in the heart wherein breath consisting of five species rests. The

[1] See Ward, vol. ii. p. 30.

mind being perfectly freed from impurity, God, who spreads over the mind and all the senses, imparts a knowledge of himself to the heart." [1]

In point of fact the language of the Buddhist mystic is very like that of all other mystics. Thomas à Kempis, in his "Soliloquy of the Soul," has a chapter headed, "On the Union of the Soul with God." [2] Indeed, all the Christian mystics sought this "union" quite as earnestly as Buddha. St. Theresa had her *oraison d'union.* [3] St. Augustine based all his mysticism on the text (John xiv. 23), "Jesus answered and said unto him, If a man love Me, he will keep My words: and My Father will love him, and We will come unto him, and make Our abode with Him." [4]

Clement of Alexandria sketches the end to be kept in view by the "Christian Gnostic:" "Dwelling with the Lord He will continue His familiar friend, sharing the same hearth according to the Spirit." [5]

Madame Guyon renewed her mystical "Marriage with the Child Jesus" every year.

The mystics of all religions sought this union with God by means of extasia. The method is described in the Persian Sharistan and the Zerdusht Afshâr; and

---

[1] Rajah Rammohun Roy, "Translation of the Veds," p. 36.
[2] Chap. xiii.
[3] Madame Guyon, "Discours Chrétiens," vol. ii. p. 344.
[4] Cited by Madame Guyon. [5] Misc., p. 60.

the processes are completely similar to those of the Indian yogi. He whom the ancient Persian called Izad, and the modern Persian Allah, is thus described by Maulâvi Jami :—

"Thou but an atom art, He, the Great Whole. But if for a few days thou meditate with care on the Whole thou becomest one with it." [1]

Mr. Vaughan, in his "Hours with the Mystics," shows that the motto of the Neo-Platonist was, "Withdraw into thyself; and the Adytum of thine own soul will reveal to thee profounder secrets than the cave of Mithras." He asserts that a mystic, according to Dionysius the Areopagite, is not merely a sacred personage acquainted with the doctrines, and participator in the rites called mysteries, but one also who, exactly after the Neo-Platonist pattern, by mortifying the body attains the "divine union." [2] Cornelius Agrippa and Behmen held the same views.

I may mention, as an interesting fact, that catholic mysticism has very nearly the same terminology as Buddhism. Madame Guyon and the mystics have their "states" likewise, the "mystic indifference," [3] "l'anéantissement," [4] the mystical "death." [5] When Buddha was performing his "Dhyâna," it is said that

[1] Olcott, "Yoga Philosophy," p. 271.
[2] Vaughan, vol. i. p. 22.
[3] L. Guerrier, Madame Guyon, p. 342.
[4] Ibid., p. 112.   [5] Ibid., p. 116.

the " Chakravâla " (visible universe) became invisible,
and the azure domains of the Buddhas (the spirit
world) "luminous."[1] Madame Guyon, in her "Moyen
Court," cites Revelations iii. 7, 8, to show that the
mystic " key of David " consists in "shutting the eyes
of the body and opening the eyes of the soul."[2] Of
course this " annihilation," this " death," this " indifference " only refers to the lower life with St. François
de Sales and Madame Guyon. And I think we must
say the same of early Buddhism, in spite of Schopen-
hauer. What strikes one most is the total discre-
pancy between the life of Buddha and his teachings,
supposing they were atheistic and agnostic.

The Buddha of Dr. Rhys Davids was a young man
of genius, who perceived that the theology of his contemporaries was utterly wrong. They believed in an
infinite eternal God. They also believed that the
death of the body was not the death of the soul.
The young prince determined to devote his life to
the teaching of " nobler and simpler lessons."[3] These
lessons were flat atheism, and the flat denial of the
soul's immortality. All this is very good ; but let us
see how the young man of genius set to work to
propagate these lessons. He was the son of an Âryan

[1] Lalita Vistara, p. 267.   [2] "Moyen Court," p. 10.
[3] "The nobler and simpler lessons of the founder" ("Buddhism,"
p. 207).

king, who volunteered to abdicate in his favour. He had thus an army of soldiers and an army of ductile priests at his disposal. He had palaces and wives and diamonds. He was bold, active, intelligent. What did he do? On the surface two prominent courses seemed open to him :—

1. He might issue an edict that his soldiers would chop off the head of any one who believed in Brahma.

2. He might corrupt some of the avaricious and pliant priesthood, and introduce his atheism more subtly under the guise of orthodoxy.

But, if we turn to the biographies, we find that the proceedings of the young atheist were quite different from this. The young atheist gave up his useful instrument, the army of soldiers. The young atheist gave up his still more useful instrument, the army of insincere priests. The young atheist renounced his palaces, his wives, and indeed all the joys that the ordinary philosophy of materialism recognizes. The young atheist went and placed himself for years under a teacher of theism. The young atheist swept this theist's cell no doubt. The young atheist brushed the flies from the theist's nose. The young atheist washed the theist's feet and drank the water afterwards. Then, under the directions of the theist, the young atheist squatted under a tree, and rammed a cotton cloth, about the size of a window curtain, constantly up and down his throat to suppress his breath. The young atheist sat between the "five fires." The young atheist exposed himself to the cold of winter and the great heat of summer to gain a knowledge of that God whom he had, according to modern teachers, made it the special mission of his life to deny and disprove.

It may, perhaps, be said that the "nobler and simpler lessons" of atheism came to him during this initiation. If so, his inconsistencies are greater than ever. His father constantly urged him to return and take up the government. Instead of this, he announced that the ordinary teachers of religion were gross and material. They could not know Brahma, because that pure God was essentially different from them. Holy men in the past had known him, because they had led blameless lives. The young prince announced that he would restore this lofty creed. Patiently he trained an army whose self-abnegation has never been paralleled, an army that he himself named The Teachers of God (Brâhmaṇas). Under his directions they marched all over India and eventually over Asia, making known the Buddhi, the Brahma, the omnipresent intelligence, to poor and great.

CHAPTER IX.

BUDDHA BEGINS TO PREACH.

WHEN Buddha has become a perfect Buddha, a great struggle takes place in his mind. Shall he impart to others his important knowledge? shall he preach the law? This struggle, in the Scriptures of both North and South, is imaged as a dialogue between him and Brahma the Ineffable. The Brahma in his breast at length is victorious; and Buddha goes off to the deer forest, near Benares, and converts five disciples, who abandoned him as a heretic when he took the nourishment of Sujâtâ. This incident seems historical.

Before we can get at Buddha's real teachings, we must clear away the mystifications of the " Carriage that drives to the Great Nowhere." I will consider briefly four epochs of Buddhism :—

1. Buddhism from the first sermon of Buddha to the date when King Asoka made it the official creed in India.

2. The Buddhism of Asoka, commencing B.C. 257.

3. The Buddhism of the "Great Vehicle," the "Carriage that drives to the Great Nowhere." It was made paramount at the convocation of King Kaniśka, a few years after the commencement of the Christian era.

4. Buddhaghosa and the atheism of Ceylon, about A.D. 410.

A writer in the *Indian Antiquary* has charged me with "crass" ignorance and other unkind things, because I assert that Buddhism, in the first instance, made its progress as a secret society. The critic points triumphantly to the abundant chronicles of the Southern Buddhists, where every step of the reformer and his movement is set down.

I wish I could agree with my critic, and accept these chronicles without critical sifting. My present task would then be much simplified. The Lalita Vistara stops at the first preaching of Buddha, but other narratives continue the story. The Ceylon version, as given by Dr. Rhys Davids in his "Birth Stories," is considered by him the "original" history.

Buddha, as we know, first preached the law in a deer forest, about four miles to the north of the holy city of Benares. The spot is called Sârnâth (Sârug-ganâtha, the "Lord of Deer") to this day. Aśoka built a splendid temple in this wilderness. The dome is ninety-three feet in diameter, and its imposing mass still dominates the plain. Pilgrims from China have visited it ; and pilgrims from all countries in the world go to it still. It is called Dhamek, a corruption for the Temple of Dharma. Now, the Cingalese historian, evidently writing long after this temple of Dharma had become famous, makes Buddha put up in a fine temple and vihára in a " suburb of Benares "[1] during the first rainy season after his conversion.

Benares was already the most holy city of the Hindoos, and yet it is recorded that Buddha preached openly against the Brahmin religion, and made sixty-one converts.

He then proceeded to the powerful Brahmin kingdom of Magadha, and arrived at the capital, Râjâgriha, attended by over a thousand followers. The king at once became a convert, with a large proportion of his subjects ; and handed over to Buddha the grove in which the celebrated Veṇuvana Monastery was afterwards situated. The Cingalese writer does not take the trouble to say a word about the building of it, being evidently under an impression that it was already there. Five months after Buddha had attained the Bodhi, he started off to Kapilavastu, a distance of sixty leagues, to see his father. He was accompanied by twenty thousand yellow-robed shaven

[1] " Buddhist Birth Stories," p. 91.

Bhikshus ; and he marched along the high-roads of the various Brahmin kingdoms, that were on his road, without any molestation. At Kapilavastu he found another fine vihâra ready for him ; and the bulk of the nation and the king became converts to his religion. He returned shortly to Râjâgriha to find a convenient merchant ready at once to hand over to him the rich vihâra, or monastery, of Jetavana at Śrâvasti (Sahet Mahet). Buddha went at once to the spot ; and this time the chronicler allows a vihâra to be built, a *new* one, he again fancying apparently that one was there. There was " a pleasant room for the sage," separate apartments for " eighty elders," and " other residences with single and double walls, and long halls and open roofs ornamented with ducks and quails ; and ponds also he made, and terraces to walk on by day and by night." [1]

When Buddha arrived at Śrâvasti, this convent was dedicated to him by the merchant, who went through a formula well known in the ancient inscriptions of Ceylon. He poured water out of a bowl, and made over the land to the monks. Then a gorgeous festival took place, which lasted nine months. Exactly five hundred and forty millions of gold pieces were expended on this feast and on the convent ; so that we may presume, I suppose, that

[1] " Buddhist Birth Stories," p. 130.

most of the inhabitants of the powerful Brahmin kingdom of Śrâvasti had become converts. Thus, in less than a year, Buddha had practically converted the Brahmin kingdoms that stretch from Śrâvasti (Sahet Mahet) to Gayâ.

In a word, his creed had already won what is called the Holy Land of the Buddhists.

Is all this true? Even by lopping off Eastern exaggerations and accretions, can we reduce it in any way to a plausible story? If the Buddhism set forth by Dr. Rhys Davids, or even by M. Barthélemy St. Hilaire, be the real Buddhism that was preached by Buddha, I say that the task is impossible. If in the holiest city of the Hindoos Buddha had proclaimed that there was no God, and in a complete and categorical manner had announced that man had no soul, nor anything of any sort that existed after death, the cruel laws of the Brahmins against heresy would have been put in force against him. Dr. Rhys Davids contends that it is proved by the Upanishads that "absolute freedom of thought" existed in ancient India.[1] But the Upanishads were secret—he forgets that. They were whispered to pupils who had passed through a severe probation. Megasthenes, the Greek ambassador to Patna, bears witness to this.[2]

[1] "Hibbert Lectures," p. 26.
[2] Cory, "Ancient Fragments," p. 225.

L

The laws against heresy, although there is a controversy as to their date, must certainly have been framed before Buddhism became the official religion. Besides this, ancient priesthoods were sometimes tolerant of abstract discussions about the nature of God, but they resented fiercely all attacks on religion viewed as a political system. Buddha, in every sermon, assailed this root and branch. He denounced the caste system, the bloody sacrifice, the use of wine in the Soma sacrifice, the lucrative pilgrimages. In a word, the principal sources of priestly revenue and ascendency were fiercely assailed.

Another great difficulty about the early years of Buddha's ministry is this monastery (vihâra) question. It is plain that Dr. Rhys Davids's biography is the work either of a pious knave giving the sanction of Buddha to large donations for convents, processions, etc., or of a pious fool too dull to draw any picture except that of the late and corrupt Buddhism that was under his nose. The real question is, Did the earliest disciples dwell in any vihâra at all?

From the North we get an important set of Buddhist rules—the "Twelve Observances." The "Mob of Beggars," as Buddha called his followers, are expressly forbidden to have any covering over them except a tree. Their "one seat" is to be mother earth. Their clothes are to be rags from the

dust-heap, the dung-heap, the graveyard. The tree
that covers the beggar must be, if possible, in a graveyard. He is to be called Durkhrodpa (" He who lives
in a graveyard "). He is not allowed to sleep twice
under the same tree.[1]

These rules, if genuine, put the Cingalese chronicles
out of court. Let us consider the vihâra as an
apparatus of propagandism. Could it have conquered India ? Could it have conquered Asia ?

Buddha in person, in Dr. Rhys Davids's translation,
tells us the functions of vihâras :—

> " Cold they ward off, and heat ;
> So also beasts of prey
> And creeping things and gnats,
> And rains in the cold season ; [2]
> And when the dreaded heat and winds
> Arise they ward them off.
> To give to monks a dwelling-place
> Wherein in safety and in peace
> To think till mysteries grow clear,
> The Buddha calls a worthy deed.
> Let, therefore, a wise man,
> Regarding his own weal,
> Have pleasant monasteries built,
> And lodge there learned men.
> Let him with cheerful mien
> Give food to them and drink,
> And clothes and dwelling-places
> To the upright in mind.
> Then shall they preach to him the truth." [3]

---

[1] Burnouf, Introd., pp. 269, 274.

[2] I cannot say whether the doctor or the chronicler is responsible for
this displacing of the ordinary epoch of the Indian rains.

[3] " Birth Stories," p. 132.

If this translation of Dr. Rhys Davids gives us, as it professes to do, the truest and most authentic account available of a vihâra in the first year of Buddha's preaching, we gather that the chief objects of a vihâra were—

1. To afford shelter, clothes, food, and comfort to a recluse whilst he developed his individual spiritualism.

2. To keep off from the monks the floods of the rainy season, the great heats of the hot season, the fiery blasts of the season of the hot winds, and the cold of winter. Moreover, the vihâra was to be "pleasant."

Now, if the monk resided in his vihâra in the hot season, and during the rains and hot winds and in the cold season, it is difficult to see when he acted as missionary, for a monk in a monastery is called the silent one (Muni). In his walks abroad he may present his begging-bowl, but must not speak. A regulation exists that the monk should devote himself to silent meditation during the rainy season (Varshâ);[1] but this rule must have been issued long subsequent to the issue of the "Twelve Observances," as it stultifies them.

Vihâra propagandism may be good for a country which is already Buddhist; but I fail to see how it could make a country of Buddhists. And yet some

[1] Hwen Thsang, "Mémoires," vol. i. p. 64.

very active propagandism must have leavened India
from one end to the other before Aśoka made Buddhism the official creed. The Holy Land of the
Buddhists—and it is to that that Buddha's own
preaching was almost completely confined—was an
insignificant portion of Aśoka's vast dominions. He
tells us that Gândhâra (Peshawur), to the north, and
Chola and Pândiya, the extreme southern provinces
of Hindostan, had become converted. On the extreme west, at Girnâr, near the Gulf of Cutch, a
rock inscription was cut. On the eastern coast, at
Ganjam, were the Dhauli and Jaugada inscriptions.
To Ceylon, and to Bactria, and to Egypt the
Buddhist missionaries, as he announces, had also
gone.

Bishop Bigandet's history, the Burmese Scripture,
gives a different colouring to these early days. It
makes Buddha go, not to a suburb of Benares, where
there was a vihâra, but to Mṛigadava, the "deer
forest," near Benares. When he leaves Benares he
makes his way towards the "desert of Uravilva." It
is under a tree in a forest that he is found by the
profligate young men whom he converts on his journey.
At Gayâ it is on a mountain that he preaches. When
he nears Râjâgriha he repairs to a "palm grove."
The king presents to him, not the vihâra, but the
"garden of Bamboos" (Veṇuvana). When he visits

Kapilavastu he goes to the "Grove of Banyan Trees," and so on.

Buddha's instructions also to his disciples are more in harmony with the account given of early Buddhism in the "Twelve Observances" than in the Cingalese version.

"A great duty is yours—to work for the happiness of men and spirits. Let us separate and go each in a different direction, no two following the same road. Go and preach Dharma."[1]

At the risk of getting a subtle thinker like Dr. Oldenberg also charged with "crass ignorance" by the masked critic of the *Indian Antiquary*, I must mention that he also considers that there is little in this portion of Buddha's life that deserves even the name of "tradition," but "merely collections of countless real or feigned addresses, dialogues, and sayings of Buddha."[2] The doctor affirms, also, that from the Cingalese books, the "tarrying of ascetics under trees might be multiplied *ad libitum*."[3] Where else, he says, could they sit in Buddha's time? The following citation he gives from the Cûlahatthi pado pama sutta :—

"He dwells in a lonely spot, in a grove, at the foot of a tree, on a mountain, in a cave, in a mountain grotto, in a burial-place, in the wilderness, under an

---

[1] Bigandet, p. 126.   [2] "Buddha," p. 138.   [3] Ibid., p. 88.

open sky, on a heap of straw." That was plainly early Buddhism.[1]

Bishop Bigandet accounts for the rise of Buddhism by supposing that it was at once adopted as the official religion in Magadha. Then there are theories abroad that some of the kingdoms of India were Turanian, and their creeds were Jinism, or some non-Brahminic religion. And it is affirmed that some of these monarchs befriended Buddha. In the way of all these theories stand the Asoka stones. They distinctly record that the Brahminism of the animal sacrifice was the official creed all over India until Asoka superseded it. It is to be remembered that Patna was his capital, which is in the very heart of the Holy Land of the Buddhists ; so the king could no more make a mistake about the official creed of the neighbouring Magadha, than the Archbishop of Canterbury be wrong about the official creed of Sussex. The Atthakathâ in tracing his history also confesses that the official religion was Brahmin up to the king's conversion.[2]

The question of the great missionary success of early Buddhism is no doubt a difficult one. The enormous area conquered by it at the date when Asoka made it an official creed seems to indicate a

---

[1] " Buddha," p. 88.
[2] Journ. Beng. As. Soc., vol. vi. p. 731.

victory already won. Aśoka was a politician. He had swum to the throne in the blood of many slaughtered brothers. He seems scarcely the man to have offended the powerful Brahmin priesthoods of every kingdom in India, except under the pressure - of a more potent force. If the formidable "Sons of Dharma" had silently undermined these kingdoms, and a vast organization able to make and unmake kings, united, secret, terribly in earnest, had revealed themselves to him, his proceedings are intelligible, not otherwise. The vast empires of the palmy days of Indian Buddhism were found unattainable by the most gory Mogul.

In this matter we are not quite without historical data. China was officially converted A.D. 61, by the apparition of a "golden man," "a spirit named Foe." The Emperor Mingti on perceiving this "golden man" at once made his religion the official creed. But in the notes of Klaproth and De Rémusat to their translation of the "Pilgrimage of Fa Hian,"[1] it is made quite clear that Buddhism came to China nearly two hundred years earlier. Lassen believes that it reached Babylon B.C. 250. Buddha's name is mentioned with praise in the Zend Avesta.[2] "Go ye into all the world and preach Dharma!" said Buddha.

[1] Page 40 et seq.
[2] M. Haug, "Religion of the Parsis," p. 208.

The " Sons of Śâkya," as they were called, seem to have taken him at his word.

But the question is, Was this done secretly or openly ? Did the preacher call aloud in the market-place—" Sacrifice no bulls to Rudra ! Make no pilgrimages to the Tîrtha of Vyâsa ! Contemn Soma and his intoxicating drink ! Laugh at caste privilege !"? My intelligent critic in the *Indian Antiquary* seems to answer this in the affirmative. I think it quite impossible.

From the moment that Buddha left the palace he had been undergoing an initiation into what the ancients called "the Mysteries." These in India, as we learn from Megasthenes,[1] were guarded with the extreme of jealousy. Mr. King in his able work, " The Gnostics," asserts that the Therapeuts, the disciples of the bloodless altar of Mithras, and similar adepts of the " mysteries " in the West, were due to Buddhist propagandism. He considers them also akin to modern Freemasonry. Mr. Mackenzie gives from Lassen's " Indische Alterthumskunde " an account of the Indian initiation into the Mysteries. It has this advantage, that it is written by a Freemason to show how close a likeness there is between the Indian initiation and that of Freemasons.[2]

---

[1] Cory, " Ancient Fragments," p. 225.
[2] " Royal Masonic Cyclopædia," *sub voce* " Mysteries of Hindostan."

At eight years of age the child girded on the sacred cord. For the "Fellow-craft degree of the Mason," as Mr. Mackenzie calls it, the disciple "was led into a gloomy cavern in which the aporrheta were to be displayed to him. Here a striking similarity to the Masonic system may be found." Three chief officers or hierophants "are seated in the east, west, and south, attended by their respective subordinates. After an invocation to the sun, an oath was demanded of the aspirant to the effect of implicit obedience to superiors, purity of body, and inviolable secrecy. Water was then sprinkled over him, he was deprived of his sandals or shoes, and was made to circumambulate the cavern thrice with the sun. Suitable addresses were then made to him, after which he was conducted through seven ranges of caverns in utter darkness, and the lamentations of Mahâdevî or the great goddess for the loss of Śiva, similar to the wailings of Isis for Osiris, were imitated. After a number of impressive ceremonies the initiate was suddenly admitted into an apartment of dazzling light, redolent with perfume and radiant with all the gorgeous beauty of the Indian clime, alike in flowers, perfumes, and gems. This represented the Hindu paradise, the acme of all earthly bliss. This was supposed to constitute the regeneration of the candidate, and he was now invested with the white robe and the tiara. A peculiar cross was marked on his forehead and the Tau cross on his breast; upon which he was instructed in the peculiar signs, tokens, and doctrines of his order. He was presented with the sacred girdle, the magical black stone, the talismanic jewel for his breast, and the serpent stone which guaranteed him from the effects of poison. Finally, he was given the sacred word, A.U.M."

To obtain the third degree it was necessary to practise tapas in a forest. In the "fourth degree the Brahmin was, by peculiar ceremonies, conjoined with the divinity."

It is evident that we get here, in pantomimic form, a struggle similar to that which Buddha carried on with Mâra, or his lower nature. The "mysteries," in point of fact, were a dramatic representation of the struggle. By-and-by in all countries they degenerated into histrionics. At first the struggle was in the mind of the mystic.

I think that geography is also in favour of my view. The caves and steeps and jangals selected for Buddha's teachings show that he wished to train his Bhikshu Sangha, his "Mob of Beggars," in secret. When they were trained he launched them forth, a conquering force that has never been matched.

By the aid of the monuments, and also the

inscriptions, we can throw some light on the Buddhist cultus before Aśoka's conversion.

In the British Museum are the marbles of the Amarâvatî Tope. I see strangers, with puzzled look, stop before certain tablets that represent marble worshippers crouching before a small throne or table placed before a marble tree. On the altar are often two footprints. More learned inquirers have been equally puzzled. But the recent exhumation of the remains of the Stûpa of Bharhut (B.C. 250) has placed the meaning of these emblems beyond the region of controversy. Similar designs have been there discovered, and they are furnished with explanations incised in the Pâli character. One, it is said, is the throne and tree of Kaśyapa, another the throne and tree of Kanaka Muni, and so on through the list of the Seven Great Buddhas. Every great Buddha has his tree and his worship. And here I must mention a curious piece of Chinese-puzzle adjustment, which shows how closely the ritual fits the ancient temple and the temple the ritual. In vol. xvi. of the "Asiatic Researches," Professor Wilson gives a ritual from Nepâl, called the Praise of the Seven Buddhas.[1] Each Buddha is "adored" in a separate paragraph, and it is announced that he found emancipation under a special tree. Comparing the list of these

[1] Page 453.

trees with that of the Bharhut Stûpa, as given by General Cunningham,[1] we find that five of the trees exactly correspond. The sixth, that of Visvabhû, is obliterated. Śâkya Muni's tree in one list is the aśvattha, and in the other the pippala—synonyms for the *Ficus religiosa*. This seems to give great antiquity to the litany.

I will copy down one or two of these addresses :—

"I adore Jinendra, the consuming fire of sorrow, the treasure of holy knowledge whom all revere, who bore the name of Vipasvi, who was born in the race of mighty monarchs in the city of Bandumati, who was for eighty thousand years the preceptor of gods and men ; and by whom endowed with the ten kinds of power, the degree of Jinendra was obtained at the foot of a pâṭala-tree."

This is the praise of Śâkya Muni :—

"I adore Śâkya Siṁha the Buddha, the kinsman of the sun, worshipped by men and gods, who was born at the splendid city Kapilapura, of the family of the chief of the Śâkya kings, the life of which best friend to all the world lasted one hundred years. Having speedily subdued desire, unbounded wisdom was acquired by him at the foot of the aśvattha-tree."[2]

---

[1] Stûpa of Bharhut, p. 46.

[2] "Asiatic Researches," xvi. p. 454.

But before folks worship trees sculptured in marble, we may presume they worshipped them in the forest. Each Buddha has his tree, because that tree was his earliest symbol. The Seven Great Buddhas are the Seven Rishis, or Prophets, taken on from the Brahmins. They are the seven stars of the Great Bear, which constellation, probably, in days of crude astronomy roughly represented the apex of heaven. Allusions to the Seven Tâla Trees that surround the mystic Lion Throne occur more than once in the Lalita Vistara.[1] It is possible that seven trees in a forest formed the first rude Buddhist cathedral. The sculptures of all the earliest topes attest this tree-worship. And in several of them a spirit is represented coming down to receive the offerings.

The stones of Aśoka here also give us their invaluable testimony. There is no mention of the costly chaityas and "great vihâra halls" that we read of in Dr. Rhys Davids's history. "Whenever devotees shall abide round the holy fig-tree for the performance of pious acts, the benefit and pleasure of the country and its inhabitants shall be in making offerings ; and according to their generosity, or otherwise, they shall enjoy prosperity or adversity, and they shall give thanks for the coming of the faith. Whatever villages with their inhabitants may be

[1] Pages 263, 269, etc.

given or maintained for the sake of the worship, the devotees shall receive the same, and for an example unto my people they shall exercise solitary austerities. And likewise whatever blessings they shall pronounce by these, shall my devotees accumulate for the worship. Furthermore, the people shall in the night attend the great myrobolan tree and the holy fig-tree. My people shall accumulate the great myrobolan tree. Pleasure is to be eschewed as intoxication.

" My devotees doing thus for the profit and pleasure of the village, whereby they coming around the beauteous and holy fig-tree may cheerfully abide in the performance of pious acts " ("Delhi Pillar," Edict IV., Prinsep).

It must be remembered that the *Ficus religiosa* was the tree which was dedicated to Śâkya Muni. The paragraphs just cited show, I think, for certain, that the deification of Buddha had already taken place. Indeed, another passage on the Delhi pillar sets this beyond the region of doubt :—

" And he who acts in conformity with this edict will be united with Sugato."

Union with the Supreme was, as we have shown, the highest object of Indian worship, and here we see it confused already with union with Sugato (the "God of the present happy advent "), a name of Buddha.

But a second piece of pure history gives to this deification of Buddha a still earlier date. Seleucus Nicator sent an ambassador, named Megasthenes, to King Chandragupta (B.C. 302 to 298). He visited that monarch at his capital, Palibothra, or Patna. His account of the India of that day is unfortunately lost ; but through Diodorus Siculus, Strabo, Arrian, and Clement of Alexandria, some valuable fragments have come down to us. Patna, it must be remembered, was in the very heart of the Buddhist Holy Land. Clement of Alexandria cites a passage from Megasthenes, "On Indian Affairs." On the same page he thus describes the Indian " philosophers : "—

" Of these there are two classes, some of them called Sarmanæ and others Brahmins. And those of the Sarmanæ who are called Hylobii neither inhabit cities nor have roofs over them, but are clothed in the bark of trees, feed on nuts, and drink water in their hands. Like those called Encratites in the present day, they know not marriage nor begetting of children. Some, too, of the Indians obey the precepts of Buddha, whom, on account of his extraordinary sanctity, they have raised to divine honours."

The importance of this passage is this, that from Strabo we get the description given by Megasthenes of the Indian philosophers, and it is made certain that the earlier part of this passage is from the same source.

Strabo describes the Brahmins and the "Germanes," also called, he says, "Hylobii." He gives the same details as Clement of Alexandria, about their feeding on wild fruits and wearing the bark of trees. He, too, draws a distinction between the Germanes and the Brahmins on the subject of continency, the Brahmins being polygamists.[1]

From this it seems certain that Clement of Alexandria was writing with the original work of Megasthenes before him. We may therefore conclude that this passage about Buddha, sandwiched as it is between two genuine citations, was also in Megasthenes. Strabo has handed down to us another statement of Megasthenes about the Hylobii :—

" By their means the kings serve and worship the Deity." [2]

There can be no doubt that the Sarmanes (Śramaṇas) and Brahmins of Megasthenes were the Brahmins and the Buddhists. To the first, according to Megasthenes, were confided sacrifices and ceremonies, for the dead as well as the living. They were a caste apart, and none outside this caste could perform their duties. The gods would not accept the sacrifices of such an interloper. Their ideas on

---

[1] Cory, "Ancient Fragments," pp. 225, 227. All that can be recovered of Megasthenes is given in this work in Greek and English.

[2] Ibid., p. 227.

M

life and death were very similar to those of Plato and the Greeks. The Brahmins ate flesh and had many wives. Every new year there was a great synod of them. They dwelt in groves near the great cities, on " couches of leaves and skins."

The Hylobii, on the other hand, insisted on absolute continence, and strict vegetarianism and water-drinking. Clitarchus gives us an additional fact. Megasthenes, we learn from him, has also recorded that the Hylobii "derided the Brahmins."

This confirms Aśoka, who has placed on record the fact that the official creed of India, until he changed it, was Brahminism. It proves, too, that Buddha was already deified 170 years after his death. This, as it seems to me, quite settles the atheistic question, as the deification of a mortal could scarcely have proceeded from a body of professing atheists. Dr. Rhys Davids is invaluable as a Pâli translator; but I feel convinced that if he had lived amongst natives on the peninsula of Hindostan, he would have been saved many errors. God, speaking through the holy man, is still and ever has been the leading Brahmin religious idea. "What is God?" said the missionary Robson. "He is speaking to you!" replied a Brahmin. Trance obsession was the root of the fancy ; and to this day in India the Brahmin is treated as God Almighty walking on the earth. His feet are

kissed, and offerings of flowers, scents, etc., are made
to him, because this is the homage paid by man to
God. A little female Brahmin child is often placed
on a throne and worshipped as Bhagavatî. At the
great festival of Durgâ, a female is tricked out with
the fine muslins and jewels and symbols of the great
goddess, and placed on an altar to receive flowers and
homage and incense and garlands, all through the
festival. The susceptibility of the female to Sibylline
frenzies, no doubt, was at the bottom of these customs ;
but these facts, combined with the early Buddhist
sculptures, suggest a pregnant question. Why was
Buddha, when alive, honoured with prostrations, feet-
kissing, offerings of food and flowers and incense ?
Why was Buddha, when dead, honoured with similar
offerings ? There is but one answer to this. Divine
homage was paid to Buddha because God (call him
Buddha, or Brahma, or what you will) was supposed
to speak through him.

CHAPTER X.

KING AŚOKA.

THERE are two distinct histories that record the events immediately after Śâkya's death, and these radically contradict one another. The first is the Mahâparinirvâṇa Sûtra, which affirms that the Buddhist world was exclusively agitated with this great question : What is to be done with the sacred relics of Tathâgata ? The second narrative, derived by Buddhaghosa from the early chronicles of Ceylon, is admitted by all scholars to be a much later one ; and according to it the Buddhist world was exclusively agitated by a totally different question, namely, with an alleged council, summoned three months after Buddha's death, to settle the voluminous Buddhist canon. Dr. Oldenberg sensibly deduces from this that the second narrative is pure fiction. "It shows," he says, "that the author of the Mahâparinibbâna Sutta did not know anything of the first council." Dr. Rhys Davids, in opposition to this, suggests that the first writer ignored the first council, "because he considered it unnecessary to mention an event which had no bearing on the subject of his work." Why had it no bearing on the subject of his work? In any case, to assume that a fact is genuine because we can invent a fanciful theory to show why it is *not* recorded in history, is scarcely pure Comtism.

Bishop Bigandet's history throws serious doubts on the first narrative likewise. It shows that there are two histories of the disposition of Buddha's relics differing radically.

The first narrative, that contained in the Mahâparinirvâṇa Sûtra records that after the cremation of the body, the King of Magadha demanded a portion of the relics, with a view to build a tope in their honour. The same request was made by the inhabitants of Vaiśâlî, Kapilavastu, Allakapa, Râmagama, Vithadipa, and Pâvâ. The men of Kusinârâ refused ; but to avoid strife, the relics were at length divided into eight portions. Each claimant carried away his share and erected a tope over it. The second narrative affirms that Kaśyapa, the head of the Buddhist faith after the death of Buddha, being opposed to the superstition of relic-worship, persuaded the eight kings to give back their portions. He then furtively carried them off to the south-east of Râjâgṛiha, and caused a cavern to be excavated. In the centre was

a rich chaitya of brass, "in form and proportions
exactly similar to the great Vihâra of Ceylon." In
six caskets of solid gold the relics were deposited.
And the gold caskets were in the centre of seven
caskets of silver, and the silver ones in the centre
of seven caskets of precious stones, etc. Five
hundred and five statues, representing Buddha in his
five hundred and five previous existences, were ranged
around. Five hundred and five lamps flickered
in the cavern. The whereabouts of this cavern was
kept a secret till the days of King Aśoka; when it
was discovered, together with a scroll of gold, in
which was found a prophecy, written by the hand of
Kaśyapa himself (two hundred years at least before
the introduction of the alphabet into India). It contained these words :—

"In days to come a young man named Piyadasi
will mount the throne and become a famous king,
called Aśoka. By him Buddha's relics will be distributed all over Jambudvîpa [India]." [1]

Before commenting on all this it is as well to give
the Northern account from an early narrative, entitled
the "Twelve Acts of Śâkya." That work states that
the relics were divided into eight portions. They
were then deposited in a pyramidal building in
"Kuśa, or Kâma Rupa." The princes in Central

[1] Bigandet, p. 331.

India demanded that the relics should be divided, but it is expressly ˌstated that the people of Kuśa refused.[1]

If we snip off from the second Southern narrative the silly accretion about Kaśyapa getting back the relics from the eight kings, which is plainly a clumsy expedient to make the two stories tack together, it harmonizes substantially with the Northern account. Buddha's body was cremated, and the relics deposited in a *single* sepulchral mound. This was what he expressly ordered to be done according to the Parinirvâṇa Sûtra, as I shall shortly show.

I have shown from the Mahâbhârata that pilgrimages to the dead Ṛishi in his stûpa constituted the prominent religious rite at about the date of Buddha's advent. We know from the anthropologists that after cremation was adopted a vase of ashes represented the dead saint in his temple domicile. We know from history that when Aśoka made Buddhism the official creed, he had costly stûpas erected to Buddha in every part of his wide domains, and in each stûpa a tiny fragment of Buddha's relics, a tooth, a pinch of ashes, was deposited. The explanation I take to be this. Aśoka had to change a simple theosophy into a creed fit for a vast empire. Reverence to Buddha's tomb and Buddha's tree

---

[1] Csoma Korösi, " Asiatic Researches," vol. xx. p. 297.

seemed the chief tangible features of that religion, viewed from the outside. This saint-worship was also the Brahminical creed at the date of Aśoka. That monarch made the tope-worship the main feature of his new official religion. But the prominence given to Śâkya Muni over all other saints required a novel expedient, relic distribution. This seems to have been the originality of Aśoka.

From Hwen Thsang's "Mémoires" we can restore this tope-worship. At Mathurâ the "heretics" of the "Little Vehicle" still carried it on. Śâriputra, Maudgalyâyana, Ânanda, Upali, and other saints of Buddhism had each his stûpa. At certain fixed fast days the worshippers collected in crowds. Jewelled banners and parasols were reared aloft. Clouds of incense and quite a "rain" of flowers were offered. Once a year the relics were exposed to the crowd. Those who went fasting to the spot could often see a miraculous coruscation round the relic exposed. Miracles worked by a relic are crowded into the narrative of the Chinese pilgrim. Even walking three times round a stûpa within the rails would produce a certain cure at some stûpas.[1]

The rule of the good King Aśoka was a very noteworthy attempt to establish on cold earth the rule

---

[1] Hwen Thsang, "Mémoires," vol. i. pp. 109, 208; vol. ii. pp. 13, 49. "Histoire," pp. 103, 104, 216, etc.

of the sky. War was forbidden, and executions and torture. Slavery was condemned, and the orgies of blood at the autumn festival. For the benefit of both beast and man, gardens of healing shrubs and herbs were to be cultivated everywhere. Shady trees were to be planted along the high-road, wells sunk, serais, or inns, erected. He records on his rocks that previous kings had found delight in " gambling," and " hunting the antelope " in "convivial meetings," when, for the purpose sometimes of food and sometimes of " false gods," many harmless animals were put to death. But for these a great Festival of Dharma was to be substituted, with many " fireworks," " elephant processions," parade of " chariots," and much "beating of drums." A feast of the pattern instituted by Aśoka was witnessed by Hwen Thsang on the " Plain of Munificence " (Dânamaṇḍala) at Allahabad. Four hundred thousand people were collected together, with countless elephants and chariots and men-at-arms. King Śîlâditya pitched his splendid pavilion on the north bank of the Ganges. King Kumâra had a fine tent in a grove on the banks of the Jumna. Eighteen other kings attended. The accumulated wealth of five years in Śîlâditya's vast empire was given away in presents and food. For eight days the festival lasted; and on the eighth the king, having given his last diamond necklace and silken robe, appeared in the rags of a pauper. Under a fine canopy a golden image of Buddha presided, [1] flanked by statues of Indra and Brahmâ. When this golden Buddha moved about, as we see, on another occasion,[2] Silâditya disguised as Indra with a white fly-whisk, and Kumâra disguised as Brahmâ with a dainty parasol, waited humbly upon him. This custom throws light on many passages of the Lalita Vistara. In the Mahâwanso it is announced that King Asoka instituted a seven-days' "festival of the Sight offering," during which a "miraculous figure" of Buddha was constantly visible. The two histories throw light the one on the other.

The Buddhism of Asoka was a Buddhism of stûpas, processions, pilgrimages, feasts for the poor. His rule was a very noteworthy attempt to introduce the rule of the "Other Bank" on this side of the Vaitaraṇî. But by designing a new and lower Buddhism for the people, he undermined the purer faith.

[1] "Histoire," p. 254.   [2] Ibid., p. 244.

CHAPTER XI.

THE "CARRIAGE THAT DRIVES TO THE GREAT NOWHERE."

THE Buddhism of the "Great Vehicle," as it was called by its disciples, and the "Vehicle that drives to the Great Nowhere," as it was called by the earlier school, was first officially recognized at a great convocation summoned by King Kaniśka about A.D. 10.[1]

The controversy between the "Vehicles" was illustrated by an allegory. Three vehicles, the first drawn by a sheep, the second drawn by a stag, and the third drawn by an elephant, once crossed a river. The sheep, drawing the little vehicle, looked selfishly in the direction of the "other bank." The stag looked backwards, after the manner of stags when the hunter's arrows are assailing their does. The noble elephant, drawing the great vehicle, marched on sure ground. This fable was invented by the dis-

---

[1] Hwen Thsang, "Mémoires," vol. i. pp. 173 et seq.

ciples of the Great Vehicle,[1] and the moral it
intended to inculcate was this. The selfish disciples
of the Little Vehicle look forward to the "Other
Bank," look forward to a future life. The disciples
of the Great Vehicle disdained such selfishness. It
was called the "Pride of Individuality" (Âtma-
mada); and Hwen Thsang records how a foolish
monk of the Little Vehicle was sternly rebuked in
the heaven Tuśita by Maitreya himself, for holding
it.[2] The disciples of the Little Vehicle worshipped
the Buddha of the past ; the disciples of the Great
Vehicle worshipped "Bodhisatwa" Maitreya, the
Coming Buddha.

The worship of a Bodhisatwa seems at first sight
the worship conceived by a madman. The main
design of the Lalita Vistara is to show how a
Bodhisatwa is to develop into a Buddha. The
Bodhisatwa is in the heaven Tuśita. He is still in
the Kâmaloka, or Domain of Appetite. His "Divine
eye" is still closed. Far from being the Governor of
the Universe, for it was thus Maitreya got to be
viewed, he can do no good thing. And yet the great
allegory is full of interpolated passages which call the
"Buddhas of the Ten Horizons" the "Bodhisatwas
of the Ten Horizons," and so on. The absurdity

---

[1] Fa Hian, p. 10.
[2] Hwen Thsang, "Mémoires," vol. i. p. 222.

reaches its culminating point when, in the Nepâlese litany, although it is entitled the "Praise of the Seven Buddhas," an address to an eighth Buddha, Maitreya, is added. And as ritual is a more conservative institution than metaphysic, some other marked inconsistencies were found necessary. The corpse-worship of the old Buddhism had to be retained, because that was the outward rite of Buddhism. But as the prophet that has not yet come to the world is not yet available as a corpse, sepulchral mounds had to be erected, that contained neither corpses nor relics. The Bodhisatwa, or future Buddha, had many stûpas erected to him. They contained no relics, but the disciples of the "Vehicle that drives to the Great Nowhere" offered flowers and food to the non-existent relics. They marched three times round the stûpa, within the mystic altar rails. This "Bodhisatwa" was sometimes called " Bodhisatwa Mańjuśrî," the architect of the heavens.[1] He was sometimes called "Bodhisatwa Avalokiteśvara," the "God who looks down upon us." On the Ganges, Hwen Thsang was seized by pirates. These, struck by his splendid physique, prepared to sacrifice him to the goddess Durgâ. The pilgrim prayed to Maitreya, and suddenly, aloft in the sky, "in the palace of the Tuśita heaven," the dazzling

---

[1] Klaproth, "Travels of Fa Hian," p. 113.

form of the Bodhisatwa appeared. He was seated on a throne with legions of spirits around him. A mighty tempest suddenly arose, which whirled the dust into huge spiral clouds, and sank all the pirates' boats. They repented, and released the pilgrim.[1] Fa Hian, in a mighty storm at sea, also nearly lost his life. He prayed to Bodhisatwa Avalokiteśvara, and the ship was saved.[2]

At Mathurâ, during his visit, as the pilgrim Hwen Thsang shows, this rival stûpa-worship was very marked. The disciples of the Little Vehicle paid homage to the relics of Śâriputra, Maudgalyâyana, Ânanda, and the other great Buddhist saints, who had each one a handsome stûpa in that city. But the disciples of the Great Vehicle worshipped the Bodhisatwas, says the Chinese pilgrim.[3] Fa Hian bears similar testimony.[4]

If a vast nation of subtle thinkers were suddenly called upon to choose between the teachings of a prophet of the past, and those of a prophet yet unborn, one would think that the teachings of the former would have the preference, as they would certainly be better available to the general public. How the quaint cultus of a man who was only to attain the spiritual enlightenment some thousands of

---

[1] Hwen Thsang, "Histoire," p. 118.   [2] Fa Hian, p. 359.

[3] Hwen Thsang, "Histoire," p. 104.   [4] "Pilgrimage," p. 101.

years hence arose, it is very difficult now to say
precisely. We see from the writings of Hwen
Thsang, that from its political side the movement
was aimed against the authority of the Âchârya of
Magadha, the Rome of the Buddhists. Kaniśka, a
powerful Kashmîri, had conquered vast territories
that included Hindû Kush, and Kabul, Yarkand and
Khokan, Kashmîr and Ladâk, the plains of the
Upper Ganges as far as Agra, the Punjâb, Rajputâna,
Guzerat, and Scinde. Such a large Buddhist empire
would require a strengthened discipline amongst its
great army of monks. Magadha was not included in
this empire, and the two leading monks of Kaniśka,
Pârśvika and Vasubandhu, may have wished to
establish an ecclesiastical authority independent of
the " High Priest of all the world," as the Âchârya
of Magadha is called in the Mahâwanso.[1] Perhaps
the authority of the latter was ill defined ; and perhaps
it had also become weakened now that Magadha was
no longer the head-quarters of a large empire. If a
strong religious controversy were raging, it would be
the manifest policy of the king's head ecclesiastics to
take the side that opposed the Âchârya ("Teacher"
par excellence) of Magadha. The leader of the
religious movement was a monk of the convent of
Ayodhyâ—a visionary, one Asangha, who was trans-

[1] Mahâwanso, p. 21.

ported one night to the heaven Tuśita, and received the Yoga Śâstra, the principal Scripture of the new faith, from Maitreya himself. Vasubandhu, his pupil, was also an author. He indited many of the chief Śâstras of the innovating Buddhism.[1] He presided at the convocation summoned by King Kaniśka to introduce it. The king wanted to hold the convocation at Magadha :—

"He wished to repair to Râjâgriha, to the stone palace where Kaśyapa had formed the collection of sacred books. But the honourable Pârśvika (his senior monk) said to him : 'Take care, in that city are many heretics ! Many conflicting opinions will be expressed, and we shall not have time to answer and refute them. Why compose Śâstras ? The whole convocation is attached to this kingdom. Your realms are defended on all sides by high mountains, under the guardianship of Yakshas.' "[2]

It is plain from this that the new creed was established in the teeth of the High Priest of Magadha and the official Buddhism ; but Magadha afterwards took it up, as its tendency was plainly in the direction of strengthening the priesthood. At the date of King Śîlâditya the Âchârya of Magadha, in his head-quarters at Nalanda, was the chief exponent of the new creed.

---

[1] Hwen Thsang, " Histoire," p. 114 et seq.
[2] Ibid., "Mémoires," vol. i. p. 174.

I will copy down two passages from Hwen Thsang. This is what the disciples of the Little Vehicle said of their opponents :—

"They answered that the heretics of the Carriage that drives to the Great Nowhere [Śunyapushpa],[1] residing at the monastery of Nalanda, differed in nothing from the Kâpâlikas."[2]

They said, too, that the doctrine of the Great Vehicle did not come from Buddha at all.[3]

A Kâpâlika was a Brahmin, cunning in Tântric rites. A drama—the Prabodha Chandra Udaya—gives us a sketch of him when Buddhism was the official religion of India. Talking to a Buddhist he speaks thus :—

> " With goodly necklace decked of bones of men,
> Haunting the tombs, from cups of human skulls
> Eating and quaffing, ever I behold,
> With eyes that meditation's salve hath cleared,
> The world of diverse jarring elements
> Composed, but still all one with the Supreme.

The Buddhist. This man professes the rule of a Kâpâlika. I will ask him what it is (*going to him*). O ho, you with the bone and skull necklace ! what are your hopes of happiness and salvation ?

The Adept. Wretch of a Buddhist ! Well, hear what is our religion :—

> With flesh of men, with brain and fat well smeared,
> We make our grim burnt offering—break our fast
> From cups of holy Brahmin's skull, and ever
> With gurgling drops of blood that plenteous stream

---

[1] Pushpa means "flower" as well as "carriage." Eitel prefers this rendering.

[2] Hwen Thsang, "Mémoires," p. 220.   [3] Ibid.

N

From hard throats quickly cut ; by us is worshipped
With human offerings meet the dread Bhairava.

*   *   *   *   *   *

I call at will the best of gods, great Hari,
And Hara's self and Brahma.   I restrain
With my sole voice the course of stars that wander
In heaven's bright vault ; the earth, with all its load
Of mountains, fields, and cities, I at will
Reduce once more to water ; and, behold,
I drink it up ! " [1]

The Kâpâlika, or Adept, plainly thought that he was God on earth ; that at will he could restrain the movement of the stars and destroy the universe. Plainly, in the view of the early Buddhist school, the movement entitled the Great Vehicle was in the direction of turning the humble "Son of Śâkya" into a pretentious Kâpâlika.   In early Buddhism any one, without the intervention of any other mortal, could make a direct appeal to the supreme Buddha merely by walking three times round a relic stûpa.   But Hwen Thsang plainly tells us that the apostles of the Great Vehicle discouraged this worship of Śâkya Muni and the dead saints.

In the view of the disciples of the Little Vehicle the movement entitled the Great Vehicle was manifestly in the direction of Brahmin sacerdotalism. Seydel thinks that the passage in the Lalita Vistara where Buddha hands over his authority to

---

[1] Journ. Beng. As. Soc., vol vi. p. 15.

Maitreya in the heaven Tuśita is a veiled description of Buddha handing over the headship of the
visible Church ; and that Maitreya may have been
accepted in the first instance like the Christian " Com-
forter" by sacerdotalists, as a vague Being that was
practically the Visible Church deified. Here Fa
Hian, the other Chinese pilgrim, may be cited. He,
too, makes Maitreya-worship the key-stone of the
new creed. "Without the assistance of Maitreya,
who could have continued the labours of Śâkya and
reduced his laws to practice?"[1] Maitreya, to the
pilgrim, was plainly something akin to the principle
of Church development enunciated by Cardinal
Newman.

Details of the convocation of Kaniśka are given by
Hwen Thsang. The number of monks was fixed
at four hundred and ninety-nine. The ambitious
Vasubandhu presented himself at the door, but the
traditions of early Buddhism were still strong. Some
of the monks desired him to depart, as none but
Arhats (the fully enfranchised) could remain near the
building.

"I care little for the enfranchisement of study" (the
rank of Arhat),[2] said Vasubandhu. Then, with some
inconsistency, he performed a great miracle to prove
that he had attained that dignity. He flung into the

---

[1] Fa Hian, p. 37.   [2] Hwen Thsang, "Histoire," p. 104.

air a ball of thread, and one end remained fixed in
the sky. A similar prodigy was witnessed by Marco
Polo and other old travellers. Vasubandhu was
chosen president, and the convocation commented on
the Three Baskets.[1]

Bishop Bigandet has an interesting chapter on the
" Hierarchy of the Buddhists."[2]   Dr. Rhys Davids, in
opposition to this, tells us that there was no hierarchy
until the Buddhists set one up in Tibet;[3] which they
did about the fourteenth century A.D.   I have no
space to adjudicate between these rival authorities;
but a bishop of the Roman Catholic Church might
be expected *a priori* to be the better informed on
such a subject.   Certainly, too, there was a " High
Priest of all the world " as early as the second convocation, according to the Mahâwanso;[4] and this
Âchârya, as he was also called, was always the pupil
of his predecessor, as General Cunningham has pointed
out.[5]

Hwen Thsang throws some light on the status of
the Âchârya in his day.   He gives him the same
title as is given to him in the Mahâwanso.   It must
be mentioned that India at this time was governed
by a powerful monarch, Śîlâditya, whose dominions,

---

[1] Hwen Thsang, " Mémoires," pp. 176, 177.
[2] Bigandet, p. 447.　　　　　　　[3] " Buddhism," p. 246.
[4] Mahâwanso, p. 21.　　　[5] " Bhilsa Topes," p. 72.

according to Dr. Hunter, extended from the Punjab to North-East Bengal—from the Himalayas to the Narbada River.

But the centre of the Buddhist spiritual power and the centre of the imperial power were many miles apart. The emperor's capital was Kanouj. The Rome of the Buddhists was still in Magadha, and their largest ecclesiastical centre on a mountain at Nalanda (Baragaon). It would seem as if this spot was not in the actual territory ruled by Śîlâditya, for a king named Kumâra, in Eastern India, sent a message to the Mahâthêrô that if he did not send Hwen Thsang to him he would come to Nalanda and make it a heap of ruins. As a nod from King Śîlâditya brought this king fawning along the Ganges in a superb travelling palace to pay his homage, we may presume that Śîlâditya's soldiers were not actually posted at Nalanda. If they had been, King Kumâra would no more have thought of threatening to lay it in ruins, than the King of the Belgians would propose to go and burn the palace of the Archbishop of Paris.

Hwen Thsang's visit to Nalanda and its convents throws some light on the sunny days of Buddhism. These convents were built by King Śakrâditya and his five successors. There were eight courts surrounded by a long brick wall. Lines of tall towers pierced

the sky. Pavilions adorned with coral were surmounted some with domes and some with graceful
pinnacles, amongst which floated the mountain mists.
The houses of the Men of Pure Life were four storeyed.
The temples had pillars ornamented with dragons
and rafters shining with rainbow tints. Precious
jade adorned the red columns and the richly carved
roof. The pilgrim tells us that Indian architecture
was exactly like the Chinese. " Carved balustrades
allowed the light to shine through them," says the
worthy pilgrim. We can easily conjure up the scene.

Vast tanks outside the convents were spread with the
blue lotus. The spot had once been a mango garden,
and as such was given to Buddha by a rich merchant.
The fine mango plantations still gave shade to the
Men of Pure Life. Inside or attached to the convent,
when Hwen Thsang visited it, were no less than ten
thousand monks. Amongst the many convents in
India, he adds, were none as rich and as grand as
this.[1]

The Âchârya was so respected that "nobody dared
even mention his name."[2] He was alluded to as
the Treasury of Dharma (Saddharmakośa).

Hitherto, in India kings and monks had always
paid their reverence to the Chinese pilgrim. As his
adventures are given to us by two of his disciples,

[1] Hwen Thsang, vol. i. pp. 150, 151.   [2] See p. 144.

this may be a little exaggeration to gratify Chinese susceptibilities. But when Hwen Thsang is presented to the Âchârya in the Nalanda convent there can be no mistake as to who paid the homage on that occasion. Twenty old monks introduced the pilgrim to Dharmakośa.

"When he was in the presence of the superior he paid him all the duties of a disciple, and exhausted every token of homage. In obedience to the sacred regulations and the official etiquette, he [the Chinese pilgrim] moved forwards on his knees, supporting himself on his elbows. He struck the ground with his forehead, and made it resound with the tappings of his feet."[1]

The Convocation of Kanouj took place shortly after this, and its details were fixed by the High Priest of all the World.

The Grand Lâma of Tibet seems to me to be the representative of the Âchârya of Magadha, who, on the sacking of the great vihâra of Nalanda, took refuge first of all in North India, and on the expulsion of the Buddhists from that quarter escaped to Tibet. The traditions that we possess, though scanty, seem to point to this conclusion. In 1417 there was already a Grand Lâma in Tibet, one Tsonkhapa, a Buddhist from India. Like the earliest Âchâryas he appointed

[1] Hwen Thsang, vol. i. p. 144.

his successor to the office, one Dharma Rancha.[1]   It is worthy of remark that the Lâma is recognized as the head of the Buddhist Church by the Chinese and Japanese.   M. Abel de Rémusat, in his "Origine de l'Hierarchie Lamaïque," cites the literature of the latter to show that it was conceived that at the death of Buddha he at once reappeared on earth in Bengal as a "teacher" of kings.   That seems to be as the Âchârya ; and it is stated that Buddha as the Grand Lâma is always on earth.[2]   Gengis Khan patronized the Buddhists ; and his grandson officially designated the "Master of Doctrine" in Tibet, the "Living God," the "Self-existent Buddha," etc.[3]   Intolerant Mussulmans could only have proceeded to such extremities on the supposition that a vast body of Buddhists in their dominions believed that the Grand Lâma was the Âchârya, and that it was politic to conciliate them.

Dr. Rhys Davids draws a parallel between Lâmaism and the Roman Catholic religion, and comes to the conclusion that "natural causes" produce the same priestly developments.[4]   I own that I fail to see the close parallelism of conditions.   Lha Sa is a half-starved village amongst the glaciers of the Himalayas. What are the "natural causes" that could evolve a

---

[1] Schlagintweit, "Buddhism in Tibet," p. 153.   [2] See pp. 24, 25.
[3] See pp. 27, 28, 29.   [4] "Buddhism," p. 247.

"pope," "cardinals or chutuktas," "cathedrals," a
"hierarchy," "mystic sacraments," "gorgeous processions"[1] in desolate uplands? When a Constantine
in Europe, or an Aśoka in India rules a large army
of priests, it is conceivable that a spiritual general
and his lieutenants would be a necessity. I can
understand Lâmaism rising at Magadha, but not at
Lha Sa.

Bishop Bigandet shows that in Burmah there
are "novices," "professed members," "heads of
monasteries," a "provincial" who rules over the
monks of an entire district, and a "supérieur général,"
or "grand master," residing in the capital. This
looks very like a "hierarchy."[2]

---

[1] "Buddhism," p. 250.   [2] "La Vie de Gaudama," p. 478.

CHAPTER XII.

BUDDHAGHOSA AND THE ATHEISM OF CEYLON.

ABOUT the beginning of the fourth century A.D., there came to Magadha a young Brahmin who excelled in religious disputation. Near the bo-tree there was a convent where the youth obtained shelter. And thanks to the good-natured toleration of the Buddhists, he was allowed day after day to rehearse his fiery speeches, " clasp his hands," and otherwise get up his logic and gestures. He attracted the attention of the Mahâthêrô, who by-and-by converted him.

The eloquence of the new convert soon became more renowned than ever. He was called Buddhaghosa, the "Voice of Buddha," because he was as " eloquent as Buddha himself." These details are from the Mahâwanso, and so are the significant passages that follow.

One day the head of the Buddhist Church, one Rewato, came to the young man, and said—

" In the island of Ceylon is a commentary on the

Buddhist holy books. It is called the Aṭṭhakathâ, and was written in the Cingalese language by Mahindo, the son of Aśoka. Outside Ceylon this commentary does not exist. Go thither and translate this commentary into Pâli."

Supposing that we were to hear that the Archbishop of Canterbury had learned that a fifth Gospel existed in Gaelic in the Isle of Skye, and that he had sent his chaplain to translate it into English, for the purpose of bringing it into the lectionary, such a story would be equally probable.

Buddhaghosa repaired to Ceylon, to the convent at Anurâdhapura, and commenced his task. A miracle authenticated his qualifications. The Aṭṭhakathâ in its present form contains more than one life of Buddha, lives of the six previous Buddhas, and long-winded commentaries on all the Cingalese Scriptures. These in turn were "recompiled" by the young convert. The Buddhist Scriptures of Ceylon, " if translated into English," says Dr. Rhys Davids, " would be about four times as long as our Bible." [1] Yet when this colossal task was completed, the spirits (devas) conjured away the manuscript, and the painstaking convert went to work a second time. Again his completed work was spirited away, and again he finished it. The mischievous spirits then restored the two previous

[1] " Buddhism," p. 20.

translations, and lo and behold, in the three great compilations, not a "verse," a "meaning of a word," a "letter," or a transposition differed.   By this miracle Buddhaghosa proved his powers.   "Of a truth," said the monks of Ceylon, " this is the coming Buddha, Maitreyo!"

In the long and elaborate article in the *Journal of the Asiatic Society of Bengal,* from which I have been quoting,[1] Turnour makes patent a wholesale falsification of the ancient Cingalese chronicles by Buddhaghosa.

The main objects of this, in his view, were—

1. To show that Wijayo, who figures in these chronicles as the first King of Ceylon, was a disciple of Buddha ; that he was sent by Buddha to Ceylon ; that he arrived there at Buddha's death (B.C. 593 in the annals of Ceylon).   As the historical Wijayo, according to Turnour, did not appear on the page of history until about one hundred years later, the lives of some of the kings who ruled in Ceylon prior to Aśoka have to be spread out like niggard butter on abundant bread to make up these one hundred years. One dies over a hundred years of age.   Another "commences a turbulent reign " at ninety.   A third seems to have been 147 years of age.[2]   The two dates that can be checked by Western chronology, the date of

---

[1] Journ. Beng. As. Soc., vol. vi. p. 725.   [2] Ibid., p. 721.

Alexander's expedition and that of Megasthenes to King Chandragupta at Patna, are both dislodged by these changed dates. Alexander, according to the Ceylon chronology, must have visited India in the days of Aśoka, and not " during the commotions which preceded the usurpation of the Indian empire by his grandfather Sandracottus." [1] And the embassy of Megasthenes to Patna would have to be set down in Aśoka's reign likewise.

2. The story of Wijayo is only one of many fictitious incidents, all designed to invest the spread of Buddhism in Ceylon with paramount importance. Prophecies about a branch of the great bo-tree being planted at Anurâdhapura, about Buddha's collar-bone going to the dagoba in the same place, are put into the mouth of the dying Tathâgata in Buddhaghosa's Atthakathâ.

3. To fill up the same gap preposterous ages have to be given also to the monks, who take part in the three convocations that Buddhagosa describes. One is 107 years of age, another 140, according to the unrelenting arithmetic of Turnour.[2]

The minutely adjusted dates of the Cingalese kings, he says, " are found only in Buddhaghosa's Pâli version of the Atthakathâ and in the Mahâwanso." [3]

---

[1] Journ. Beng. As. Soc., vol. vi. p. 716.   [2] Ibid., p. 723.
[3] Ibid., p. 717.

As the second work was composed by Mahanâma at least fifty years after the Buddhaghosa's visit,[1] Mr. Turnour plainly fixes the forgeries on the latter.

In the account in Buddhaghosa's Aṭṭhakathâ of the three great convocations, a leading feature has to be noticed. It is recorded that eight monks who had seen Buddha were present at the second convocation, which occurred one hundred years after the first.

We possess two histories of the three Buddhist convocations, that of the North and that of the South. These are utterly at variance the one with the other.

The Northern account seems to me the most plausible. Buddha's early disciples were required to sleep under trees and never enter a house. They were also required, for missionary purposes, to shift this rude domicile every night. Wandering beggars (Bhikshus) of this sort could scarcely be expected to collect a large literature. A "convocation," as it is called, is said to have taken place just after Buddha's death. " The first compilers," says Csoma Korösi, "were three individuals of his principal disciples. Upali compiled the Vinaya Sûtram ; Ânanda the Sûtranta ; and Kaśyapa the Prajñyâ Pâramitâ."[2]

Buddhism struggled in obscurity until the reign of Aśoka, when it was fortunate enough to make a

---

[1] " History of Ceylon," p. 27.
[2] " Asiatic Researches," vol. xx.

convert of that powerful monarch. This was the cause of its outside success. In the Northern account, after the three disciples had collected the scanty scraps of remembered precepts, there is no convocation until Aśoka summoned one at Patna. The third convocation is fixed in the reign of Kaniśka, four hundred years after Śâkya.

The motive of Buddhaghosa in cramming one hundred fictitious years into the narrative has been not quite appreciated by Turnour. I shall be able to make it plain as I proceed, that Buddhaghosa has condensed the three convocations into the space of time that elapsed between the death of Buddha and the conversion of Ceylon to Buddhism, and that his hundred fictitious years were wanted for this purpose. His motive was, as Turnour suggests, the exaltation of Ceylon Buddhism ; but on the theological side it went deeper. He was about to push the " Carriage that drives to the Great Nowhere " into flat atheism, and sap the authority of the High Priest of Magadha in Ceylon. It may be asked, if the last were his object, why he did not fall back on the Little Vehicle, the original Buddhism. The answer, gathered from Hwen Thsang, is plainly that Ceylon was already saturated with the teachings of the Great Vehicle and its chief Scripture, the Yoga Śâstra. Buddhaghosa, too, learnt all his Buddhism from the

Mahâthêrô of Magadha. From Fa Hian we know that the great monastery of Magadha in his day was the head-quarters of the disciples of the Great Vehicle.[1]   Fa Hian and Buddhaghosa were nearly contemporaries.   Thus we see that both in Ceylon and from the Mahâthêrô of Magadha, Buddhaghosa could have learnt only one Buddhism, the Buddhism of the " Carriage that drives to the Great Nowhere." Besides this, Buddhaghosa was a Brahmin, a more or less converted Brahmin.   He was, perhaps, of the type Kâpâlika ; at any rate, he wished to make his own status as priest more exalted and more Brahminic.   In early Buddhism Buddha forgave sins ; in Cingalese Buddhism the priest is knelt to as God, and he forgives sins.   In North Buddhism the supernal triad grant the mystic grace that comes with the Parivrajyâ Vrata when the monk is ordained ; in Cingalese Buddhism the superior of the convent grants it.   Buddha had been dethroned in the sky to make way for the Church Militant deified, and Buddhaghosa wanted a Buddhism of his own.

I am aware that all this goes completely counter to the teachings of Dr. Rhys Davids.   He contends that the Buddhism of Ceylon was the Buddhism of

[1] He calls it " the very lofty and very beautiful Great Vehicle Monastery," meaning no doubt the Monastery of Nalanda (" Pilgrimage," p. 254).

the Little Vehicle; and that the Little Vehicle the original Buddhism, denied any after-life, and was in fact the "Carriage that drives to the Great Nowhere." But surely Hwen Thsang is a better authority on the point than Dr. Rhys Davids, considering that he was chosen expressly by the Âchârya of Magadha to conduct the great convocation of King Śîlâditya, which was summoned specially to consider the metaphysical dispute between the disciples of the Great Vehicle and the disciples of the Little Vehicle.

"In Ceylon," he says, "are about ten thousand monks who follow the doctrines of the Great Vehicle."[1] He says, moreover, that the controversy raged fiercely for a long time before the Great Vehicle was successful over the Little Vehicle. He tells us that one of the chief apostles of the Great Vehicle was Deva Bodhisatwa, a Cingalese monk.[2] At Kanchapura the Chinese pilgrim came upon three hundred monks that had just fled across the water from Ceylon, to escape the anarchy and famine consequent on the death of the king there.[3] Hwen Thsang was a sort of Lord High Inquisitor at the Convocation of Kanouj, that suppressed the Little Vehicle a short

---

[1] Hwen Thsang, "Histoire," p. 192.
[2] "Mémoires," vol. i. p. 218, 277
[3] Hwen Thsang, "Histoire," p. 192.

time afterwards. If a vessel containing three hundred mixed Christians from the Low Countries had been wrecked on the coast of Spain in the reign of Philip II., we may fairly presume that any of them released after due inquiry by the Holy Office might be considered Catholic, and not Protestant.

That a foreigner like Hwen Thsang should have been chosen to conduct the Convocation of Kanouj argues the possession by him of much metaphysical subtlety; whereas Dr. Rhys Davids seems to me a confused thinker though invaluable as a translator. He says Buddhism is an "atheism;" but he says that in the South the Buddhists "worship Buddha."[1] He says, moreover, that the Buddhists of Ceylon "think Brahma the Highest God."[2] He says that the Buddhists "take as their ultimate" the world of matter,[3] and yet that they believe in a "Messiah" like the Christians—a "Word of God made flesh." He says that Buddha rejected the idea of the soul, or of "anything of any sort that exists in any manner after death," and yet that he would have rejected the "title Agnostic with indignation."[4] I shall show as I

---

[1] "Buddhism," p. 170.   [2] *Indian Antiquary*, vol. i. p. 331.
[3] "Buddhism," p. 87.
[4] This is qualified, it is true, by an explanation that by *gnosis* the doctor means knowledge of the seen and not of the spirit world. This would make Clement of Alexandria an Agnostic, and Professor Clifford a fervent Gnostic.

proceed that Fa Hian confirms Hwen Thsang on important points.   And Dr. Rhys Davids himself tells us that in Ceylon the "White Statue" of Maitreya is everywhere.[1]   This is, in fact, the kernel of the question.   The worship of Maitreya is, in brief, the Buddhism of the Great Vehicle.

[1] "Buddhism," p. 201.

CHAPTER XIII.

THE FIRST CONVOCATION.

BUDDHA died miserably under a tree ; but, according to the Aṭṭhakathâ, there were near Râjâgṛiha, at the moment of his death, eighteen great vihâras (monasteries) all "filled with rubbish," because the monks had gone off to be present at the saint's cremation. The monks determined to repair these monasteries, for fear of the reproach that the "enormous wealth" bestowed for religious purposes was misapplied. Five hundred of them got together, and said, "Let us employ ourselves in the first month of Wasso (the Buddhist Lent) in repairing the monasteries. In the middle month of Wasso we will hold a convocation on Dhammo and Winayo." At the end of the first month these repairs were completed.

The monks then went to the King of Râjâgṛiha and said, "Mahârâja, we propose to hold a great convocation on religion and discipline. On the Webhara

Mountain is a cave called Sattapanni. Be graciously pleased to prepare that cave for us!"

The king at once gave orders that a mighty cave-temple should be scooped out of the rock. A "hall," with "pillars" and "walls," was executed as if by the hand of Viśvakarma, the architect of heaven. "Flights of steps, embellished with representations of festoons of flowers and of flower-creepers, rivalling the splendour of the decorations of his palace, and imitating the magnificence of the mansions of the devas," were constructed. Five hundred carpeted seats were prepared for the monks, and a pulpit for the principal. A preaching desk, "for the sanctified Buddha himself," in the centre of the hall facing the east was erected, and an ivory fan placed upon it. This incident shows, I think, that the early sermon-monger was supposed to get his inspiration direct from the dead Tathâgata.

In two months this great cave-temple was completed; and the monks were summoned. A difficulty arose about Ânanda, who had not acquired the miraculous powers that stamp the adept in the knowledge of Prajñâ Pâramitâ, the wisdom of the unseen world. Thus, as first constituted, the convocation consisted of 499 members, and a vacant carpet was spread for Ânanda. During the night he meditated on the Kâyagastâ Satiyâ, and in the morning these

powers came; and in proof he reached his seat
through the medium of the floor of the temple.

Mahâ Kaśyapa was the chief Thêrô, and he opened
the proceedings by requesting Upali, to detail Buddha's injunctions on discipline. Upali before answer-
ing, sat in the pulpit of Buddha, and held the mystic
ivory fan. Three hundred and four Sikkhapadini on
form and rites were wearily gone through. After
Upali detailed each section the monks at once chanted
it forth. When Upali took the mystic fan in his
hand the mighty earth quaked. As the narrative
announces that this was done to give the assembly
a greeting similar to the one that Buddha used to
give his Arhats, I think the idea plainly was that,
instead of being annihilated, the great teacher was
present, obsessing Upali in his chair. After Upali had
revealed all that he recollected from Buddha's lips on
the subject of discipline, Ânanda stepped into the
" pulpit of the sanctified Buddha himself," and detailed
all the utterances that he could call to mind about
Dharma. The Northern account gives to Ânanda the
Sûtras, and to Kaśyapa the department of Prajñâ
Pâramitâ, or Dharma. The convocation sat for seven
months. Earthquakes and other miracles greeted its
finish.

Now it seems to me we are here in the presence of
a piece of pure history. The details of the great cave-

temple with its mats, pulpits, ivory fan, chanting monks, etc., are too lifelike to be absolute invention. The incident of the eighteen tumble-down vihâras filled with rubbish, but hastily got ready, is not the sort of incident that would have suggested itself to a Cingalese writer of fiction. The Mahâwanso, describing the great banquets during Aśoka's inauguration, announces that elks, wild hogs, and winged game came to the king's kitchen of their own accord, and then expired ; that parrots daily brought nine hundred thousand loads of hill paddy, and mice husking that hill paddy converted it into rice. The fine fancy of a Cingalese historian, if left to itself, would have gone off into similar flights.

But if the convocation described is a *bonâ fide* convocation, it cannot be the first convocation of the Cingalese records ; nor yet the second, nor even the third. The cave which is thought to be the Sattapanni cave (though its identity is questioned by Mr. Fergusson) is, according to that authority, a natural cave " slightly improved by art." [1] In Aśoka's day the cave-temple was a small cave without sculpture, and with merely a polished roof. Even in Kaniśka's day there was no cave-temple of the gorgeous pattern here described. This gives a very modern date to the narrative. It gives us, I think, without any doubt, some details of

[1] " Indian Architecture," p. 108.

Kaniśka's convocation. Observe that the number of monks in Kaniśka's convocation, and the number of monks in the first convocation as recorded by Buddhaghosa, are in each case exactly four hundred and ninety-nine. In each case, also, this is made up to five hundred by a monk performing a miracle.

It must be remembered that, if in the third or fourth century of our era a writer in Ceylon were drawing up a history of the convocations, the details of the last one would naturally be the most prominent in his mind. He would see the panorama of history reversed. The last convocation would be clear, the second and first dim and shadowy. I must point out, too, that the incident of the chanting monks could not have taken place, as described in the Ceylon books. It would be quite impossible to get five hundred monks to learn by heart a voluminous canon, four times as long as our Bible, in the time given. Two contradictory narratives have been made use of—a story similar to the Northern story, which announced that three disciples collected the scanty scraps of the remembered precepts of Buddha three months after his death, and a narrative of Kaniśka's convocation, which would have had the incident of the chanting monks. At that period they *could* have sung out all the canonical books, as they knew them by heart. The incident of Ânanda's exclusion, on account of defective mystical knowledge, is also an impossible incident, as, instead of being the only monk of five hundred ignorant of Dharma, he is confessed to be the only one who knew anything about it. The incident has a meaning when applied to Vasubandhu, as he was of a school that exalted the Bodhisatwa over the Arhat. The disciples of the Great Vehicle objected to become Arhats.

But the evidence that Buddhaghosa's account of the first convocation has been largely made up from details of Kaniśka's convocation is by no means exhausted. The chief individual work discussed was the Brahmajâla Sûtra. Mahâ Kaśyapa, the president, asked Ânanda which Sûtra should be first considered.

" Lord, the Brahmajâla Sûtra," said Ânanda.

" Let us then rehearse first that Sûtra," said the president, "which triumphed over the various heretical faiths sustained by hypocrisy and fraud, which unravelled the doctrinal issue of the sixty-two heterodox sects, and shook the earth together with its ten thousand component parts." When Ânanda had explained all about this Sûtra, the earth rocked. "All the thirteen Sûtras," says the narrative, "were then rehearsed in the prescribed forms."[1]

---

[1] Turnour, Journ. Beng. As. Soc., vol. vi. p. 521.

I shall show by-and-by that the Brahmajâla Sûtra is the chief armoury of Dr. Rhys Davids. From it he has derived his "original Buddhism," the "Buddhism of the Little Vehicle." From it, too, he has derived his notion that Buddha denied the existence of the "soul" and of "anything of any sort that exists in any manner after death." The doctor is evidently not aware that the Brahmajâla Sûtra was a prominent work of the Great Vehicle. This is made patent by the Chinese books.[1] It is called Fan Kang. As its special object, according to Buddhaghosa, was to triumph over heterodox sects (who believed in soul and a future life), it is highly probable that it really was made a prominent book at the convocation which, under Kaniśka, first made official the teachings of the "Carriage that drives to the Great Nowhere." Fa Hian fully supports his brother pilgrim, Hwen Thsang. He says, very positively, that the disciples of the Little Vehicle worshipped the saints of the past, Kaśyapa, Śâkya Muni, Ânanda, Śâriputra, etc. He says, as explicitly, that the disciples of the Great Vehicle worshipped the Bodhisatwas, Manjuśrî, and Avalokiteśvara.[2] In a storm, when leaving Ceylon, the worthy pilgrim sent up a prayer to this last being,

---

[1] See Rémusat's note to " Pilgrimage of Fa Hian," p. 108. He cites Hoa Yen, the great authority on the Great Vehicle.

[2] Fa Hian, p. 101.

and the ship escaped. Dr. Rhys Davids confesses that the "Arhat," or saint idea, was the "key-note" of "early Buddhism," the Little Vehicle, and that the "Bodhisatwa" idea was the "key-note" of the Great Vehicle, the "later school;"[1] but if his conclusions are true, the disciples of the Little Vehicle worshipped the saint of the past, although they believed in his non-existence, and the disciples of the Great Vehicle made it their special tenet to leave off the worship of the saint of the past, because they had become convinced that he still lived.

I think that the additional light that Dr. Oldenberg has thrown on the building up of the Cingalese legend of the first convocation has been quite mis-understood by Dr. Rhys Davids. Dr. Oldenberg brings together two narratives, and shows that the Buddhaghosa narrative has taken long passages word for word from the first, taken many of the incidents, especially one of a foolish monk called Subhadda, who rejoiced because Buddha was no longer present to annoy them with his authoritative words, "This beseems you! This beseems you not!" "Every-thing that the legend of the First Council alleges as a motive for, and as a background to, the story about Kassapa's proposal for holding the council, is found here altogether, except that there is no allusion to

[1] "Hibbert Lectures," p. 254.

the proposal itself or to the council. . . . If anywhere, we should certainly have expected to find here some allusion to the great authentic depositions about Dhamma and Vinaya." I think no one except Dr. Rhys Davids will draw exception to Dr. Oldenberg's conclusion, "What we have here before us is not history but pure invention, and moreover an invention of no very recent date."[1]

Although Dr. Rhys Davids is the warmest defender of the authenticity of the first convocation, if we consult dates it would seem as if even he had abandoned it. He has written an article to fix the date of the death of Buddha at 412 B.C.[2] That would of course give the date of the first convocation. But in his preface to his Buddhist Suttas, he announces that their date may be "fixed without much uncertainty" about the latter end of the fourth or the beginning of the third century before Christ. As the second convocation is recorded to have taken place one hundred years after the first, this would make them fit in with the *second* convocation. In his "Buddhism" he fixed their date, also "without much uncertainty," at the third convocation. I don't quite see how it is consistent with the severe positive method to shift a date up and down in this manner.

[1] Vinaya piṭaka, Introd.
[2] Numismata Orient., 1877.

If the poems of Rowley, a priest said to have lived in the fifteenth century, can be proved to have been forged by Chatterton, a mere shifting of dates, say, to the fourteenth century or the sixteenth would not make them a bit more authentic. It must be remembered that this is a case not of gossipy history but of title-deeds. It is not in debate whether or not some convocation of Buddhist monks sat somewhere, but whether the testimony of the Cingalese chronicles about the Cingalese holy books is sufficiently strong to put all other Buddhist literature out of court.

Regarding the second convocation I have already said perhaps enough. Turnour shows that to make up the hundred odd years which, as he alleges, Buddhaghosa has foisted on the original chronicles, a line of preternaturally long-lived monks had to be added as companions to the patriarchal kings.

"If," he says, "we follow the narrative history of the Buddhist patriarchs, and which is termed the "sacerdotal succession," we shall find ample justification for throwing equal discredit on the dates of both convocations. In that narrative will be found a consecutive and detailed account of no less than six generations of preceptors having intervened from the death of Śâkya to the meeting of the third convocation, comprising a period of 235 years, and affording an average of about thirty-nine years for each

preceptor." [1] This causes impossible ages to be given
to some of the monks, 170, 140 years, and so on ; and
prophecies about Moggaliputta Tissa and Aśoka have
been foisted into the deliberations of the council.
The subjects discussed, such as whether an ascetic
may sit on seats covered with fringes, may drink whey,
whether also he is forbidden to eat after midday, or
is allowed a few minutes' grace until the shadow of
the declining sun is two inches long, plainly belong to
times when monks are fat and idle, not lean and active.
Fortunately, too, we can completely disprove this
second convocation from pure history.   Megasthenes
visited Patna B.C. 302 to 298.   As Buddha died
470 B.C.,[2] and the second convocation took place at
Vaiśâlî one hundred years after his death, it must
have taken place B.C. 370.   So Megasthenes visited
Patna, which is about twenty miles from Vaiśâlî, not
more than seventy years after the second convocation.
Instead of finding lazy Buddhist monks living in
sumptuous monasteries and entering into puerile
disputes about whether or not they were to have
fringes to their couches and so on, he found the
Buddhists with no other monasteries than the jaṅgal
and the mountain waste.   Even the rich Brahmins,
the official priests, dwelt in those days, as I have

[1] Journ. Beng. As. Soc. vol. vi. p. 724.
[2] This is the date accepted by Max Müller, Bühler, and the chief
authorities.

shown,[1] in a "grove," and slept on skins of beasts and couches of leaves.

"The second convocation," says Tiele, "said to have been held under a certain King Kâlâśoka, is as little historic as that prince himself."[2]

[1] From Megasthenes, see p. 162.
[2] "Ancient Religions," p. 139.

CHAPTER XIV.

THE THIRD CONVOCATION.

I NOW come to the third convocation said to have been held in the reign of King Aśoka. And here we are on sure ground. Buddhaghosa's account of the thirty-four books "reaffirmed" at this convocation can be proved to be pure fiction by the best of all possible evidence, the evidence of the Aśoka stones. With Buddhaghosa's third convocation, of course, his first and second depart also to the Great Nowhere. I have been considering the building up of the Buddhaghosa legend, rather than seriously arguing against his history of the three convocations.

On the Bairât rock is a list of the "religious works" which Aśoka orders the monks and nuns to get by heart. This list consists of seven tractates; and in the Dhauli Separate Edict the king expressly orders that nothing else shall be recited at his temples except what he expressly enjoins.[1]

[1] Cunningham, "Corp. Ins. Indicarum," p. 128.

1. The Summary of Discipline.
2. The Supernatural Powers of the Masters.
3. The Terrors of the Future.
4. The Song of the Muni.
5. The Sûtra on Asceticism.
6. The Question of Upatishya.
7. The Admonition to Râhula concerning Falsehood, uttered by our Lord Buddha.

Nothing can be more important than this. If the Bairât rock-inscription is genuine, the Ceylon history of the convocations is pure fiction. I brought this argument forward in my "Buddha and Early Buddhism," and only one critic, Dr. Rhys Davids, has ever attempted to meet it. I will consider his answer presently.

It must be remembered that in the old Indian creeds holy books were handed down entirely by recitation. The letters of the alphabet, according to Professor Max Müller, General Cunningham, and the chief authorities, were not known in India until Asoka's day. We know from the Mahâwanso[2] that the holy books of Ceylon were not committed to writing until the reign of King Wattaganini (104 to 76 B.C.). So the books that Asoka ordered to be handed down by the recitation and chantings of his monks must have plainly constituted the entire body

[1] Chap. xxxiii.

P

of the recognized Scriptures. In what way could any other Scriptures come down? Dr. Oldenberg talks of these seven books as if they were " passages " only, he believing that the large body of Pâli Scriptures of Ceylon was in existence as early as the second convocation.[1] But if they were "passages," who was to remember and recite the rest of the voluminous canon? Aśoka's monks were expressly forbidden so to do. In an article in the *Saturday Review*, generally attributed to Dr. Rhys Davids, reviewing my book " Buddha and Early Buddhism," is a second argument. The authorship perhaps is immaterial ; but I give it the additional importance that it may derive from the doctor's name. This is what he writes of my argument :—

" His argument from the titles on the Aśoka monuments cannot be seriously urged when we know that they are rather descriptions of contents than fixed titles, and may be easily varied."[2]

This means, if I read it aright, that the titles refer to groups of books, not individual volumes.

But will this theory bear discussion any more than the other? The Muni Gâthâ, or Life of Buddha, in the only form that the doctor sanctions, is not a library, but a work that has in his view brevity for its most

---

[1] " Buddhism," p. 134, note.
[2] *Saturday Review*, Nov. 5, 1881.

conspicuous merit. "The Admonition to Râhula concerning Falsehood, uttered by our Lord Buddha," has been restored to us, thanks to the activity of Professor Beal. It occupies two pages of the Chinese Dhammapada. "The Supernatural Powers of the Masters" and "The Terrors of the Future" can scarcely be considered by Dr. Rhys Davids generic titles of large groups of the "original Pâli" Scriptures, because he has so often pointed out to us that the distinctive feature of those Scriptures is that they ignore "supernatural powers" and "the future" altogether.

"The Question of Upatishya" had reference to the acquisition of the amrita, the "food of immortality."[1] Upatishya is a name of Sâriputra, Buddha's chief disciple. This, again, could scarcely be a felicitous motto for a large section of volumes which deny immortality altogether. "The Question of Upatishya" and Buddha's answer to it occupy leaf forty-one and leaf fifty of the Tibetan Dulvâ. Far from there being a sacred literature four times as voluminous as the Bible at the date of Aśoka, it is possible that up to his date there were no holy books at all.

I will now briefly consider the rites, the symbols, the cosmology, etc., and some of the holy books of Buddhism, to see what light they throw on the great

---

[1] Korösi, "Asiatic Researches," vol. xx. p. 51.

change of front effected by the movement entitled the Great Vehicle. And on account of its factitious importance at the present moment, I will consider chiefly the literature of Ceylon.

CHAPTER XV.

BUDDHAGHOSA'S CONDENSATION OF THE LALITA VISTARA.

An analysis of the Lalita Vistara seems to show portions due to at least three distinct schools, and, I may add, periods of Buddhism.

1. When Brahma was recognized as the Supreme God.

2. When Śâkya Muni had been promoted to the rank of Supreme God.

3. The Buddhism of "the Carriage that drives to the Great Nowhere."

It is patent that in its main lines and framework the Lalita Vistara is an allegory, exhibiting a fallible man working up from the lower to the divine life. It is not pretended that he is without sin :—

"I have known the lusts of man, O charioteer, and my joy is fled!"

In the Chinese Life of Wung Puh there is a picturesque expression that the prince revelled in the

"five dusts ;" and if the story means anything, its
main purpose is to show how a mortal, subject to the
chief miseries of existence—age, disease, and death—
can find a mode of escape.   Much ingenuity of alter-
ation has been shown by later Buddhists, but the ribs
and backbone of the story have proved too stout for
them.

The historical Buddha was a Brahmacharin.   To
know Brahma was the main object of these solitary
mystics ; and in the Lalita Vistara is much that is in
harmonious keeping with such an historical character.
Buddha constantly alludes to the "world of Brahma "
and to Nirvâna, as if the two ideas were synonymous
in his mind.   Before his last birth he was in the
heaven Tuśita, the sixth of the Devaloka, and therefore the nearest, according to Brahmin ideas, to the
indestructible heaven of the immortal spirits, the
Brahma heaven.   The prince is constantly described
as being well versed in the "way of Brahma."   He
is "eminently raised by his prayers."   In the great
competition for pretty Gopâ he excels all rivals in his
knowledge of theology and worship, and also in
"joining his hands in prayer."   He certainly prays
to Him of the Ten Hundred Eyes before riding away
through the Gate of Benediction ; and it is to be
observed that Brahma is the title given to the father
when Buddha as the Golden Germ is in the womb

of his mother. And finally, in the great crisis of Buddha's struggle with the Wicked One, the ascetic invokes Brahma, and at once the hellish legions are dispersed. An important subtlety has to be noticed here. All the influences that push the prince along the higher pathway are from spirit-land. The king, the court, the pious priests, and even poor Gopâ, all mortals, persistently attempt an opposite urging. And in the Lalita Vistara these unseen guides all belong to the Brahma heavens; and a moment's reflection shows that this subtlety was a logical necessity to the original author of the allegory. None of the denizens of earth and of the six lower heavens had attained the great spiritual enlightenment; and the prince, having reached the Tuśita heaven, was as instructed as they. The Southern Canon, by banishing the ministering Jinas and Buddhas of the Northern Lalita Vistara, has completely stultified the whole original story. It was a mighty conflict between two great camps, the indestructible heaven of the immortal spirits and the domain of Kâma or Eros, whence the prominence given to the erotic principle in the struggle.

To one who holds that Buddhism started as a pure atheism, this question of Brahma is vital. In the Buddhist books there are two Brahmas—one a kind of body-servant to Buddha, and the other the supreme

Father. "Mahâ-Brahma offers flowers to the cloth that cleans my feet," says Buddha in one of the Cingalese versions.[1]

Thus the question arises : Did Brahma develop from the Supreme Being into a worshipper of foot-cloths, or was this last ideal the first in point of time ? Those who boldly avow that the Brahmin ideas in what is called Northern Buddhism are a modern addition must really accept the latter almost inconceivable hypothesis. Buddha without doubt called his followers Brâhmaṇas, or seekers after Brahma. We have the evidence of the Ceylon Scriptures that he said that he came to restore the pure Brahma religion. We have the same evidence that he said, in answer to certain Brahmins, that there was a supreme Brahma ; but that it was only pure-minded ascetics like his own disciples that could know him. The Lalita Vistara makes Buddha pray to Brahma in the crisis of his conflict with the Very Wicked One. Buddhaghosa brings in Brahma to do what in the green-room is called some "funny business" with an umbrella at the same critical period. When Buddha hesitates to preach, both Buddhaghosa and the Lalita Vistara make Brahma over-persuade him.

But to make Brahma into a Polichinelle Brahma was not enough. Buddhaghosa and the other apostles

[1] Hardy's "Manual," p. 185.

of the Great Vehicle found it necessary also to leave out the "Buddhas of the Ten Horizons," the "Buddhas of the past," the " Jinas of the past," that figure every-where as the "guides of mortals" in "the Lalita Vistara. He has changed them into devatâs, and Dr. Rhys Davids into " fairies."

But in the pathway of the new school there was an obstacle—the ritual. Here we detect the falsifi-cations.

In the modern ritual of Tibet are these words : " I adore the Tathâgatas of the three periods who dwell in the ten quarters of the world, the Jinas [triumphant spirits], the perfect Buddhas, I offer to them and confess my sins." [1]

In the Chinese ritual these words occur : " All hail, Buddhas of the ten quarters ! " [2]

In the Ceylon ritual we find this : " I worship continually the Buddhas of the ages that are past. . . . I worship the Buddhas, the all-pitiful—I worship with bowed head." [3]

Dr. Rhys Davids considers his version of the Life of Buddha as given in the " Birth Stories " the " original " Life of Buddha, the " best Life we have." Preference is claimed for this biography on the ground that it is briefer and more free from marvel than the

[1] Schlagintweit, " Buddhism in Tibet," p. 126.
[2] Beal, " Catena," p. 409.   [3] Pâtimokkha, p. 507.

other biographies, points that denote an earlier
Scripture.

But the plea completely falls to the ground, because
Buddhaghosa, its compiler, confesses that it is a mere
abridgment of several other biographies, the Pabbajâ
Sutta,[1] an "older Cingalese Commentary,"[2] the
"Mahâpadâna," etc.[3] Other versions of the biography
are alluded to as existing in the "Jataka Commentary,"[4]
and as given by the "Repeaters of the Dîgha Nikâya."[5]
In Dr. Rhys Davids's version are also to be found
fictitious lives of many previous Buddhas. After the
death of each one of these, three convocations always
sat. As I have shown the Convocation of Vaiśâlî to
be pure fiction, it is plain that the work could not
have been composed until after the third historical
convocation held by King Kaniśka.

---

[1] "Birth Stories," p. 89.   [2] Ibid., p. 82.   [3] Ibid., p. 77.
[4] Ibid., p. 82.   [5] Ibid., p. 78.

CHAPTER XVI.

THE BRAHMAJÂLA SÛTRA.

ONE great obstacle to viewing Buddha, as the French philosopher Comte, born two thousand years too soon, is the Buddhist doctrine of Karma, and the Skandhas (Pâli, Kandhas). The Buddhists took over from the Brahmins the notion that a man's actions in one existence regulated his fate in subsequent births. My idea is that it was invented by the priesthood to account for the caste system. Certainly the prolonged life of the individual was the key-note of the idea. You groan and sweat under the weary life of a Sûdra, because in your last birth you were a brigand! I am allowed to seek union with Brahma, because for many existences my life has been pure! Regarding what the Buddhists call the Five Skandhas, some difference of interpretation prevails amongst scholars. Some think that the skandhas are what the individual takes with him to each new birth. Some think that they are that which he leaves behind him. Burnouf calls them the "intellectual attributes;"[1] Goldstücker, the "means of conception;" Schröter, in his Bhotanta Dictionary, the "five bodies;" Judson, in his Birman Dictionary, the "living animal." But all agree in this, that the Buddhists teach that individuality and its karma continue, at least till the Bodhi, or great emancipation.

Childers's explanation is this: "When a man dies the khandhas of which he is constituted perish, but by the force of his kamma [Sanscrit, Karma] a new set of khandhas instantly starts into existence, and a new being appears in another world, who, though possessing different khandhas, and a different form, is in reality identical with the man who has just passed away."[2]

Spence Hardy, in his "Manual," takes the same view. He cites a dialogue between Buddha and Sabha.

"A woman or a man takes life. The blood of that which they have slain is continually on their hands. They live by murder. They have no compassion on any living thing. Such persons, on the breaking up of the elements (the Five Khandas), will be born in one of the hells, or if on account of the merit received in some former birth they are born as men, it will be of some inferior caste."[3]

---

[1] "Introduction," p. 513. [2] Pâli Dictionary.
[3] "Manual," p. 463.

Of this teaching, Dr. Rhys Davids gives a version which differs *in toto* from these authorities. He affirms that the Buddhists teach that each individual is annihilated at death, but that the causation of his deeds is handed over to another distinct individual.[1] If A leads a thoroughly wicked life, B will take up the remorse and moral deterioration that result from A's misdeeds. If B conquers his fate and reforms, C will be happy because B neutralized the errors of A. This, says the doctor, avoids the "irreligious extreme of those who do not believe in moral justice and retribution,"[2] and illustrates the text: "Whatever a man soweth, that shall he also reap."[3] Perhaps B might answer that he was reaping what somebody else had sown. But one thing is certain, Dr. Rhys Davids differs not only with Beal, Hodgson, Burnouf, Colebrooke, etc., but also with Oldenberg, Childers, Spence Hardy, and other writers on Cingalese Buddhism.[4]

His sole authority for his views is the Brahmajâla Sûtra, mentioned at page 201. This Sûtra he considers the great exponent of early Buddhism, whereas I have already shown that it is the main Bible of the Great Vehicle teaching. Three speeches put into the

[1] Buddhism, p. 101.   [2] Page 103.   [3] Ibid.
[4] Oldenberg, "Buddha," p. 48; Hodgson, pp. 44, 45; Beal, "Romantic History," p. 10; Colebrooke, "Essays," vol. i. p. 397.

mouth of Buddha must now be considered. These three speeches may be considered the backbone of Dr. Rhys Davids's many lectures, treatises, and magazine articles, all of which on the strength of them charge Buddha with denying a life after death. As so much importance is attached to the speeches, I will give them at length:

"Priests among these Samanas and Brahmins are some who hold the doctrine of future conscious existence, and in sixteen modes teach that the soul consciously exists after death. But the teaching of these Samanas and Brahmins is founded on their ignorance, their want of perception of truth, their own personal experience, and on the fluctuating emotions of those who are under the influence of their passions.

"Priests among these Samanas and Brahmins are some who hold the doctrine of future unconscious existence, and in eight modes teach that the soul exists after death in a state of unconsciousness. But the teaching of these Samanas and Brahmins is founded on ignorance, their want of perception of truth, their own personal experience, and on the fluctuating emotions of those who are under the influence of their passions.

"Priests among these Samanas and Brahmins are some who hold the doctrine of a future state of being neither conscious nor yet unconscious, and in eight modes teach that the soul will hereafter exist in a state between consciousness and unconsciousness. But the teaching of these Samanas and Brahmins is founded on ignorance, their want of perception of truth, their own personal experience, and on the fluctuating emotions of those who are under the influence of their passions."

Plainly, says the doctor, conscious existence after death, unconscious existence after death, and existence in a state that is "neither conscious nor unconscious" are here flatly denied. "Would it be possible," he adds triumphantly, "in a more complete and categorical manner to deny that there is any soul, or anything of any kind which continues to exist in any manner after death?"

Now, considering the enormous superstructure that has been built upon this Sûtra, the first remark that I have to make is: "Has Dr. Rhys Davids read it?" I will continue the passage quoted. It gives a fourth speech of Buddha on the same subject:

"Priests among these Samanas and Brahmins are some who affirm that existence is destroyed, and who in seven modes teach that existing beings are cut off, destroyed, annihilated. But the teaching of these Samanas and Brahmins is founded on their ignorance, their want of perception of truth, their own personal experience, and on the fluctuating emotions of those who are under the influence of their passions."[1]

Now, it would be possible here for a disputant to obtain a cheap victory over the somewhat contradictory doctor; but I think that these difficult discrepancies merit closer study. We have before us a genuine Scripture of the Gospel of the " Carriage that drives to the Great Nowhere," and we see how that gospel was superposed on the earlier faith. It was deemed impossible to annul and change the vast literature of Buddhism, so the innovating school contented themselves with placing in the mouth of Buddha a few new speeches contradicting the earlier theology. In the present Sûtra, Buddha is brought on the scene to contradict and condemn every form and aspect of every conceivable question. Burnouf remarked this long ago, and Buddhaghosa praises these "conflicting" passages as being good for " discipline " (Vinaya).[2]

It is to be added that many of the arguments of the Brahmajâla Sûtra are very obscure, and it is difficult to know, at times, whether a view is being praised or condemned. Every possible aspect of such questions as soul, the eternity of matter, etc., is stated, and then Buddha is brought in to announce that, from his

[1] " Sept Suttas Pâlis," p. 107 (Grimblot).
[2] Turnour, Journ. As. Soc. Beng., vol. vi. p. 524.

unaided wisdom, he thoroughly knows the subject, and then he enunciates no opinion at all.

Dr. Rhys Davids, 'I must mention, cites one other passage from it, to prove the non-existence of the individual after death. It is a passage in which Buddha is made to declare that "after death neither gods nor men will see him."[1] But Dr. Rhys Davids's inference is distinctly confuted by another portion of the Sûtra, where Buddha gives his adhesion to the transmigration theory,[2] and says, moreover, that souls after death will go to a portion of the Brahmaloka which is never destroyed by fire.[3] It is to be remembered that Buddha, when he made the speech cited by the doctor, had already been born on earth five hundred and fifty times, and Dr. Rhys Davids himself, with patient labour, has translated a work entitled the "Five Hundred and Fifty Rebirths of Buddha." Childers affirms that after the Bodhi, when enfranchised Buddhas reach the Arupaloka, four out of five of the Skandhas still exist. The Lalita Vistara draws a line between the aggregations (Skandhas) of the true and the aggregations of the false.

[1] "Buddhism," p. 99.   [2] "Sept Suttas Pâlis," p. 76.
[3] Ibid., p. 78.

CHAPTER XVII.

THE MAHÂPARINIRVÂNA SÛTRA.

WHAT we may call the gospel of flat contradiction, the gospel of the later Buddhism, is well illustrated in a Sûtra from Ceylon, which describes the death of Buddha.   It is called the Mahâparinirvâna Sûtra ; and seems an instructive jumble of many epochs of Buddhism.

The Northern Life, the " Twelve Acts of Sâkya," records that after Buddha's death, at his dying request, his body was cremated with rites in use for secular emperors, and that his ashes were deposited in a chaitya.   A proposal was made that they should be divided, but this was refused.   The Mahâparinirvâna Sûtra has for groundwork *precisely the same story.*

" What should be done, Lord," said Ânanda to the dying reformer, " with the remains of a Tathâgata ? "

" As men treat the remains of a king of kings, so, Ânanda, should they treat the remains of a Tathâgata."

"And how, Lord, do they treat the remains of a king of kings?"

Buddha gives explanations about placing the body in a coffin of iron, and the proper mode of cremating it; he then proceeds :—

"And as they treat the remains of a king of kings, so, Ânanda, should they treat the remains of the Tathâgata. At the four cross-roads a dâgaba [sepulchral mound] should be erected to the Tathâgata, and whosoever shall there place garlands or perfumes or paint, or make salutation there, or become in its presence calm in heart—that shall long be to them for a profit and joy."[1] He explains, a sentence or two afterwards, that a "true hearer of the Blessed One, the Arahat Buddha," is to be buried in a similar mound.

Nothing can be more explicit than this. Buddha plainly leaves injunctions that his relics are to be kept in one chaitya, not divided. Great chiefs in India and North Europe had each his solitary mound or haug. The Brahmin Rishi had his solitary haug. All that was mortal of Sâriputra, Buddha's chief Arahat, had already been deposited in a chaitya, and a yearly festival instituted in his honour.[2] A chaitya was also erected to Maudgalyâyana. It is plain that the earliest Cingalese writer, like the Northern one,

---

[1] "Buddhist Suttas," p. 93.   [2] As. Res., vol. xx.

was well aware of the fact that Buddha's undivided remains had been deposited in a single chaitya. This gives us a date for the earlier tradition.

On the top of the first narrative is the account of the distribution of the relics clumsily put in; and a later accretion still, I think, is one recommending pilgrimages to four special spots, made holy in connection with Buddha's life. These were the spots where Buddha was born, where he attained the Bodhi, where he first preached Dharma, and where he died.[1] Buddha's special aversion was pilgrimages. He called the Brâhmins Tîrthakas, "men of tank and shrine pilgrimages," so it must have been a long time before an institution so hateful to him could have crept into his own religion. But Dr. Rhys Davids has given us a rare opportunity of checking the date of a portion of the narrative. In the mouth of the dying Tathâgata is put a long disquisition about what spoken teachings are to be considered orthodox and what not. The rule laid down is that the spoken words are to be "put beside the Scripture and compared with the rules of the Order."[2] Now, we know that the Cingalese books were not written down at all earlier than B. C. 104,[3] so here we get a valuable date.

---

[1] "Buddhist Suttas," p. 90.   [2] Ibid., p. 68.

[3] In the reign of King Wattaganini, according to the Mahâwanso (Journ. Beng. As. Soc., vol. vi. p. 506).

Dr. Rhys Davids quoted three speeches from this Sûtra in his " Hibbert Lectures." I think they are very instructive, as they show us once more how the apostles of the " Carriage that drives to the Great Nowhere " dealt with a well-known Scripture. They did not change it. They simply interpolated it.

" So long as the brethren shall live among the saints in the practice of those virtues . . . which are untarnished *by the desire of future life.*"

" The mind set round with intelligence is free from the great evils, that is to say from sensuality, from *individuality.*" [1]

" So long as the brethren fall not under the influence of that craving which, springing up within them, would give rise to renewed existence, . . . so long may the brethren be expected not to decline, but to prosper." [2]

Side by side with these three passages which Dr. Rhys Davids cited to prove his favourite theories, are other passages which flatly contradict them. Thus Buddha, contrasting the fate of the " wrong-doer " and the " well-doer " to give his hearers a strong incentive to do good, announces that the former after death will be reborn in some " unhappy state of suffering." [3] The well-doer, on the contrary, gains good report, the

---

[1] Page 38. "Hibbert Lectures," pp. 178, 179.
[2] "Hibbert Lectures," p. 175.   [3] "Buddhist Suttas," p. 17.

love of the worthy, and so on. "Fourthly, he dies without anxiety; and, lastly, on the dissolution of the body after death he is reborn into some happy state in heaven."[1]

This is the second passage: Buddha is explaining why a sepulchral tumulus is put up to the Arahat Buddha :—

"At the thought, Ânanda, 'This is the Dâgaba of that Blessed One, that Arahat Buddha,' the hearts of many shall be made calm and happy; and since they there had calmed and satisfied their hearts, they will be reborn after death when the body is dissolved in the happy realms of heaven.[2]

Mention is made, too, of a holy woman, Nandâ, who had "become an inheritor of the highest heavens,"[3] and was never to return to earth, showing that existence was not put an end to even by Mahâ-parinirvâna.

This gives us the secret of the apostles of the "Carriage that drives to the Great Nowhere," when dealing with an ancient Scripture. They put in a speech or two illustrating their own teachings, and relied on being able to mystify a simple disciple by the aid of these. In this they have been but too successful, and their mystifications have even succeeded in learned Europe.

[1] "Buddhist Suttas," p. 17.   [2] Ibid., p. 94.   [3] Ibid., p. 25.

Both the Mahâparinirvâna Sûtra and the Brahmajâla
Sûtra are placed amongst the Chinese Scriptures of
the "Great Vehicle" in the official catalogue recently
drawn up at the Indian Office by Bunyiu Nanjio.

THE PRAISE OF THE SEVEN BUDDHAS.

The worship of the seven Buddhas in Northern
Buddhism has come down to us in the shape of a
litany, the Sapta Buddha Stotra (The Praise of the
Seven Buddhas). In Tibet, in addition to the seven
mortal Buddhas, a number of minor saints are now
invoked. In the Cingalese Scriptures we have this
litany also, but a clumsy fable has been invented to
explain it away. It is recorded that when Buddha
was on the mountain called the Eagle's Peak, near
Râjâgriha, a demon, named Vessavana, visited him,
and gave him a charm to be recited by his male
and female disciples as a "defence" against all the
demons of the universe. I will cite a few paragraphs:

"Adored be the all-seeing and glorious Vipassi
[Vipassissanam].

"Adored be Vessabhu the subjector and destroyer
of the passions!

"Worship Gautama the Conqueror! We worship
Gautama the Conqueror, the Buddha endued with all
knowledge!"[1]

[1] Atânâtiya Sutta, in the "Sept Suttas Pâlis" (Grimblot, p. 323).

Here we catch Dishonesty in his workshop. The litany has been explained away by the innovating school because it confuted their theories of annihilation. The words "Adoration to Buddha," by a silly story, have been changed from a prayer used after his death to an address made to him whilst he was alive. The litany was in the hands of the people, so it was thought more prudent to stultify it than to suppress it. The invaluable Stûpa of Bharhut, as I have shown, enables us to expose the cheat, as it gives us in marble the seven trees with the name of each great Buddha incised on each.

I give a list of these seven Buddhas and their trees: Vipaśyi, pâtala (*Bignonia*); Śikhi, puṇḍarîka (*lotus*); Viśvabhû, śâla (*Shorea robusta*); Krakuchch'handa, śirisha (*Acacia sirisa*); Kanaka Muni, udumbara; Kaśyapa, nyagrodha (Banian tree); Śâkya Muni, asvattha (*Ficus religiosa*).[1]

In the sacred literature of Tibet is a Sûtra of the Seven Buddhas (Sapta Buddhaka), who are invoked by a saint, and who appear in succession in the air, and give him charms against evil.[2] It is plainly a Sûtra of the earlier Buddhism.

---

[1] A similar list of trees and Buddhas can be extracted from the Southern Scriptures, "Birth Stories," pp. 48, 49, etc.

[2] Csoma Korösi, "Asiatic Researches," vol. xx. p. 469.

THE DHAMMAPADA.

The same dishonesty is to be detected in Buddha-ghosa's version of the Dhammapada, the collected sayings of Buddha. Professor Beal has translated for us the Chinese version of this work. In it we see that Buddha preached that the Bodhi, or emancipation, transported the saint to the "heaven of Brahma."

"There are eleven advantages which attend the man who practises mercifulness, and is tender to all that lives. His body is always in health. He is blessed with peaceful sleep; and when engaged in study he is also composed. He has no evil dreams. He is protected by devas, and loved by men. He is unmolested by poisonous things, and escapes the violence of war. He is unharmed by fire or water. He is successful wherever he lives, and when dead goes to the heaven of Brahma."[1]

This is another passage :—

" He who is humane does not kill. He is ever able to preserve life. This principle is imperishable. Whoever observes it no calamity shall betide that man. Politeness, indifference to worldly things, hurting no one, without place for annoyance, this is the character of the Brahma heaven. Ever exercising love towards

[1] Beal's "Dhammapada," p. 58.

the infirm ; pure according to the teaching of Buddha ; knowing when sufficient has been had ; knowing when to stop,—this is to escape the recurrence of Birth and Death."[1]

Buddhaghosa's version has left out these passages, but the cheat is a silly one, because in his Aṭṭhakathâ, in giving a Life of Kaśyapa Buddha, he has allowed the following passage to remain :—

"They [certain holy persons] do not possess the qualification which would involve their reproduction in the Suddhâvasa Brahmaloka, from whence they would never return to the human world."

On the same page it is announced that in the great cataclysms that at the end of a Day of Brahma, or dispensation, destroy the seen world, the Heaven of Brahma is untouched.[2]

THE TWELVE OBSERVANCES.

Perhaps the most barefaced piece of falsification in Ceylon is to be found in the Southern manipulation of these well-known edicts of Buddha. According to the Northern account he required each Son of Śâkya to lodge under a tree, and to have no other roof. He enjoined also that his disciples should wear

---

[1] Beal's " Dhammapada," p. 57.

[2] Turnour, Journ. Beng. As. Soc., vol. vii. p. 728.

nothing but rags from the graveyard, dung-heap, etc. As the Lalita Vistara is in brief the Book of Yoga, or mystical training, the incident of Buddha digging up a shroud to hide his nakedness carries the custom to the earliest Buddhism. Buddhaghosa's school have coolly copied down the edicts, and then explained them away in this fashion :—

" Robes made of pieces of rag are a requisite for a priest.

" The following exceptions are allowed—robes made of linen, of cotton, of silk, of wool, of hemp, or of these five materials together."

" Lodging at the foot of a tree is a requisite for a priest. So lodged it is good of you to strive as long as life shall last. The following exceptions are allowed: monasteries, large halls, houses of more than one storey, houses surrounded by walls, rock caves."

This quotation is from Mr. Dickson's translation of the form of Ordination of a Buddhist Priest.[1]

Mr. Clough tells us that in spite of modern permissions to dwell in three-storeyed palaces, the Cingalese Son of Śâkya is still called Abhyâvakâsika (he whose covering is the heavens).[2]

By a silly legend the innovating party have

---

[1] Journ. R. As. Soc., vol. vii. p. 12.
[2] " Ritual of the Buddhist Priesthood," p. 15.

attempted to countermarch history. The rigorous edicts are set down to an innovating Devadatta (the Buddhist Judas), and the silken robes and three-storeyed palaces to Buddha.[1]

BUDDHAGHOSA'S CHANGES IN THE ORDINATION SERVICE.

In the Tibetan ordination service the novice calls upon the triad of Divine Personages to bestow upon him the priestly unction. "I salute Buddhanâth, Dharma, Sañgha, and entreat them to bestow on me the Parivrajyâ Vrata (lit., Ceremony of the Wanderer)."[2]

In Ceylon the novice kneels to the president of the chapter, and speaks thus :—

"Lord, graciously grant me the parivrajyâ vrata. Lord, I pray for admission as a deacon. Again, lord, I pray for admission as a deacon. A third time, lord, I pray for admission as a deacon!"

And when the yellow robes are granted, he thus addresses his guru, or spiritual instructor :—

"I make obeisance to my lord. Lord, forgive me all my faults," and so on.[3]

This lets in a flood of light on Buddhaghosa's

---

[1] Oldenberg, "Buddha," p. 161.   [2] Hodgson, p. 140.
[3] Dickson, "Ordering of Priests," Journ. R. As. Soc., vol. vii. p. 7.

movement. In early Buddhism Buddha forgave sins.
In Ceylon the monk forgives sins.

The island of Ceylon, from its geographical position,
could laugh at the threats of even Śilâditya. It
possessed, moreover, the famous left canine tooth of
Buddha, to which was attached a legend that its
possessor was invariably to be the ruler of the world.
All this gives a conceivable motive to Buddhaghosa's
patient painstaking elaborate falsifications. It was
necessary to directly connect the independent
Buddhism of Ceylon with the great Tathâgata.
Hence the mission of King Wijayo. In the
Mahâwanso it is expressly stated that Buddhaghosa's
Atthakathâ was not in existence outside Ceylon at
the date of Buddhaghosa's visit to the island. Mr.
Childers draws attention to the "astounding fact"
that Buddhaghosa coolly declares that even his commentary was in existence before Buddha's death.[1]
Moreover it was seen and approved of by Buddha.
The fictitious hundred years, I think, inserted into
the Cingalese chronicles were plainly put in to make
room for the fictitious second convocation, and to
compress the three convocations into the time that
elapsed between Buddha and Aśoka.

[1] "On the Origin of the Buddhist Arthakathâ," Journ. R. As.
Soc., vol. v. p. 289.

CHAPTER XVIII.

RITUAL.

THE Buddhist ritual has been pronounced very like that of the Roman Catholics. The early Christian rites are divided into two portions, the "Mass of the catechumens," and the "Liturgia mystica" when the latter were expelled.

In Buddhism a procession of chanting monks in the first instance effects what is called the "Lesser Entrance." They march into what the Buddhists call the "main court of the temple," and each monk "reverently bows his head." They have in China what Professor Beal calls a "Prayer of Entrance." They then advance to the "sanctuary," and solemnly march round it three times. Then follows a "Prayer of Incense."

This is the Prayer of Incense in the Liturgy of St. Mark :—

"We offer incense before Thy glory, O God. Do Thou receive it to Thy holy and super-celestial and

intellectual altar. Do Thou, in its stead, send down
the grace of Thy Holy Spirit, for Thou art blessed,
and do Thou send forth Thy glory." [1]

Now let us listen to the Chinese Prayer of
Incense :—

> " Hail, diffusive Incense Cloud,
> Bright mirror of the divine excellences !
> Far-spreading boundless is the Heart of Wisdom.
> Wherever lights one single ray,
> There is worship, there is praise
> To honour him who reigns as King in the midst of all.
> (*Invocation*) All hail, Incense Cloud Canopy !" [2]

This is followed in the Greek Church by what
doctors call an "Ascription of Praise to the Trisagion," a word very like the Buddhist Triratna
(three jewels). This is the Buddhist invocation :—

"In close communion we adore the everlasting
Buddha, and everlasting Dharma, and everlasting
Sañgha" (one bow after each ascription). "This
whole assembly prostrate in adoration, holding flowers
and incense, presents this bounden sacrifice."

In the Liturgy of St. Chrysostom, before the
address to the Trisagion, they sing : "Let us who
majestically. represent the cherubim, and sing the
holy hymn to the quickening Trinity." [3] This completely shows that early Christian worship was a

---

[1] Neale, "Liturgies of the Greek Church," p. 7.
[2] Beal, "Catena," p. 400.   [3] Neale, p. 106.

drama, like the Brahmin worship as exhibited in the Aitareya Brâhmana, or the Buddhism of the Life of Buddha.

Worthy of remark is the treatment of "Wisdom," "Dharma," "Heart of Wisdom," etc., in the Buddhist ritual. Here is another address to her:—

"Thou who art possessed of great mercy, and who in virtue of thine infinite power and wisdom art manifested throughout the universe for the defence and protection of all creatures, and who leadest all to the attainment of boundless wisdom, and teachest therein the connection of divine sentences. Thou who protectest us ever from the evil ways of birth, who grantest us to be born in the presence of Buddha, who dispellest all troubles, evil diseases and ignorance, and who, by thy power of spiritual perception, art able to appear always to answer prayer, causing that which is desired to be brought about, who removest all doubt and art able to cause speedy acquirement of the three degrees of merit and rapid birth in the land of Buddha; possessed of infinite spiritual power beyond the capability of language to express, we therefore adore thee, and worship with one heart and mind." [1]

It has been suggested that, as the name selected for the Universal Mother (Kwan Yin) existed in

[1] "Catena," p. 404.

China before Buddhism, this litany is not a Buddhist litany at all. But both in the ritual of Ceylon, and in the chants of the monks of Nepâl, Dharma or Prajñâ, the great "Mother of Buddha," the great "Mother of Saints," is worshipped. Aditî in India was thus worshipped quite as early as Kwan Yin in China. Let us listen to a hymn in the Rig-Veda :—

"Aditî is heaven. Aditî is air. Aditî is the Mother, the Father, the Son. Aditî is all the gods, and the five species of beings. Aditî is all that is born, and all that will be born."

The similarity of the Buddhist and Christian liturgies has induced other writers to jump to the conclusion that the Chinese ritual, at any rate, was borrowed from some ritual brought to China by early Christian missionaries. In the path of this theory is the fact that incense, processions, an address to the Triratna, and the other points of similarity traced by Professor Beal, exist in all Buddhist countries. And the evidence of the early Buddhist sculptures might be adduced, and also the early Brahminical rituals, to give these practices an antiquity far greater than that of Christianity. General Cunningham [1] gives us, side by side, the ground plan of Sanchi, one of Aśoka's topes (B.C. circa 250), and the ground plan of Ajanta, one of the later Buddhist cave-temples (about A.D.

[1] "Bhilsa Topes," plate ii.

R

500). For all purposes of worship they are identical.
In each is the "sanctuary." This at Sanchi is represented by the tumulus and rails. In each the
main court is marked off by a rectangle rounded at
one end, like the Christian apse. At Sanchi this is
effected by lines of monoliths. At Ajanta there
are columns cut out of the rock. All this means
that in the earliest Buddhist monuments, the temple
was already an apparatus for Buddhist rites as we
know them. Those rites, like all early rites, consisted
in a dramatic representation of what the ancients call
the "Mysteries." "It was feigned," says Clement of
Alexandria, speaking of them, "that the soul was
buried in the body as in a sepulchre."[1] This was
the pastos, or bed, the mystical Hades.

"For to be plunged in matter, is to descend to
Hades, and there fall asleep." This is a citation from
Plotinus, by the celebrated mystic, T. Taylor.[2] This
"Hades," this "sepulchre" in the temple, was an
actual cemetery. It will be remembered that Constantine found great difficulty in inducing the
Christians to forsake the catacomb worship for a
cathedral above ground. In Buddhism the choristers
come first into this sepulchre to represent birth in
the lower life; they then march within the mystic
rails, and make three turns round the chaitya

---

[1] Strom., lib. iii.   [2] "Ennead," i. lib. 8.

(heaven figured as a dome or umbrella).   The bloodless oblation is also, as I have shown, a symbol of
the soul, like Buddha leaving the "cemetery" for the
" Other Bank," the birth of the spiritual man.

It has been said that by ritual the earlier form of
a creed is best ascertained.   I will copy down a
sentence or two from the ritual of Ceylon.

"I worship continually the Buddhas of the ages
that are past,

"I worship the Buddhas, the all-pitiful,

"I worship with bowed head."

"May Buddha forgive me my sin."

It is plain here that the worship of the non-God
is an after-thought, stultified by the ritual.

CHAPTER XIX.

THE BUDDHIST TRIAD.

IN the Indian religion it was feigned that the ecliptic, or circle of the year, was a great serpent with his tail in his mouth—Ananta, the Endless.

This serpent was supposed to be cut in half, and to become two serpents which represented Summer, or the period of life, and Winter, or the period of death. These two serpents, as Ketu and Râhu, also represented good and evil with the Buddhists and Brahmins.

The word " Union " is the key-stone of all ancient mysteries. With the Brahmins this was Yoga. With the Buddhists it was Sañgha. In early Christianity it was the mystic " marriage." Buddha (heaven, spirit, the universal father) was allied to Dharma (earth, matter, the universal mother), and from the union was born the mystic child, the " Voice of Brahma," as the Lalita Vistara calls it. Sañgha, in the Scriptures of Nepâl, is said to be the " Creator of the world," and

PLATE II.

Fig. 1.

Catacombs.

Fig. 2.

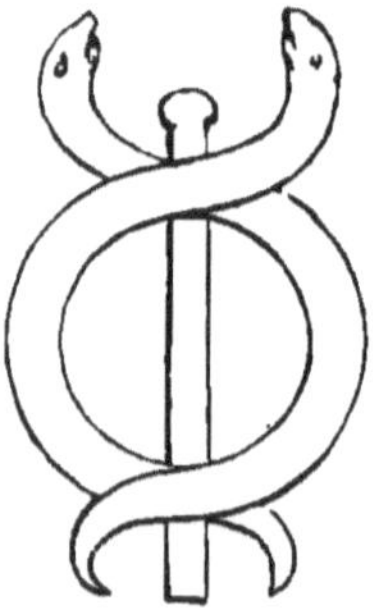

Sanchi.

Fig. 3.

Triratna.

Fig. 4.

Sanchi.

Fig. 5.

Burmah.

Fig. 6.

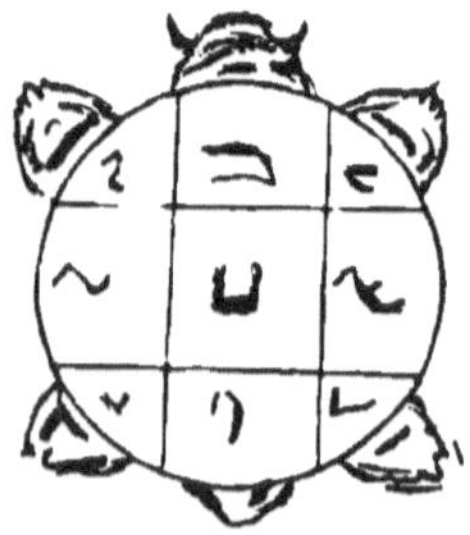

Tibet.

TRIRATNA OUTLINE.

[Page 245.

the Lord of the visible Kosmos.[1] Those who have
mastered the Adwaitam philosophy will not be surprised at this.   The "Voice of Brahma" in the
prophet is the real ruler of the world.

The favourite way of representing these two mystic
serpents was as twined round the "Rod of Hermes"
(Fig. 2, Plate II., from the early Buddhist tope of
Sanchi). In an ornamental form (Fig. 3 and Fig. 4) this
became the Triratna outline, the most holy symbol of
Buddhism. Buddha's head (Fig. 5) has, I think, its very
long ears to make up the same outline.   Fig. 6 is a
magic tortoise from Tibet, and here we have the same
outline in another form.   In Buddhism it is everywhere.
Fig. 1 from the Catacombs, whether by accident or
design, makes up the same symbol of the mystic
"Union."   In Greece it was feigned that Jupiter and
Rhea disguised as serpents had produced this symbol.
This was the explanation of the Rod of Hermes.

The Swastika, or Indian cross, is also two serpents
making up the same "Union."   This is the only cross
in the Catacombs, and the only symbol in the text of
the Aśoka inscriptions. Did space permit, I could
show from the Indian epics that this Swastika was the
zodiacal symbol for the Fish.

The two serpents in Alexandrian Gnosticism were
the legs of the mystic I. A. ω.   Compare Fig. 2,

---

[1] Hodgson's "Essays," p. 88.

Plate III., with Fig. 1, from the Buddhist tope of Jamal-giri. In Fig. 4 and Fig. 5 we see Buddha's symbol of the elephant as one limb of the triad. Later Buddhism changed this Buddha Dharma Sañgha into Śâkya Muni, " Canon Law," and the " Congregation," but it is evident that if Buddha and Dharma are not personifications the whole force of the mysticism is nullified.

" Know that when in the beginning all was void, and the five elements were not then the Supreme Buddha [Âdi Buddha], the stainless was revealed in the form of flame or light."

This is from the "Wisdom of the Other Bank" (Prajñâ Pâramitâ) in the Scriptures of Nepâl. We learn from the same source that the Supreme Buddha "delights in making happy all sentient creatures," that " by the aid of Prajñâ or Dharma he made the world." [1]

" I bow my head to the ground and worship Buddha," says the ritual of Ceylon.

" I salute that Dharma who is Prajñâ Pâramitâ, pointing out the way of perfect tranquillity to all mortals, leading them into the paths of perfect wisdom." (Baptismal Service in Nepâl.)

" The external and internal diversities of nature are produced by her, Mother of Buddha." (Scriptures of Nepâl.)

[1] Hodgson, p. 85.

PLATE III.

Fig. 2.

I. A. ω.

Fig. 3.

Serapis.

Fig. 1.

Jamalgiri.

Fig. 4.

Father, Mother, and Mârttânda.

Fig. 5.

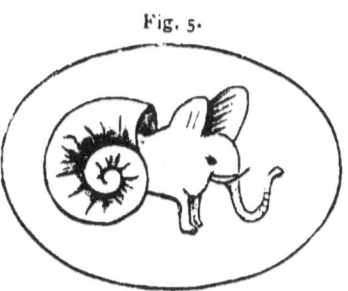

Serapis Shell and Mârttânda.

THE GNOSTIC TRIAD.

"I bow my head to the ground and worship Dharma."

"May Dharma forgive me my sin."[1]

The word Âdi Buddha, the first Buddha, was never used, according to Dr. Rhys Davids, until the tenth century A.D. This may be true; although a statue of him[2] in Western India seems to carry back the name to a period before the expulsion of the Buddhists. Âdi Buddha is only a word ; and the discussion seems very like entering into an inquiry, at what date in the last century the worship of "God" ceased, and the worship of "the Deity" commenced.

I will cite an address, probably chanted during the the bloodless oblation in Ceylon :—

"Whatever spirits have come together here, either belonging to the earth or living in the air, let us worship Tathâgata Buddha, revered by gods and men. May there be salvation !

"Whatever spirits have come together here, either belonging to the earth or living in the air, let us worship Tathâgata Dharma, revered by gods and men. May there be salvation !

"Whatever spirits have come together here, either belonging to the earth or living in the air, let us

---

[1] Ritual of Ceylon.
[2] Tod's "Travels in Western India," p. 276.

worship Tathâgata Sañgha, revered by gods and men. May there be salvation ! "[1]

The meaning of Tathâgata is simply tathâ "thus," agata "come." It was used at first, I think, with another word, as in the present Sûtra. Tathâgata Buddha would thus mean the present advent of Buddha ; Tathâgata Dharma, the present advent of Dharma ; Tathâgata Sañgha, the present advent of Sañgha. It is plain that each limb of the triad means, and can only mean a divine personage, as in Northern Buddhism. No man in his senses could "worship" and expect "salvation" from Sañgha in the sense of "the Congregation."

My second citation shall be from Dr. Rhys Davids's "Birth Stories : "—

> "Those who have put their trust in Buddha,
> They will not go to a world of pain ;
> Having put off this mortal coil,
> They will enter some heavenly body.

> "Those who have put their trust in Dharma,
> They will not go to a world of pain ;
> Having put off this mortal coil,
> They will enter some heavenly body.

> "Those who have put their faith in Sañgha,
> They will not go to a world of pain ;
> Having put off this mortal coil,
> They will enter some heavenly body."[2]

"Sañgha," the doctor renders by "the Order ;" but

---

[1] Fausböll, Sutta Nipâta, p. 39. [2] Page 137.

it is plain that a " Refuge," a power that can put an end to rebirths, cannot be an order of lazy monks, but God imaged as the vicegerent of the seen world.

By substituting the modern rendering of the triad in the phrases of the Ceylon ritual its nonsense becomes more plain :—

" May Congregation forgive me my sin ! "

" I have no other refuge ! Canon Law is my refuge."

" I bow my head to the ground and worship Canon Law ! "

" Śâkya Muni is the best refuge ! "

" May Canon Law forgive me my sin ! "

I have attempted to draw up a table, more or less accurate, of this triad idea in the old creeds.

	Father.	Mother.	Solar God-man.
Rig-Veda, . .	Varuṇa, . .	Aditî, . .	Mitra.
Manu, . .	Brahma, .	Mâyâ, . .	Brahmâ.
Buddhism, . .	Buddha, . .	Prajnâ or Dharma,	Sañgha.
Zoroastrianism, .	Zervan Akáréné,	Ardvi Cura,	Ahura Mazda (Ormuzd).
Egypt, . .	Amen-Ra, .	Neith, . .	Osiris.
Old Greece, .	The Serpent, .	Ceres, . .	Bacchus.
Plato, . . .	Father, . .	Mother or Nurse,	Logos.
Woden, . .	All-Father, .	Frigga, .	Woden.
Cabbala, . .	Ensoph, . .	Sophia, .	Logos.
Gnostics, and perhaps Essenes,	Abraxas, . .	Sophia, .	Gnosis or Christos.
China, . .	Yn, . . .	Yâng, . .	Taiki.
Babylonia, . .	Bel, . . .	Melissa, .	Tammuz.

CHAPTER XX.

COSMOLOGY.

PERHAPS the most prominent contradiction which has resulted from Dr. Rhys Davids's displacement of the two Buddhist "Vehicles" is his treatment of the Buddhist cosmogony. "The earlier Buddhism," he says, "teaches that above the worlds of the gods are sixteen worlds of Brahma," that mortals will successively reach.[1]

To make the full force of this admission plain, I give a sketch (Plate IV.) of the heavens as conceived by the Buddhists of Ceylon.[2]

The Devaloka, the "worlds of the gods," as Dr. Rhys Davids calls them, are six in number, the highest being the heaven Tusita. It will be remembered that this heaven is the highest that mortals who have not become Buddhas, and emancipated themselves from returns to earth, can reach.

---

[1] "Buddhism," p. 204.   [2] Upham, p. 74.

PLATE IV.

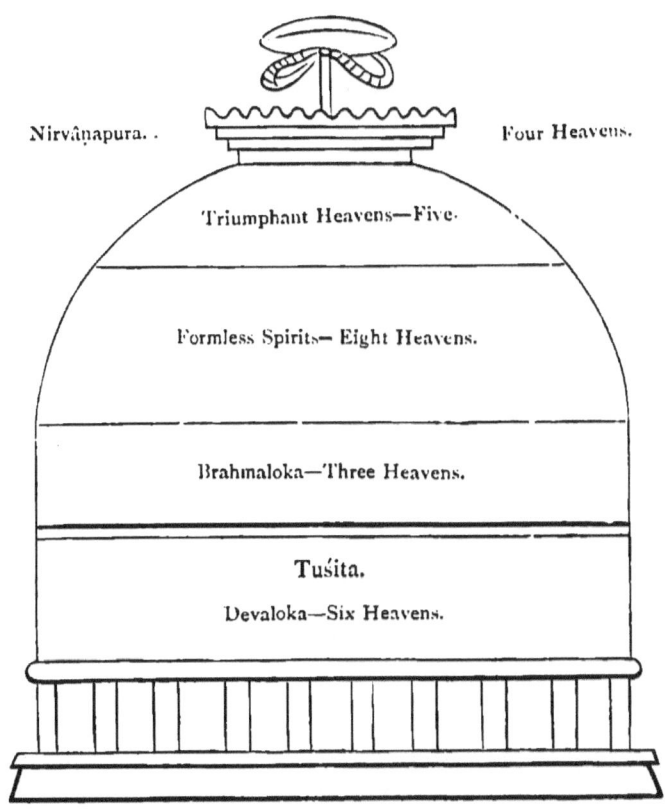

Nirvânapura. .

Four Heavens.

Triumphant Heavens—Five.

Formless Spirits— Eight Heavens.

Brahmaloka—Three Heavens.

Tusita.

Devaloka—Six Heavens.

THE HEAVENS AS CONCEIVED BY THE BUDDHISTS OF CEYLON.

[*Page* 250.

The sixteen worlds of Brahma in my dome (copied from an early tope) are subdivided into the three heavens of the Brahmaloka, eight heavens of the Arûpaloka or Formless Spirits, five heavens of the Buddhas or Jinas (Victorious Ones). Above is Nirvâ-napura, the city of Nirvâna, in four compartments, which latter fact militates against the notion that Nirvâna means annihilation. This is plainly the cosmology of the "Little Vehicle." In Nepâl the heavens of the Jinas have been swept away, and the heavens above Tuśita are tenanted by Bodhisatwas. This is a plain piece of absurdity, for the Bodhisatwa, as all know, cannot advance higher than the heaven Tuśita until he becomes a Buddha. But the "Carriage that drives to the Great Nowhere" was driven to this folly.

If souls visit in succession sixteen heavens of Brahma after becoming Buddhas, it is plain that the cosmology makers knew nothing of the theory of annihilation, still less of Dr. Rhys Davids's fancy that the Buddhists deny any after-life.

I will strengthen my position with a few passages culled from the doctor's translations :—

"As a man fond of gay clothing, throwing off a corpse bound to his shoulders, goes away rejoicing, so must I, throwing off this perishable body and freed from all desires, enter the city of Nirvâna."[1]

[1] "Birth Stories," p. 6.

" As a man carrying various sorts of jewels, and going on the same road with a band of robbers, out of fear of losing his jewels withdraws from them and gains a safe road, even so this impure body is like a jewel-plundering robber—if I set my affections thereon, the precious spiritual jewel of the sublime path of holiness will be lost to me, therefore ought I to enter the city of Nirvâna, forsaking this robber-like body." [1]

"The lake of the great deathless Nirvâna for the washing of the defilement of sin." [2]

"And the angels are manifested, the Formless alone excepted." [3]

"The whole world, up to the realms of the immaterial angels, will pass away." [4]

"Dying, I shall be born in the Formless World" (speech of Asita).[5]

The man having thrown off his dead body goes away rejoicing, not annihilated. Then, too, Asita, a mortal, goes to the Formless Heavens, or, as Dr. Rhys Davids puts it, the "realms of the immaterial angels," which shows that these angels are simply enfranchised mortals. Another passage asserts that Buddha was like "one who, using Mount Meru for a churning-rod,

---

[1] "Birth Stories," p. 7. [2] Ibid., p. 5.
[3] Ibid., p. 17. [4] Ibid., p. 59.
[5] Ibid., p. 70.

churns the great Cakkawâla Ocean."[1] The favourite
fable of Brahminism setting forth the gift of immortality to man, is a legend of Vishṇu churning the
ocean (uncreated matter).

[1] " Birth Stories," p. 26.

CHAPTER XXI.

SHAMANISM.

I NOW come to the Buddhist supernaturalism. In
the view of Dr. Rhys Davids, early Buddhism relegated
such ideas "to the region of legend and fairy tale." [1]
Sweeping negation was Buddha's " answer to the
mystics." [2] If he were Comte, the Positivist, born two
thousand years too soon, this theory would of course
be a necessity.

A priori there are difficulties in the way of this
view. In every Buddhist temple there are hundreds
of statues of Buddha. Each is sitting in the attitude
prescribed by the Brahmins for producing yoga. All,
even the rudest, manage to give the calm dreaminess
of yoganidrâ. Every Buddhist idol is seeking dhyâna.
And every Buddhist Śramaṇa has given up father,
mother, wealth and worldly joys ; and he mumbles
his mantras, a hundred thousand a day,[3] to gain the

---

[1] " Buddhist Suttas," p. 208.   [2] "Buddhism," p. 177.
[3] Schlagintweit, " Buddhism in Tibet," p. 54.

very dhyâna or mystical vision that his prophet sought to " relegate to the region of fairy tale."

And I must say that when I read the doctor's translations I am very much puzzled. The ideal Northern Buddhist, in his view, is a man of many superstitions, a miracle-monger. The ideal Southern Buddhist is what we should call a scientific freethinker. The Northerns have six magical powers (Shaddhâbhijñâ), which they believe to be acquired by the recluse when the divine vision is attained. I will copy them down from the Lotus of Dharma :—

1. The ascetic must be able to rise into the air.

2. He must rain down fire from his body.

3. He must rain down floods of water from his body.

4. He must make his body expand indefinitely and then grow infinitely little.

5. He must make it disappear and return to earth.

6. He must rise again into the sky.

But when I turn to the literature of the Southerns I find six magical powers likewise :—

1. The ascetic, being one, must become multiform.

2. He must become invisible.

3. He must pass through walls, mountains, solid ground as if through water.

4. He must be able to walk on the water without dividing it.

5. He must be able to travel cross-legged through the sky.

6. He must be able even to reach the world of Brahma.

Really the only difference between the freethinkers of the South and the miracle-mongers of the North, that I can see, is that the Southerns fly through the air "cross-legged," and the Northerns without crossing their legs. I must mention that these magical powers are given to us by Dr. Rhys Davids in a Sûtra written, in his view, as early as the fourth century before Christ.[1] They are detailed by the freethinker Buddha himself.

Another question arises : What was the meaning of the tope-worship, relic-worship, image-worship of early Buddhism ? Why did powerful kings fight for a tooth or a lock of hair of the great Tathâgata ? If Dr. Rhys Davids had carefully read the Mahâbhârata he might, I think, answer the question. The chaitya to which the pilgrimages were made, and at which sacrifice was offered, was supposed to contain the dead prophet, the dead Vyâsa, or the dead Kaśyapa. And with all old races the dead saint was believed to be more potent than the living one. The cave, the dolmen in the tumulus, the rude log, the unhewn monolith encased the soul when fire had consumed its mortal envelope.

[1] "Buddhist Suttas," p. 214 ; also Preface, p. x.

I will here cite an incident witnessed by Father Borri, and narrated by him in his "Account of Cochin-China."[1] A Buddhist of rank, the governor of Pulu Cambi, died. This official had been very friendly to the Jesuit Fathers, and the missionary Borri attended at all the funeral ceremonies of the dead man. One day several "necromancers" gathered round the corpse, and prayed that some of the governor's kindred who were also gathered around might receive a message about the deceased. After a while, an elderly lady, a sister of the governor, became possessed, and skipped and raved, although she was quite decrepit until the fury seized her. The stick that she threw from her "hung in the air all the while that the devil was in her body," says the Father. A huge palace, far more splendid than that inhabited by the governor during life, was erected for him. In the middle of this was a "stately temple with a fine altar." Here the corpse was by-and-by placed, surrounded by wooden horses, wooden elephants, huge wooden galleys running on wheels, and other emblems of his wealth and state. Then all was burned amid much pomp, and the calcined remains were buried.

This tomb-worship is also illustrated by certain customs still retained by the Chinese Buddhists,

[1] Page 807.

S

although they are quite out of harmony with modern agnostic tenets. The dead man is held to have more influence over mundane affairs than the living man, and he is conciliated with many rites. The belief being retained that the next world is the counterpart of this, wives and servants, a house and money, are sent to him, chiefly by burning effigies and models of these in tinsel paper. At stated periods food and money sufficient for a fixed time are offered at his tomb amidst much burning of crackers and offerings of flowers and little flags. And as the ghosts of the poor must have their influence also and their wants, the Buddhist priests celebrate every year a great nocturnal feast of the dead, summoning the hungry ghosts by beat of gong and sound of bells.

A paper in vol. xviii. of the "Chinese Repository," entitled the "Worship of Ancestors amongst the Chinese," throws much light on this subject. The poor are buried in the ground, the better classes in family mausoleums. A lonely spot is, if possible, chosen for a tomb, near a river or lake. Over it waves a solitary tree. The uncremated corpse is placed in a sitting posture upon a throne. Apparitions of Buddha in the Sûtras are always "seated on a throne." A pompous procession of illuminated boats carries the rich man to his sepulchre, a lofty column of lanterns being conspicuous in the prow of the leading boat, and the water all aglow with innumerable floating lights.

This is part of a hymn to the dead :—

> " The beauty of a thousand hills is centred here,
> And the dragon coils around to guard it ;
> A winding stream spreads far and wide—
>   Rest here in peace !
> The sighing firs above will make you music—
> For ever rest in this fair city !
> Friends and kin in crowds collect to salute you ;
> Our poor libation with humble mind we offer,
> And looking up, your favour we implore ! "

It is to be observed that the dragon represents the Indian cobra as a symbol in China for the Supreme. The tree is also conspicuous in this Pái Fan (grave-worship) ; indeed, the tomb is called the " fir hall." The dead man carries jewels, talismans, coins, etc., with him to the tomb, and the " pearl," so sacred in Buddhism, is put in his mouth to keep off evil influences. The bells and gongs that it is still the custom to sound when food is offered to the ghost prove, I think, that there was no idea that the spirit resided continuously in the " fir hall." He came back when summoned to animate his effigies, his body, or his relics.

It must be mentioned also that in the Mahâ-wanso,[1] Buddha, seated " on a throne on which he had obtained Pari-Nirvâna," is made more than once

---

[1] Journ. Beng. As. Soc., vol. vi. pp. 717, 718.

to take an interest in mortal affairs centuries after his death.

This brings me to a very singular incident narrated in the "White Lotus of Dharma," one of the oldest Buddhist books. One day when Śâkya Muni was preaching, a colossal sepulchral mound (stûpa) of the seven precious substances—of diamonds, emeralds, red pearls, etc.—suddenly appeared in the heavens ; and a Buddha of the past, Prabhûtaratna, who was seated in the midst of it, approved of Buddha's words, and cried, "It is well! it is well!"[1] This Buddha and this stûpa remained present whilst Buddha uttered many sermons. It is explained away, evidently, by some modern emendator, who records that the stûpa and its occupant were non-existent, and due only to the miraculous power of Buddha. But it is evident that Prabhûtaratna is really present to confirm the teaching of Śâkya Muni. Indeed, at one period he is appealed to by the latter to perform a miracle in order to influence the Bodhisatwa Gadgadeśvara ;[2] and a short time after the first stûpa has disappeared, another stûpa and a fresh Buddha appear in the sky.[3]

I think these stûpas tell their own story. So clumsy an apparatus as a sepulchral mound could never have been used as a carriage for a saint unless

---

[1] "Lotus de la Bonne Loi," p. 151.   [2] Ibid., p. 255.
[3] Ibid., p. 274.

the saint was obliged to be in his sepulchral mound to be considered a transcendental authority. Śâkya Muni in the Lotus himself says, "I will appear after I have obtained Pari-Nirvâna."[1] Also, he himself appeals to the authority of the Buddhas: "I call to witness the beatified Buddhas who exist," etc.[2]

The religion of the Ṛig-Veda, like most early creeds, sprung also from this ancestor-worship. The sun-god, the active and anthropomorphic god, as distinguished from Brahma, is identified in more than one hymn with Yama and with Manu, two names for the Indian Adam. This circumstance tends to show that what Tiele calls the "poly-demonism," the worship of tree spirits, fountain spirits, cloud spirits, etc., was an after-growth of the earlier faith. I will first of all describe the simple rites of this ancestor-worship. They are called the Śrâddha, and are still the chief rites of the Brahmins. They were probably practised in the same form three thousand years ago, before our ancestors, the western Âryas, left the parent stock.

After smearing the ground with cow-dung, the presiding Brahmin raises a square altar of sand one or two fingers high, and about a span in each direction. He washes his hands and feet, sips water, and puts a ring of kuśa-grass on the ring finger of his hand. He sits down on a blade of kuśa-grass, lights

---

[1] "Lotus de la Bonne Loi," p. 144.   [2] Ibid., p. 247.

a lamp, recites a prayer or two, and sprinkles holy water on the assembled worshippers. He then invites the gods and manes of ancestors to the feast.

Two little cushions of kuśa-grass are placed near the altar for the gods, and six in front of it for the ancestors. Each cushion consists of three blades of grass folded up. Barley and oblations of water in little vessels of leaves are offered. Kuśa-grass is put into each vessel, and water sprinkled on it. In the vessels intended for the ancestors Sesamum Indicum is added. I quote some of the invocations made use of :—

" Eagerly do thou [O fire] call our willing ancestors to taste our oblation! May our progenitors who eat the moon-plant, who are sanctified by holy fires, come by paths along which gods travel. Satisfied with ancestral food at this solemn sacrifice, may they applaud and guard us."

" Thou art barley sacred to Soma. Framed by the divinity, thou dost produce celestial bliss. Mixed with water, mayst thou long satisfy with nourishment my several progenitors, whose mouths are full of blessing !"

" May the demons and giants who sit in this con-secrated spot be dispersed !"

Passing from the present to very old times, I will cite portions of one of the hymns of the Rig-Veda.

It is addressed to Agni, the god of fire, on the occasion of a funeral.

" Full of pious wishes we place thee on the hearth and light thy fires. Accept our offerings, and bring the ancestors eager as thou to consume them.

" Burn not this corpse. Tear not his skin, his body, O Jâtavedas [Agni]! Surround him with the ancestors. He comes to obtain the [subtile] body which will transport his soul. Give to the water, and trees, and heaven, and earth that of his body which belongs to them.

" But there is in him an immortal portion. Light up that with thy rays, and warm it with thy fires, O Jâtavedas! In the favoured body formed by thee, transport him to the world of the saints.

" O Agni, let him descend again amongst the ancestors ; let him return in the midst of invocations and offerings." [1]

Here is another hymn, addressed to Yama, at first the Indian Adam, and afterwards the Indian Pluto :—

" Yama, place thyself on the altar of the sacrifice with the ancestors. King, let the prayers of the saints summon thee. Accept our sacrifice.

" Come, Yama, with the honourable Angirases [seven great saints]. Seated on the grass I invoke Vivaswan.

[1] Langlois' translation, p. 520.

"We have amidst our ancestors, the Angirases, the Navagwas, the Atharvans, the Somyas; may we obtain their favour, their benign protection! O dead man [the corpse], come to us! Come by the ancient roads that our fathers have traversed before thee. Behold these two kings, Yama and the divine Varuṇa, who rejoice in our oblations.

"Come with the ancestors. Come with Yama to this altar which our piety has dressed. Thou hast cast off all impurity. Come to this domain and don a body of brilliance.

"O ancestors, disperse! Go every one to his own side. A place has been set apart for the departed one. Yama permits him to come down and enjoy our libations morning and night.

"Give our libation to Yama with Agni as a messenger. Offer to Yama a holocaust sweet as honey.

"Honour to the First Ones, the ancient Ṛishis who have shown us the way." [1]

This ancestor-worship is still prevalent in India, and the dead man much propitiated. An English magistrate of hasty temper died some time ago. He was much feared by the natives, and to calm his spirit they kept it constantly supplied with glasses of strong brandy-and-water and very large cheroots.

---

[1] Langlois, p. 518.

In the pages of Hwen Thsang we see that, in spite of the tenets of the disciples of the " Carriage that drives to the Great Nowhere," ancestor-worship, relic-worship, and corpse-worship prevailed even amongst the agnostic school ; but they refined away the idea by a theory that the marvels were due to a sort of eidolon left behind by the miraculous power of the annihilated Buddha.

At Bhîma was a statue of Sâkya. " It is thirty feet in height, beautiful in form, of aspect severe and dignified. It performs many miracles in favour of those who invoke Buddha. If a man suffers in any part of his body, a sheet of gold leaf fastened to the precise spot on the body of Buddha causes an instant cure. The prayers addressed to him are almost always granted." [1] At Buddhośnichapura was a portion of Buddha's skull. Votaries were wont to place perfumed paste near it, and the paste assumed forms which symbolized the votary's future. Hwen Thsang wrapped his perfume in silk. It assumed the shape of a bo-tree, and one of his companions got a beautiful figure of Buddha [2] The worthy pilgrim seemed to have forgotten for the moment that Buddha had gone to the Great Nowhere.

Near a stûpa at Benares, erected by King Kaniśka, was a statue in white stone, eighteen feet high, which

---

[1] Hwen Thsang, " Histoire," p. 289.   [2] Ibid., p. 177.

performed many marvels, and sometimes moved about at night.[1] The pilgrim's travels are full of coruscating relics and nodding statues, and also of rival apparitions of the Bodhisatwas and the dead Buddhas. In a cave near Jelalabad, in Affghanistan, he saw an apparition of Śâkya Muni.

Professor Beal gives us from the Chinese the prayers to be used by a monk on entering a temple, bowing to a statue of Buddha, etc. It is explained, in reference to the last act, that "the object worshipped ʳand the worshipper are both in their nature spiritual."

In my frontispiece I give Buddha appearing at the altar during worship, from a sketch taken from the Amarâvatî bas-reliefs at the British Museum. In front is an incense-burner. The following passage from the Chinese ritual explains, I think, the design:—

"I regard the sacred altar as a royal gem on which the shadow of Śâkya Tathâgata appears."[2]

This brings me to a very valuable Cingalese poem, written exactly one hundred years [3] before the date of Buddhaghosa. The writer of legends gives often a truer picture of men and their creeds than the sermon-monger and the chronicler. Buddhaghosa did not consider this legend worthy of his manipula-

[1] "Histoire," p. 84.   [2] "Catena," p. 243.
[3] A.D. 310. See Turnour, Journ. Beng. As. Soc., vol. vi. p. 858.

tion. We therefore get an honest picture of Ceylon, exactly one hundred years before Buddhaghosa's "original" Buddhism was manufactured. The legend relates to Buddha's left canine tooth. I will condense it.

When Buddha's relics were distributed, it is recorded that one Brahmadatta, a king of Kalinga, was fortunate enough to get Buddha's canine left tooth. A fine temple was erected at Dantapura, to contain it. A yearly festival was established in its honour. For eight hundred years after this, the chronicler of the deeds of the kings of Kalinga seems to have had little to tell.

Towards the close of the third century, A.D., it was reported to the Râja of Râjas (the king of kings), at Patna, that the King of Kalinga was guilty of an act of strange superstition :

"Whilst Pându, Emperor of all India, worships the deity adored by all the devas, Gûhasîwo, a râja, subordinate to his authority, reviling those gods, worships a piece of human bone."

The Emperor Pându, incensed, orders another king, named Chittayâno, to fetch both the bone and the bone-worshipper, and bring them to the capital.

Chittayâno, with a large army, arrives promptly before Dantapura. King Gûhasîwo, greatly alarmed, sends out tribute and many elephants. Chittayâno is received inside the city, and his army feasted. The commands of the emperor are detailed, and received by poor Gûhasîwo with a satisfaction the sincerity of which the chronicler plausibly throws doubt upon.

But the capture of a bone, even with an army of one hundred and fifty thousand men, seems a military exploit more difficult than the capture of a bone-worshipper. Chittayâno is told all about the bone, and all about the religion of Buddha. He is then taken to the pagoda, with his principal officers, and shown the priceless treasure. Gûhasîwo prays to the relic, rehearsing the miracles performed by it, and asking it for a repetition of these miraculous exhibitions. The relic graciously complies, and the powerful leader of armies, Chittayâno, instead of capturing the "bone," is captured by it. It is settled, however, that the emperor's orders cannot be disobeyed, and the relic, escorted by the two kings, starts for Patna.

The account of its journey throws light on many passages in the Lalita Vistara, where the infant Buddha moves about on level roadways, escorted by pompous processions. It throws light also upon Buddhaghosa's biography of Buddha, which shows us the reformer entering Śrâvasti and Râjâgriha in the same magnificent manner. The real Buddha was a ragged beggar, spreading his doctrines silently and

humbly. But when his creed became the official
religion, much of the outside cultus of Brahminism
was taken over. It has always been the custom to
carry the Indian gods about at certain seasons, in
sumptuous processions. The celebrated car of Jag-
gannâtha is merely the carriage of Krishna, in which
the god is supposed to be making an excursion to
his summer palace. Buddha, in the Buddhist processions, was represented by a relic, or a statue, the
idea, as I have shown, being that the spirit of Śâkya
Muni was actually present. As relic processions are
in the earliest bas-reliefs of Aśoka's topes, the custom
plainly is as early as these monuments. Mr. Fergusson thinks that Dantapura was Puri in modern
Orissa, and that the celebrated temple of Jaggan-
nâtha in that city was erected on the site of the
ancient relic-temple.

From Dantapura the procession set out with great
pomp. Large awnings, stretched right across the
street, shaded the tooth relic from the sun. Incense
smoked, banners waved, the streets were levelled
and spread with flowers. The relic rode in a fine
chariot, drawn by horses white as conch-shells ; and
folks wept as they bade it adieu. Above the chariot
was a splendid white umbrella. The distance from
Dantapura to Patna is at least four hundred miles ;
yet all along this road white sand was strewn and

raked, and vases of flowers liberally posted. The spirits in the jangals sang hymns to the relic, and danced before its chariot to the sound of drum and flute. The Emperor Pându, incensed at this pomp, ordered the relic, on its arrival at Patna, at once to be destroyed in a charcoal crucible. Willing Brahmins of the court proceeded to carry out this edict, when, lo and behold, a marvel was visible! The relic remained unconsumed in the crucible, and in the smoke a miraculous lotus became apparent. The emperor, still more angry, had an anvil brought; and his servants attempted to pulverize the relic with a mighty hammer. But at the first blow, the relic penetrated the anvil, and remained imbedded within it. It emitted, moreover, a miraculous coruscation, which incited the Brahmins to claim it as a relic of Râma. The Emperor Pându ordered them to try and extract it. They sprinkled holy water over it, and hymned it as Vishnu, but the relic would not stir. A holy Buddhist, named Subaddho, was summoned from his extasia in the jangal. He recounted the sublime acts of the great Tathâgata, and prayed to the relic to attest them. It flew aloft into the air. It raced round a bowl of perfumed water. Buried, it emerged in the form of a lotus. Thrown into the city sewer, it changed it to a beautiful lake, with swans and lotuses. These miracles converted many courtiers; and they addressed the Emperor Pându in the following terms:—

"Râja, if a person, having witnessed such a manifestation of the power of the Supreme Muni as this is, experience not the slightest joy, can he be endowed with wisdom? Râja, forsake not the path that leads to heaven by following the doctrines of these ignorant persons. What man, not an idiot, who is on his travels, would seek his way employing a blind man for a guide? Ruler of men, do thou, in order that thou mayst follow the path that leads to heaven and eternal emancipation, quickly incline thine heart towards the supreme rules of Dharma, the Vanquisher of the five deaths, the Déwo of Déwos."

I think this passage is important. The Dathâwanso is the popular Bible of Ceylon. And here, at least a hundred years before Buddhaghosa and his atheistic changes, we see a Buddhism that believed that Buddha was the "god of gods;" that miracles performed by relics were "manifestations of the divine power of the Supreme Muni" himself; and that eternal emancipation in heaven should be sought, not shunned. All this is immensely valuable. This speech converted the good Emperor Pându. He felt that in his previous Brahmin creed he had been "blowing at a firefly to produce heat." He repaired to the cesspool which had been converted into a

lovely tank, and addressed the Spirit who was supposed to be able to manifest itself through the
agency of the relic, in these terms:—

" Universal Intelligence, practised traffickers assign
a value to gold after having tried it on a touchstone.
Supreme Muni, in the present instance it was for the
purpose of putting thy divine attributes to the test,
that all this has been done by me. Infinite Wisdom,
forgive my great sin ! and instantly adorn the crown
of my head."

The relic immediately made its way to the king's
head. It is plain that Śâkya Muni was supposed
to have joined this fragment of his ancient body.
The Sanscrit term for relic is Dhâtu, which means
" primary matter," the idea being no doubt that the
cremation reduced the matter of the body to its
primary element. Soon a powerful king, Khîrâdâro,
attacks the Emperor Pâṇḍu to get the relic. And after
Pâṇḍu's death, when the relic returns to Dantapura,
another attack is made upon it by the nephews of
Khîrâdâro, who was slain in the first campaign.
These battles for Buddha's relics, recorded so constantly in Indian history, show that a relic was really
believed to have some special tutelary power.

Gûhasîwo is killed ; but his daughter Hemamâlâ,
who was married to Prince Danta, escapes with the
relic. The fugitives disguised themselves as Brahmins,

and buried the relic for security in the "Diamond Sands," at the mouth of the Kistna. Mr. Fergusson, in a learned article,[1] identifies these "Diamond Sands" as the spot where the celebrated Amarâvatî tope was afterwards erected to commemorate the event. Its marbles are now in the British Museum ; and on one of the tablets is a bas-relief of Danta and Hemamâlâ sailing with the relic in a vessel to Ceylon. The waves during this trip were in the form of "mountain peaks ;" violent winds raged as at that grim time when a Kalpa is violently put an end to. The welkin was disturbed by terrible noises. Men cried out in fear. But at dawn a marvel took place. The ship became as immovable as "a divine mansion in the sky." Around the sea was as still and as translucent as a large emerald. Nâgas sported around the ship. And the relic, which had been hid in the hair of the princess, "emitted rays resembling straight darts of silver." The King of Lankâ (Ceylon) was soon informed that "two Brahmins, husband and wife, carrying the tooth relic of Buddha," had reached his dominions.

Hastening to the monastery Meghagiri, where the relic was first deposited, the eager monarch did homage to it, "wetting his necklace of beautiful pearls" with tears of joy.

[1] Journ. R. As. Soc., 1867.

T

" Though I should offer to-day my head, bearing a diadem resplendent with many gems, to Buddha, the sole refuge of the world, I should not be making an offering befitting the relic.

" Wise men, planting a small seed in the earth, enjoy in due time leaves, bark, flowers, and fruits. Thus with a small offering to the Lord of Dharma I shall obtain the incomparable happiness of heaven and Nirvâna."

The relic then, in the presence of the king, performed many miracles. It was placed on a white carpet, and smothered in jessamine flowers, but it emerged and shone with milk-white rays. It was wrapped in many pieces of rich silk, but it " burst through hundreds of cloths." Earth rocked and divine flowers fell from the skies ; and the cloud-nymphs becoming visible danced with a grace unknown to earth. Songs also were sung by heavenly singers to the sound of heavenly instruments. Dazzling ropes made up of beaded rain-drops bound earth to heaven.

But it is stated that the inhabitants of the provinces, market towns, and cities felt aggrieved at not seeing the relic of Sugato. In consequence a " priest, unequalled in intelligence," suggested a great Spring festival, to show it to the people. As the priests of many monasteries disputed about the final resting-

place of the relic, the king settled that the tooth
should be placed alone in a fine chariot, drawn by
milk-white steeds, and that it should choose its own
domicile. The streets were swept and levelled.
Arches "set with images of tigers and the like" were
erected. Dancing flags warded off the heat of the
sun by their shade. Elephants trumpeted, drums
sounded, horses neighed. "New vases filled with
water indicated to good men that the wished-for
happiness of heaven and Nirvâṇa will be attained."[1]
The relic drove itself to Anurâdhapura, where a
splendid temple was erected for it. Every year, at
the Spring festival, it made a trip to the Abhayuttara
monastery with great pomp. Fa Hian, the Chinese
pilgrim, witnessed one of these festivals. "Every man
in the kingdom, enlightened by the doctrine and
anxious to promote happiness, comes from his quarter
to level the roads, adorn the highways and streets ; to
scatter all sorts of flowers and perfumes. Then, after
the chants, the king causes to be displayed on both
sides of the road representations of the five hundred
successive manifestations of Buddha. The tooth of
Foe [Buddha] is carried through the midst of the
road, and is adored wherever it passes. Arrived at
the chapel of the Mountain without Fear, they ascend
into the hall of Foe. They burn their perfumes,

---

[1] Dathâvansa, p. 76.

making accumulated clouds. They perform religious acts without intermission night and day, the whole of the ninety days. The tooth is then conveyed back to the chapel in the town. This chapel is very elegant. During the day they open the gates and perform the ceremonies according to the law." [1]

Is this the early Buddhism of Ceylon, the pure well of atheism undefiled, that we get in the works of Dr. Rhys Davids? Are these the men that are supposed to have been constantly interchanging unintelligible metaphysics about the Skandhas and the desire of death, as opposed to the desire of future life? Are these the early Ceylon Buddhists who "relegated" the supernatural to the regions of fairy tale? Would Dr. Carpenter or Mr. Maskelyne hail as a brother a man who told a story of a tooth driving a coach and four? Would Professor Clifford give the diploma of agnostic to one who called upon a "God of gods" to forgive his sin? Would George Eliot and the Positivists receive poor Dhammakitti, the singer of the poem, into her lofty "choir invisible," who sing silent psalms with fleshless lips in the cathedral of the "Great Nowhere"? [2] Recollect that the

---

[1] "Pilgrimage of Fa Hian," p. 335.

[2] In the "Hibbert Lectures," p. 110, Dr. Rhys Davids cites the following lines with pardonable admiration :—

"O may I join the choir invisible
Of those immortal dead who live again

tooth was the tooth of Śâkya Muni; and that the learned priests, as well as the ignorant king and his people had for their gospel this Daṭhâwanso.

The "rule of the entire circle of the earth" is with the possessor of the tooth relic, says that poem.[1] The British Government were obliged to humour this strong superstition of the Cingalese, and place it under a guard of English soldiers. The key of the casket was kept in the hands of an official of rank. Is not the "rule of the entire circle of the earth" with the holder of the relic, the Rânî of Rânîs?

> In minds made better by their presence ; live
> In pulses stirred to generosity,
> In deeds of daring, rectitude, or scorn
> For miserable aims that end in self."

[1] Page 65.

CHAPTER XXII.

THE TESTIMONY OF AŚOKA.

THE reader is now in a position to decide whether the gospel of the "Great Nowhere" was early Buddhism. Dr. Rhys Davids contends that it was; and his dictum has been confronted with the testimony of the old stûpas and monuments, the ritual and its food offerings to the dead Buddhas, the cosmology, the symbols—with his own translations, and the quite invaluable testimony of the Chinese pilgrims. One witness remains, Aśoka. Exactly two hundred and ten years after Buddha's death (B.C. 260) he carved his credo on rocks and stone columns, a literature that no Buddhaghosa could "recompile." It is the most valuable exponent of early Indian creeds, because all uncertainties of date and defacement are eliminated.

KING AŚOKA'S IDEAS ABOUT GOD.

"Much longing after the things [of this life] is a disobedience, I again declare; not less so is the laborious ambition of dominion by a prince who would be a propitiator of Heaven. Confess and believe in God [Îśâna], who is the worthy object of obedience. For equal to this [belief], I declare unto you, ye shall not find such a means of propitiating Heaven. Oh, strive ye to obtain this inestimable treasure." (First Separate Edict, Dhauli, Prinsep.)

"Thus spake King Devânampiya Piyadasi:—The present moment and the past have departed under the same ardent hopes. How by the conversion of the royal born may religion be increased ? Through the conversion of the lowly born if religion thus increaseth, by how much [more] through the conviction of the high born and their conversion shall religion increase ? Among whomsoever the name of God resteth, verily this is religion."

"Thus spake Devânampiya Piyadasi:—Wherefore from this very hour I have caused religious discourses to be preached. I have appointed religious observances that mankind, having listened thereto, shall be brought to follow in the right path, and give glory to God." (Edict No. VII., Prinsep.)

"In like manner, turning his mind to law in an establishment of learned men, he called together the Buddhist priests of Eastern Kalinga, who were settled there under the ancient kings . . . act of devotion . . . all equipages . . . he gives to God." (Prinsep's translation of a somewhat defaced inscription on the Khandagiri Rock, erected by the grandson of Aśoka.)

"It is well known, sirs, to what lengths have gone my respect for and faith in Buddha, Dharma, Sangha." (Second Bairât Rock, Burnouf.)

"Whatever words have been spoken by the divine Buddha, they have all been well said." (Second Bairât Rock, Wilson.)

"And he who acts in conformity with this edict shall be united with Sugato." (Delhi Pillar, Prinsep.)

"The white elephant whose name is The Bringer of Happiness to the Whole World." (Final Sentence of the Rock Edicts, Kern.)

Îsâna is the name that has been selected by the Sanscrit scholars employed recently in translating "God save the Queen." The words "Union with Sugato" imply, I think, that the Îsâna meant exoterically Śâkya Muni. But it is plain that "Buddha" and "Îsâna" mean esoterically the Supreme. It is impossible that King Aśoka could have had a religious faith in the "Congregation," the debased and brutalized herd whom it was the object of his life to elevate and spiritualize.

AŚOKA ON A FUTURE LIFE.

" On the many beings over whom I rule I confer happiness in this world ; in the next they may obtain Swarga [paradise]." (Edict VI., Wilson.)

" This is good. With these means let a man seek Swarga. This is to be done. By these means it is to be done, as by them Swarga [paradise] is to be gained." (Edict IX., Wilson.)

" I pray with every variety of prayer for those who differ with me in creed, that they, following after my example, may with me attain unto eternal salvation." (Delhi Pillar, Edict VI., Prinsep.)

" And whoso doeth this is blessed of the inhabitants of this world ; and in the next world endless moral merit resulteth from such religious charity." (Edict XI., Prinsep.)

" Unto no one can be repentance and peace of mind until he hath obtained supreme knowledge, perfect faith, which surmounteth all obstacles, and perpetual assent." (Rock Edict, No. VII., Prinsep.)

" In the tenth year of his anointment, the beloved King Piyadasi obtained the Sambodhi or complete knowledge." (Rock Edict, No. VII., Burnouf.)

" All the heroism that Piyadasi, the beloved of the gods, has exhibited is in view of another life. Earthly glory brings little profit, but, on the contrary, produces a loss of virtue. To toil for heaven is difficult to peasant and to prince unless by a supreme effort he gives up all." (Rock Edict, No. X., Burnouf.)

"May they [my loving subjects] obtain happiness in this world and in the next." (Second Separate Edict, Burnouf.)

"The beloved of the gods speaketh thus: It is more than thirty-two years and a half that I am a hearer of the law, and I did not exert myself strenuously; but it is a year or more that I have entered the community of ascetics, and that I have exerted myself strenuously. Those gods who during this time were considered to be true gods in Jambudvîpa have now been abjured. . . . A small man who exerts himself somewhat can gain for himself great heavenly bliss, and for this purpose this sermon has been preached. Both great ones and small ones should exert themselves, and should in the end gain [true] knowledge. And this manner of acting should be what? Of long duration! For the spiritual good will grow the growth, and will grow exceedingly; at the least it will grow one size and a half.

"This sermon has been preached by the departed.

"Two hundred and fifty years have elapsed since the departure of the teacher." (Rupnâth Rock, Bühler.)

How the learned have gone on maintaining that

early Buddhism was agnostic in the face of such evidence it is difficult to understand. Swarga is the Vedic paradise, and " Swarga" and " eternal salvation " are here pronounced identical.

AŚOKA ON MYSTICISM.

" Ten years after his consecration the beloved King Piyadasi obtained the Bodhi [sambodhim]." (Edict VIII., Burnouf.)

"There is no such charity as the charity which springeth from virtue [Dharma], which is the intimate knowledge of virtue [Dharma], the inheritance of virtue [Dharma], the close union with virtue [Dharma]." (Edict XII., Prinsep.)

" The beloved of the gods, King Piyadasi, honours all forms of religious faith, whether professed by ascetics [pavajitâni] or householders [gahathâni]." (Rock Edict, No. XII., Wilson.)

" Whatever villages with their inhabitants may be given or maintained for the sake of the worship, the devotees shall receive the same ; and for an example unto my people they shall exercise solitary austerities." (Delhi Pillar, Edict IV., Prinsep.)

"And he who acts in conformity with this edict shall be united with Sugato." (Delhi Pillar, Prinsep.)

I have kept the important Aśoka inscriptions to

the last that the reader might understand the full force of such phrases as " Union with Dharma," the " Sambodhi," " Union with Sugato," etc. If early Buddhism relegated all mysticism to the region of fairy tale, as Dr. Rhys Davids assures us, how is it that King Aśoka himself practised " solitary austerities " to obtain the " Sambodhi," the mystic " Union with Sugato " ?

" Buddhism does not acknowledge the efficacy of prayers," says Dr. Rhys Davids.[1] Let us test this likewise by the evidence of the Buddhist that gave Buddhism to Ceylon:—

" Devânampiya hath also said, Fame consisteth in this act, to meditate with devotion on my motives and on my deeds, and to pray for blessings in this world and the world to come." (Dhauli Separate Edict, No. II., Prinsep.)

" I pray with every variety of prayer for those who differ with me in creed, that they, following after my example, may with me attain unto eternal salvation." (Delhi Pillar, Edict VI., Prinsep.)

" Buddhism denies the existence of the soul," says Dr. Rhys Davids.[2]

" As the soul itself, so is the unrelaxing guidance of Devânampiya worthy of respect." (Dhauli Separate Edict, No. II., Prinsep.)

---

[1] " Buddhism," p. 168.   [2] Ibid., p. 3.

CHAPTER XXIII.

THE HISTORICAL BUDDHA.

HAVING cleared away the mystifications of the "Carriage that drives to the Great Nowhere," we may now look for a moment at the historical Buddha.

The movement of Buddha was a noble attempt to bring the Chakravarta Râj, the kingdom of the sky, down to dull earth. Two realms were sharply contrasted. On one side were the domains of Mâra—the domains of lust and war and selfishness and tinsel honours. On the other was the realm of Buddha, with its Pâramitâs, the "qualities of the Other Bank."[1] In the place of jewelled women and dresses of gold, the "sons of Buddha" were dowered with thirst and hunger and exposure to the elements, with beggary and reproach. The great reformer admitted that his scheme was not original; that the Brahmin dreamer in his jangal had long known that the

---

[1] Translated "perfections" by Dr. Rhys Davids, but this deprives the word of its full force.

mastery of lust brought more joy than its indulgence. But the Brahmajnâni jealously kept this knowledge to himself when he gained it, and dreamed his life away. The great originality of Buddha was that he determined to hand over the " Wisdom of the Other Bank " to the whole human family. He invented the missionary. He invented the preacher. He forged an apparatus of propagandism that has never been surpassed, that has never been equalled. " Go forth and preach Dharma ! " was his command, and the " Mob of Beggars " conquered Asia. Altars, fanes, and outside worship formed no part, I think, of the original scheme of the reformer. And if he had wanted a Bible he would have fallen back on fresh interpretations of the Indian Bible already in existence. His creed was a pure theosophy. It was based on extasia, but he swept away the Brahminic tortures, the suspension by hooks, the " five fires," etc., as being a perversion of yoga.

Buddha, the first preacher, gave vent to some of the grandest utterances that have ever fallen from human lips. Considering their date and their influence over the general happiness of the world, they are simply extraordinary. The awakening of the spiritual life of the individual was what he aimed at. Human suffering was the daughter of evil deeds.[1]

---

[1] Dhammapada, v. 117.

But these evil deeds were not due to any inherent human depravity. They were simply due to ignorance of spiritual laws.[1] And their remedy was to be found in bringing home to each individual the conviction that there was a higher life and a happier life.

"He who speaks and acts with the inner quickening undeveloped, grief follows him as closely as the chariot wheel the steed.

"He who speaks and acts with the inner quickening unvitiated has joy for his shadow.[2]

"Obey the eternal law of the heavens. Who keeps this law lives happily in this world and the next.[3]

"For the enfranchised soul human suffering no longer exists.[4]

"In the darkness of this world few men see clearly. Very few soar heavenwards like a bird freed from a net."[5]

No doubt the discipline of extasia was expected to give vitality to this inner quickening. When actual visions of the Buddhas of the ten regions were before the eyes of the fasting visionary, it was judged that he would have a more practical belief in their lapis-lazuli domains. The heart of the Eastern nations has been truer to its great teacher than their learned

---

[1] Dhammapada, v. 243. [2] Ibid., v. 1, 2.
[3] Ibid., v. 169. [4] Ibid., v. 90.
[5] Ibid., v. 174.

metaphysicians have been.   The epoch of Buddha is
called the "Era when the Milken Rice [immortality]
came into the world."[1]   This certainty of a heavenly
kingdom was not to be confined, as in the orthodox
Brahminism, to a priestly caste.   A king had become
a beggar that he might preach to beggars.   In the
Chinese Dhammapada there is a pretty story of a
very beautiful Magdalen who had heard of Buddha,
and who started off to hear him preach.   On the way,
however, she saw her beautiful face in a fountain near
which she stopped to drink, and she was unable to
carry out her good resolution.   As she was returning
she was overtaken by a courtesan still more beautiful
than herself, and they journeyed together.   Resting
for awhile at another fountain, the beautiful stranger
was overcome with sleep, and placed her head on her
fellow-traveller's lap.   Suddenly the beautiful face
became livid as a corpse, loathsome, a prey to hateful
insects.   The stranger was the great Buddha himself,
who had put on this appearance to redeem poor
Puṇḍarî.[2]   "There is a loveliness that is like a
beautiful jar full of filth, a beauty that belongs to
eyes, nose, mouth, body.   It is this womanly beauty
that causes sorrow, divides families, kills children."
These words, uttered by the great teacher on another

[1] Upham, "Hist. Buddhism," p. 48.
[2] Chinese Dhammapada, p. 35.

occasion, were perhaps retailed a second time for the Buddhist Magna Civitatis Peccatrix.[1]

The penitent thief, too, is to be heard of in Buddhism. Buddha confronts a cruel bandit in his mountain retreat and converts him.[2] All great movements, said St. Simon, must begin by working on the emotion of the masses.

Another originality of the teaching of Buddha was the necessity of individual effort. Ceremonial, sacrifice, the exertions of others, could have no possible effect on any but themselves. Against the bloody sacrifice of the Brahmins he was specially remorseless.

" How can the system which requires the infliction of misery on others be called a religious system ? . . . How having a body defiled with blood will the shedding of blood restore it to purity ? To seek a good by doing an evil is surely no safe plan ! "[3]

Even a Buddha could only show the sinner the right path. "Tathâgatas are only preachers. You yourself must make an effort."[4]

Buddha's theology made another great advance on other creeds, a step which our century is only now attempting to overtake. He strongly emphasized the remorseless logic of cause and effect in the deterio-

[1] Chinese Dhammapada, p. 159.   [2] Ibid., p. 48.
[3] "Romantic History," p. 159.   [4] Dhammapada, v. 276.

U

rating influence of evil actions on the individual character. The Judas of Buddhism, Devadatta, repents
and is forgiven. But Buddha cannot annul the
causation of his evil deeds. These will have to be
dealt with by slow degrees in the purgatorial stages of
the hereafter. He knows no theory of a dull bigot on
his deathbed suddenly waking up with all the broad
sympathies and large knowledge of the Angel Gabriel.
Unless in the next life a being takes up his intellectual
and moral condition exactly at the stage he left it in
this, it is plain that logically his individuality is lost.
This teaching of Buddha has been whimsically
enforced by some of his followers. His own words
are trenchant and clear : " A fault once committed is
like new milk, which grows not sour all at once.
Patiently and silently, like a smothered ember, shall
it inch by inch devour the fool."[1] "Both a good
action and an evil action must ripen and bear their
inevitable fruit."[2]

This teaching has been powerfully inculcated in one
or two fine parables, in which the consequences of sin
are imaged as an iron city of torment, and the sins
themselves figure as beautiful women luring man to
his ruin. On the surface all is as bewitching as a
scene of the " Arabian Nights." The palm-trees of a
soft island rustle gently, and in a delicious palace the

---

[1] Dhammapada, v. 71. [2] Burnouf, Introd., p. 87.

mean seeker of gold, the bad son, is fanned by women of a beauty unknown to earth. He has sought the unworthy prizes of the Kâmaloka, and he enjoys them for a time, because with Buddha the full basket and store of the Brahmin and the old Jew are not deemed the rewards of heaven, but of quite another region. From island to island the wanderer goes, each island being more delicious than the preceding one, but each being nearer to the iron-walled city of expiation. But the furies are cause and effect and not an eternal Ahriman. There is no devil that Buddha cannot soften.[1]

This suggests another great advance made by Buddha. In his day the beneficent God was deemed the god of a nation, a tribe; and all the gods of other nations were deemed evil demons. This creed is the real "agnosticism" and "atheism," because its main postulate implies that the reason and conscience of humanity for thousands and thousands of years have been unable to discover God, and that if He has been found at all, it is to accident alone that the discovery is due; even if the discovered god should not upon examination be found to be composed of very poor clay. But the missionaries of Tathâgata were sent to every nation, and Buddha is the first historical

---

[1] Beal, "Romantic History." Comp. Story of the Five Hundred Merchants, p. 332, and the Merchant, p. 342.

teacher who proclaimed that even in the hell Avîchi was no recess sheltered from Tathâgatha's all-pervading love.

But the crowning legacy to humanity of this priceless benefactor was his boundless compassion. "Buddha," say his disciples, "was God revealed in the form of Mercy." The theory that Buddha was a myth seems quite to break down here, for some such character must have existed, that ideas so far in advance even of modern days could have been conceived. His majestic gentleness never varies. He converts the Very Wicked One. He speaks gently to the Daughters of Sin. He clears out even the lowest hells when he visits earth, and makes devils as well as good men happy. A fool outrages and insults him: "My son," he replies, "outrage addressed to heaven is like spittle aimed into the skies; it returns upon the author of the outrage."[1] And he explained to his disciples that Tathâgata could never be made angry by foul actions and invectives. Such can only make him redouble his mercy and love.[2] When we reflect that the principle of retaliation was the rude police of the day in which he lived, and that aggregations of men were obliged to foster a love of revenge, war, plunder, and bloodshed in their midst, prompted by the mere instinct of self-preservation, such great

---

[1] Sûtra of Forty-two Sections, sect. viii. [2] Ibid., sect. vii.

sentences as the following of Buddha are indeed noteworthy : —

"By love alone can we conquer wrath. By good alone can we conquer evil. The whole world dreads violence. All men tremble in the presence of death. Do to others that which ye would have them do to you. Kill not. Cause no death." [1]

"Say no harsh words to thy neighbour. He will reply to thee in the same tone." [2]

"'I am injured and provoked, I have been beaten and plundered!' They who speak thus will never cease to hate."

"That which can cause hate to cease in the world is not hate, but the absence of hate." [3]

"If, like a trumpet trodden on in battle, thou complainest not, thou hast attained Nirvâna."

"Silently shall I endure abuse, as the war-elephant receives the shaft of the bowman."

"The awakened man goes not on revenge, but rewards with kindness the very being who has injured him, as the sandal-tree scents the axe of the woodman who fells it." [4]

I will now copy down a few miscellaneous sayings of Buddha :—

[1] Sutra of Forty-two Sections, v. 129. M. Léon Feer gives here the very words of Luke vi. 31. [2] Ibid., v. 133. [3] Ibid., v. 4, 5.

[4] This is claimed by the Brahmins likewise, but it is quite foreign to their genius. *Vide* Hodgson, p. 74.

"The swans go on the path of the sun. They go through the air by means of their miraculous power. The wise are led out of this world when they have conquered Mâra and his train." [1]

"A man is not a Śramaṇa by outward acts."

"Not by tonsure does an undisciplined man become a Śramaṇa."

"There is no satisfying of lusts with a shower of gold pieces."

"A man is not a Bhikshu simply because he asks others for alms. A man is not a Muni because he observes silence. Not by discipline and vows, not by much spiritual knowledge, not by sleeping alone, not by the gift of holy inspiration, can I earn that release which no worldling can know. The real Śramaṇa is he who has quieted all evil."

"If one man conquer in battle a thousand thousand men, and another conquer himself, the last is the greatest conqueror."

"Few are there amongst men who arrive at the other shore. Many run up and down the shore."

"Let the fool wish for a false reputation, for precedence amongst the Bhikshus, for lordship in the convents, for worship amongst other people."

"A supernatural person is not easily found. He is not born everywhere. Wherever such a sage is born that race prospers."

[1] Dhammapada.

"Call not out in this way as if I were the god Brahma" (Chinese parable).

"Religion is nothing but the faculty of love."[1]

"The house of Brahma is that wherein children obey their parents."[2]

"The elephant's cub, if he find not leafless and thorny creepers in the greenwood, becomes thin."[3]

"Beauty and riches are like a knife smeared with honey. The child sucks and is wounded."[4]

THE ONE THING NEEDFUL.

Certain subtle questions were proposed to Buddha, such as: What will best conquer the evil passions of man? What is the most savoury gift for the alms-bowl of the mendicant? Where is true happiness to be found? Buddha replied to them all with one word, *Dharma*[5] (the heavenly life).

I will now give some of the Buddhist parables, some almost unequalled for beauty.

THE PARABLE OF THE FORGIVENESS OF INJURIES.

In a previous existence, Buddha was once the ascetic Jin Juh, and he dwelt in a forest. "Forests are delightful," he subsequently declared. "Where

---

[1] Bigandet, p. 223.
[2] Burnouf, Introd.
[3] Hodgson, p. 74.
[4] Sutra of Forty-two Sections, sect. xxi.
[5] Bigandet, p. 225.

the worldling finds no delight, there the awakened man will find delight." At this time there was a king called Ko Li, who was possessed of a cruel and wicked disposition. One day, taking his women with him, he entered the forest to hunt, and becoming tired, he lay down to sleep. Then all the women went into the woods to gather flowers, and they came to the cell of the ascetic Jin Juh, and listened to his teaching. After some time the king awoke, and having missed the women, he became jealous, and drew his sword, and went in search of them. Seeing them all standing in front of the cell of the ascetic, he became very angry indeed.

"Who are you ?" he said.

"I am the ascetic Jin Juh!"

"Have you conquered all earthly passions?" pursued the king.

The ascetic replied that he was there to struggle with passion.

"If you have not attained Sheung te teng," said the king, "I do not see that you are better than the philosophers [Fan fuh] ;" and with the cruelty of an Eastern tyrant, he hacked off the hands and feet of the poor hermit.

Perceiving a majestic calm still upon the face of the tortured ascetic, the astonished monarch asked him if he felt no anger.

"None, king, and I will one day teach thee also to curb thy wild-beast passions. When, in another existence, I attain Sheung te teng [Nirvâna], thou, O king, shalt be my first convert."

In a subsequent existence King Ko Li became the disciple Kaundiliya.

In the next parable we get, I think, a protest of the Little Vehicle against the "false teachers" of the innovating "Carriage that drives to the Great Nowhere."

THE PARABLE OF THE ATHEIST.

Angati, a king in Tirhut, had a daughter, Ruchi. At first he lived piously, but one day he heard some false teachers who declared that there is no future world, and that man, after death, is resolved into water and the other elements. After this he thought it was better to enjoy the present moment, and he became cruel.

One day Ruchî went to the king and requested him to give her one thousand gold pieces, as the next day was a festival and she wished to make an offering. The king replied that there was no future world, no reward for merit; religious rites were useless, and it was better to enjoy herself in the present world.

Now Ruchî possessed the inner vision, and was able to trace back her life through fourteen previous existences. She told the king that she had once been a nobleman, but an adulterer, and as a punishment she was now only a woman. As a farther punishment she had been a monkey, a bullock, a goat, and had been once born into the hell Avîchi. The king, unwilling to be taught by a woman, continued to be a sceptic. Ruchî then, by the power of an incantation, summoned a spirit to her aid, and Buddha himself, in the form of an ascetic, arrived at the city. The king asked him from whence he came. The ascetic replied that he came from the other world. The king, in answer, laughingly said—

"If you have come from the other world, lend me one hundred gold pieces, and when I go to that world I will give you a thousand."

Buddha answered gravely—

"When any one lends money, it must be to the rich. If he bestow money on the poor, it is a gift, for the poor cannot repay. I cannot lend you, therefore, one hundred gold pieces, for you are poor and destitute."

"You utter an untruth," said the king, angrily. "Does not this rich city belong to me?"

The Buddha replied—

"In a short time, O king, you will die. Can you

take your wealth with you to hell? There you will be in unspeakable misery, without raiment, without food. How, then, can you pay me my debt?"

At this moment, on the face of Buddha was a strange light which dazzled the king.

Buddha's Parable of Kîsogotamî.

In the Savatthi country was a rich man with four hundred millions. One day all the wealth in his house turned into charcoal. The rich man took to his bed, and refused food. A friend visiting him, was told what had happened. The friend said, "All your wealth has turned into charcoal because whilst in your possession it was no better than charcoal. You hoarded it up, and gave none in alms. Will you take my advice?" The rich man promised so to do. "Then," said the friend, "spread mats in the bazaar, and pile up upon them all this charcoal, and pretend to be trafficking with it. Your neighbours, seeing the heap, will say, 'O rich man, every one else sells cloth, oil, honey; why do you sell charcoal?' Reply to them, 'I am selling my goods!' By the mâya of the devas, your money to the grosser mortals appears no better than charcoal; but if any one with the inner sense should visit the bazaar, to him or her it will appear like good gold."

The rich man spread some mats in the bazaar, and piled on them the money that had turned to charcoal. The neighbours said, "Why does he sell charcoal?"

At length a young girl named Kîsogotamî, an orphan, and miserably poor, approached the heap. "My lord, rich man," she said, "why do you thus pile up gold and silver for sale?"

The rich man said, "Madam, give me that gold and silver!" The girl took up a handful of the charcoal, and lo! it became gold once more. The rich man married her to his only son. He had argued thus in his mind: "With many gold is no better than charcoal, but with Kîsogotamî charcoal becomes pure gold."

In four years' time Kîsogotamî lost her only son. In her love for it she carried the dead child clasped to her bosom, and went about asking the neighbours to give her some medicine for it. They said, "Is she mad? The boy is dead."

At length a wise man said to her, "I cannot give you medicine for your child, but I know a doctor who can."

The girl said, "If so, tell me who it is."

He answered, "Go to Śâkya Muni, the Buddha!"

Kîsogotamî repaired to the cell of Buddha, and accosted him. "Lord and master, do you know of any medicine that will cure my boy?"

Buddha answered, "I want a handful of mustard-seed."

The girl promised to procure it; but Buddha added, "I require some mustard-seed taken from a house where no son, husband, parent, or slave has died."

Poor Kîsogotamî, with the dead child carried astride of her hip in the Indian fashion, went from house to house. The compassionate people said, "Here is mustard-seed, take it!" But when she asked if any son, or husband, or parent, or slave had died in that house, she received for a reply, "Lady, the living are few, the dead are many; death comes to every house!" At last, weary and hopeless, Kîsogotamî sat down by the wayside, and watched the lamps of the city being extinguished one by one. At this instant, Buddha, by the power of Siddhi, placed his phantasm before her, which said to her, "All living beings resemble those lamps. They are lit up and flicker for awhile, and then dark night reigns over all." The appearance then preached the law to her, and, in the words of the Chinese, he provided "salvation and refuge, pointing out the path that leads to the eternal city."

THE STORY OF PRINCE KUNÂLA.

King Aśoka had an infant boy whose eyes were so beautiful that his father called him Kunâla. There is a bird of this name that dwells amongst the rhododendrons and pines of the Himalayas. It is famed for its lovely eyes. The young prince grew up. His beauty was the talk of the king's dominions. No woman could gaze into his eyes without falling in love with him. A Buddhist Sthavira (lit. old man) spoke serious words to him one day : " The pride of the eye, my son, is vanity ! Beware ! "

At an early age Kunâla married a young girl, named Kâñchana. One day a royal lady saw the young husband, and fell desperately in love with his fine eyes. Kunâla was horrorstruck at this.

" Are you not," he said, " in the zenana of the king, my father ? " This speech changed her love to a bitter hate.

At this time the city of Taxila revolted against King Aśoka. The monarch desired to hasten thither, but his ministers counselled him to send Prince Kunâla in his place. The prince repaired to the revolted city and soon restored quiet. The people assured him that it was the exactions and oppressions of the king's officers that they had resisted, not the king himself.

Soon the king became afflicted with a revolting malady, and wanted to abdicate in favour of his son. The Queen Tishya Rakshitâ, she who hated the prince, thought in her heart, " If Kunâla mounts the throne, I am lost ! " She ordered her slaves to bring her a man afflicted with the same malady as the king. She poisoned this man and had his inside examined. A huge worm was feeding upon it. She fed this worm with pepper and with ginger. The worm was none the worse. She fed it with onion, it died.

Immediately she repaired to the king and promised to cure him if he would grant her a boon. The king promised to grant her anything she asked him. She said to him, " Take this onion and you will be well."

" Queen," said the king, " I am a Kshatriya, and the laws of Manu [1] forbid me to eat onion." The queen told him it was medicine, not food. He ate the onion and was cured.

The boon demanded by the queen as a recompense for this great cure was a week's rule of the king's dominions. The king hesitated but was over-persuaded. Immediately the queen sent an order sealed with the royal seal that Prince Kunâla should be forced to wear the garments of a beggar and have both his eyes put out. A blind prince cannot mount the throne.

[1] Mânava Dharma Śâstra, iv. st. 5.

The good folks of Taxila were thunderstruck at this command, but they said to each other, "If the king is so merciless to his son, what will he be to us if we disobey him!" Some low-caste Chandâlas were summoned; they loved the prince, and would not execute the cruel order. At last a hideous object, a man deformed and stained with eighteen unsightly marks, came forward and tore out the prince's eyes. Soon he found himself a beggar on the high-road. His wife, Kâñchana, also clad in rags, was by his side. The poor prince now remembered the solemn words of the Sthavira.

"The outside world," he said to his wife, "is it not a mere globe of flesh?"

The prince had always been sickly, and to support himself now he played upon an instrument called the vînâ. After many wanderings they reached Pali-bothra (Patna), and approached the palace of the king; but the guards, seeing two dirty beggars, thrust them out summarily.

By-and-by the king heard the sound of the vînâ.

"It is my son," he said. He sent out officers of the court to bring him in. His condition filled the king with amazement. When he understood what had happened he summoned the guilty queen to his presence and ordered her to be burnt alive.

But the Prince Kunâla was now a changed man.

When he felt himself deserted, as he thought, by his earthly father, he had become a son of Buddha (fils de Buddha).[1] His "eye of flesh" had been put out, but he felt that the spiritual vision had been for the first time awakened. In lieu of the soft clothes of Kaśi, he now wore the rags of one of Buddha's sublime beggars. He threw himself at the feet of his father, and pleaded for the queen's life: "I feel no anger, no pain, only gratitude. Kill her not."

Aśoka, the powerful sun-king, was destined to rule India with a sway more extensive than that of the proudest Mogul. He was destined also to abandon his luxurious palaces, and himself wander along the highway begging his food. He too became a Bhikshu.

A Buddha at a Marriage Feast.

King Sudarsana was a model king. In his dominions was no killing or whipping as punishment; no soldiers' weapons to torture or destroy. His city, Jambunada, was built of crystal and cornelian, and silver and yellow gold. A Buddha visited it one day.

Now in that city was a man who was the next day to be married, and he much wished the Buddha to come to the feast. Buddha, passing by, read his silent

---

[1] Burnouf, Introd., pp. 365, 366.

X

wish, and consented to come. The bridegroom was overjoyed, and scattered many flowers over his house and sprinkled it with perfumes.

The next day Buddha with his alms-bowl in his hand and with a retinue of many followers arrived; and when they had taken their seats in due order, the host distributed every kind of exquisite food, saying, "Eat, my lord and all the congregation, according to your desire!"

But now a marvel presented itself to the astonished mind of the host. Although all these holy men ate very heartily, the meats and the drinks remained positively quite undiminished; whereupon he argued in his mind, "If I could only invite all my kinsmen to come, the banquet would be sufficient for them likewise."

And now another marvel was presented. Buddha read the good man's thought, and all the relatives without invitation streamed in at the door. They, also, fed heartily on the miraculous food. It is almost needless to add that the Chinese book "Fu-pen-hing-tsi-king" (as translated by the invaluable Mr. Beal) announces that all these guests, having heard a few apposite remarks on Dharma from the lips of the Tathâgata, to the satisfaction of everybody (excepting, perhaps, the poor bride), donned the yellow robes.

The next parable is a very pretty one, and shows that a love that can pierce the limits of this narrow world and range amongst the Devalokas of the hereafter could be conceived even in the age of Śâkya Muni.

THE STORY OF THE GIRL BHADRA.

When Śâkya Muni was in a previous existence, a certain King Sûryapati invited the great Buddha Dîpankara to visit his dominions; and to do him honour he issued an edict that all his subjects within a radius of twelve yoganas from his chief city should reserve all flowers and perfume for the king and his offerings to the Buddha. No one was to be in possession of these offerings on his own account.

Śâkya was at this time a young Brahmin named Megha. He was well versed in the law, although he was only sixteen years of age. He was incomparable in appearance; his body like yellow gold and his hair the same. His voice was as soft and sweet as the voice of Brahma. He happened to reach the city at the very moment that it was adorned in expectation of the coming of the Buddha Dîpankara, and having already vague yearnings after the Buddhaship in his breast, he determined to make an offering to the incarnate Buddha.

He reasoned thus in his heart: "What offering shall I make to him? Buddhas contemn offerings of money; I will purchase the most beautiful flower I can find."

He went to a hairdresser's shop and selected a lovely flower, but the hairdresser refused to sell it. "The king has given orders, respectable youth, that no chaplets of flowers in this city are on any account to be sold!" Megha went off to a second and then to a third hairdresser's shop, and was met everywhere with the same refusal.

Now, it happened that as he was pursuing his search, he saw a dark-clad water-girl, whose name was Bhadrâ, secretly take a seven-stalked Utpala flower and put it inside her water-pitcher, and then go on her way. Megha went up to her and accosted her. "What are you going to do with that Utpala flower which I saw you put into your pitcher? I will give you five hundred gold pieces for it if you will sell it to me."

The young girl was arrested by the novel appearance of the handsome young man. She answered presently, "Beautiful youth, have you not heard that the great Dîpañkara Buddha is now about to enter the city in consequence of the king's invitation, and the king has issued orders that whatsoever scented unguents or flowers there are within twelve yoganas of the city are not on any account to be sold to any private individual, as the king will buy them all up for the purpose of presenting them to the Buddha. Now, in our neighbourhood there is a certain hairdresser's wife, who privately took from me five hundred pieces of money and gave me in return this seven-stalked flower; and the reason why I have thus transgressed the edict of the king is that I want myself to make an offering to the holy man."

Then Megha answered, "My good girl, what you have said will justify you in taking my five hundred gold pieces, and in giving me five stalks of the Utpala flower and reserving two for yourself."

She answered, "What will you do with the flowers if I give them to you?"

The young Brahmin told her that he wished to offer them to Buddha.

Now, it happened that this young girl was gifted with the inner vision, and she knew from the youth's remarkable appearance that he was destined one day to become the guide of men. She said, "Fair stranger, one day you will be a great Buddha, and if you will promise me that, up to the day of your Buddhahood, at each new birth you will take me as your wife, and that when you attain Nirvâna you will let me follow you as a disciple in your retinue of followers, then will I give you five stalks of this Utpala flower."

The Brahmin replied that an ascetic was required to give all his wealth to his fellow-men, and that if she consented to such an arrangement he was willing to contract that she should ever be his wife. She sold to him five stalks of the Utpala flower, that they might be his own special gift to the Buddha, and she desired him to present the other two stalks as her own free gift.

When Dîpañkara approached, majestic, and with a countenance like a glassy lake, the offering was thrown to him, and by a miracle the flowers remained in mid air, forming a canopy over his head.

Amongst the "Fan heavens" of the Chinese is one called Fuh-ngai (happy love). Let us hope that in that heaven the pretty Bhikshu Bhadrâ is still near her favourite teacher.

KING WESSANTARA.

Buddha once lived on earth as King Wessantara. So kind was he to everybody that it was rumoured that he had made a resolution to give to everybody whatever he was asked. He had a loving wife and two children. He had also an enchanted white elephant.

A grievous famine burst out in a neighbouring kingdom, and the poor died by thousands. Eight Brahmins were sent to King Wessantara to ask him for the white elephant; for fertile rain always falls in countries where an enchanted white elephant is staying. The benign king gave up his white elephant. This so incensed his own people that they deposed him.

Wessantara gave all his wealth to the poor, and departed in a carriage drawn by two horses, intending to repair to an immense rock in the wilderness, and there become a hermit. On his way he met two poor Brahmins, who asked him for his carriage. He complied, and the deposed king and queen, each carrying a child, made the rest of the journey on foot. Their road lay through the kingdom of the queen's father, who sought to overcome their resolution, but in vain.

Meanwhile a Brahmin named Jutaka was living very happily with a beautiful wife, until one day some envious neighbours poisoned her mind as she was drawing water at a well. They persuaded her she was a slave, and so incensed her that she attacked her husband and beat him and pulled his beard. Moreover, she threatened to leave his house unless he procured for her two slaves. A foolish king, she said, named Wessantara was dwelling as a hermit in the wilderness; let him go there and ask for two slaves. He had two children, and had made a vow to refuse no one any demand.

Jutaka departed, but found all access to the royal hermit denied by a hunter placed there by the queen's father, who, knowing Wessantara's vow, had desired to screen him from the further importunities of the greedy. Jutaka told him a lying tale and contrived to reach the hermit. He demanded the two children as slaves, and Wessantara was bound by his oath to hand them over to him. Jutaka, as soon as he was out of sight of the king, bound the royal children firmly with cords; but missing his way in the wilderness, came by chance to the territory of the queen's father, who was quickly apprised of all that had occurred.

He summoned the Brahmin before him, and offered him in exchange for the grandchildren the weight of them in gold pieces. The greedy Brahmin's end was not unlike that of Judas, for with his ill-gotten wealth he made a great feast, and from repletion his bowels also gushed out.[1]

---

[1] This parable and the two following are given by Upham from the Jâtakas of the Buddha.

KING BAMBADAT.

Buddha was in one of his births a merchant of Benares, and as he was one day passing with his wife in a carriage through the streets of Râjâgriha, the capital of King Bambadat, the monarch saw his wife and became captivated with her unrivalled beauty.

Immediately he hatched an infamous plot to gain her. He sent one of his officers to drop furtively a jewel of great value in the merchant's carriage. The poor merchant was then arrested on the charge of stealing the royal gem. He and his beautiful wife were brought before the king, who listened to the evidence with mock attention, and then ordered the merchant to be executed and his wife to be detained in the royal harem. King Bambadat was a cruel monarch, whose oppressions had earned him the hatred of his subjects.

The poor merchant was led away to be decapitated, but Indra on his throne in heaven had witnessed the atrocious transaction; and, lo! a miracle was accomplished. As the executioner raised his sword, the king, who was watching the bloody event, was suddenly made to change places with the merchant by the agency of unseen hands, and he received the fatal blow; whilst Buddha suddenly found himself exalted on the royal elephant that had brought the king to the spot. This striking interposition of Heaven awed the assembled populace, and they proclaimed the merchant their new king. It is needless to add that his rule formed a striking contrast to that of King Bambadat. It is not mentioned, but I think it is very plain also, that the beautiful wife was the girl Bhadrâ of the former story. Buddhism has done much evil by its enforced sacerdotal celibacy, but, on the other hand, it seems to have had the honour of first conceiving a love of man with woman that could pierce the skies and be prolonged after death.

THE HUNGRY DOG.

There was once a wicked king named Usuratanam, who oppressed his people so much that Buddha from the sky took compassion upon them. At this time he was the god Indra, and assuming the form of a huntsman, he came down to earth with the Deva Mâtali, disguised as a dog of enormous size. They at once entered the palace of the king, and the dog barked so wofully, that the sound seemed to shake the royal buildings to their very foundations. The king, affrighted, had the hunter brought before him; and he inquired the portent of these terrible sounds.

"It is through hunger that the dog barks," said the huntsman, and again a sound louder far than thunder reverberated through the palace.

"Fetch him food! Fetch anything!" cried the king in terror. All the food that happened then to be prepared was the royal banquet. It was placed before the dog. He ate it with surprising rapidity, and then barked once more with his terrible voice. More food was sent for, the food stored up in the city, the food of the adjacent provinces, but still the insatible dog after a brief interval ate all up and barked for more. The king could scarcely prevent himself from falling to the earth with terror.

"Will nothing ever satisfy your dog, O hunter?"

"Nothing, O king, but the flesh of all his enemies."

"And who are his enemies, O hunter?"

"His enemies," said the hunter, "are those who do wicked deeds, who oppress the poor, who make war, who are cruel to the brute creation."

The king, remembering his many evil deeds, was seized with terror and remorse; and the Buddha, revealing himself, preached the law of righteousness to him and his people. It is plain that in the original story, as in the last, Indra alone was the supernatural agent, and the clumsy introduction of

Buddha is an after-thought. Mâtali is the conventional character of Indra, which I think is an additional proof.

BUDDHA AS A PEACEMAKER.

It is recorded that two princes were once about to engage in a terrible battle in a quarrel that took place about a certain embankment constructed to keep in water. Between these kings and their assembled armies Buddha suddenly appeared and asked the cause of the strife. When he was completely informed upon the subject, he put the following questions :—

"Tell me, O kings! is earth of any intrinsic value?"

"Of no value whatever," was the reply.

"Is water of any intrinsic value?"

"Of no value whatever!"

"And the blood of kings, is that of any intrinsic value?"

"Its value is priceless!"

"Is it reasonable," asked the Tathâgata, "that that which is priceless should be staked against that which has no value whatever?"

The incensed monarchs saw the wisdom of this reasoning and abandoned their dispute.[1]

[1] Bigandet, p. 191.

THE PRODIGAL SON.[1]

A certain man had a son who went away into a far country. There he became miserably poor. The father, however, grew rich, and accumulated much gold and treasure, and many storehouses and elephants. But he tenderly loved his lost son, and secretly lamented that he had no one to whom to leave his palaces and suvernas at his death.

After many years the poor man, in search of food and clothing, happened to come to the country where his father had great possessions. And when he was afar off his father saw him, and reflected thus in his mind: " If I at once acknowledge my son and give to him my gold and my treasures, I shall do him a great injury. He is ignorant and undisciplined ; he is poor and brutalized. With one of such miserable inclinations 'twere better to educate the mind little by little. I will make him one of my hired servants."

Then the son, famished and in rags, arrived at the door of his father's house ; and seeing a great throne upraised and many followers doing homage to him who sat upon it, was awed by the pomp and the wealth around. Instantly he fled once more to the highway. " This," he thought, " is the house of

[1] This is the title adopted in the translation of M. Foucaux.

the poor man. If I stay at the palace of the king perhaps I shall be thrown into prison."

Then the father sent messengers after his son; who was caught and brought back in spite of his cries and lamentations. When he reached his father's house he fell down fainting with fear, not recognizing his father, and believing that he was about to suffer some cruel punishment. The father ordered his servants to deal tenderly with the poor man, and sent two labourers of his own rank of life to engage him as a servant on the estate. They gave him a broom and a basket, and engaged him to clean up the dung-heap at a double wage.

From the window of his palace the rich man watched his son at his work ; and disguising himself one day as a poor man, and covering his limbs with dust and dirt, he approached his son and said, " Stay here, good man, and I will provide you with food and clothing. You are honest, you are industrious. Look upon me as your father."

After many years the father felt his end approaching, and he summoned his son and the officers of the king, and announced to them the secret that he had so long kept. The poor man was really his son, who in early days had wandered away from him ; and now that he was conscious of his former debased condition, and was able to appreciate and retain vast wealth, he was determined to hand over to him his entire treasure. The poor man was astonished at this sudden change of fortune, and overjoyed at meeting his father once more.

The parables of Buddha are reported in the Lotus of the Perfect Law to be veiled from the ignorant by means of an enigmatic form of language.[1] The rich man of this parable, with his throne adorned by flowers and garlands of jewels, is announced to be Tathâgata, who dearly loves all his children, and has prepared for them vast spiritual treasures. But each son of Tathâgata has miserable inclinations. He prefers the dung-heap to the pearl mani. To teach such a man Tathâgata is obliged to employ inferior agents, the monk and the ascetic, and to wean him by degrees from the lower objects of desire. When he speaks himself, he is forced to veil much of his thought, as it would not be understood. His sons feel no joy on hearing spiritual things. Little by little must their minds be trained and disciplined for higher truths.

THE MAN WHO WAS BORN BLIND.

Once upon a time there was a man born blind, and he said, "I cannot believe in a world of appearances.

[1] Lotus, p. 45.

Colours bright or sombre exist not. There is no sun, no moon, no stars. None have witnessed such things!" His friends remonstrated with him, but all in vain. He still repeated the same words.

In those days there was a holy man cunning in roots and herbs, one who had acquired supernatural gifts by a life of purity and abstinence. This man perceived by his spiritual insight that away amongst the clouds on the steeps of the lofty Himalayas were four simples that had power to cure the man who was born blind. He fetched these simples, and, mashing them together with his teeth, he applied them. Immediately the man who was born blind was cured of his infirmity. He saw colours and appearances. He saw the bright sun in the heavens. He was overjoyed, and pronounced that no one now had any advantage over him in the matter of eyesight.

Then certain holy men came to the man who had been born blind, and said to him, "You are vain and arrogant, and nearly as blind as you were before. You see the outside of things but not the inside. One whose supernatural senses are quickened sees the lapis-lazuli fields of the Buddhas and hears conch-shells sounded at a distance of five yoganas. Go off to a desert, a forest, a cavern in the mountains, and conquer this thirst for earthly things." The man who was born blind did as these holy men enjoined, and by-and-by himself acquired the supernatural gifts.

The interpretation of this parable is that the man who is born blind is one afflicted with the blindness of spiritual ignorance. Tathâgata is the great physician, who loves him as a father loves his son, and the four simples are the four holy truths. The holy men who accosted him are the great Rishis, who teach the spiritual life in caves and in deserts, and wean mankind from the love of lower things.

PARABLE OF THE WOMAN AT THE WELL.

Ânanda, a favourite disciple of Buddha, was once athirst, having travelled far. At a well he encountered a girl named Matanga, and asked her to give him some water to drink. But she, being a woman of low caste, was afraid of contaminating a holy Brâhmaṇa, and refused humbly.

" I ask not for caste, but for water ! " said Ânanda. His condescension won the heart of the girl Matanga.

It happened that she had a mother cunning in love philtres and weird arts, and when this woman heard how much her daughter was in love, she threw her magic spells round the disciple and brought him to her cave. Helpless, he prayed to Buddha, who forthwith appeared and cast out the wicked demons.

Y

But the girl Matanga was still in wretched plight. At last she determined to repair to Buddha himself and appeal to him.

The Great Physician, reading the poor girl's thought, questioned her gently—

" Supposing that you marry my disciple, can you follow him everywhere ? "

" Everywhere ! " said the girl.

" Could you wear his clothes, sleep under the same roof ? " said Buddha, alluding to the nakedness and beggary of the " houseless one."

By slow degrees the girl began to take in his meaning, and at last she took refuge in the Three Great Pearls.[1]

THE STORY OF VÂSAVADATTA.

At Maṭhurâ was a courtesan named Vâsavadatta. She fell violently in love with one of the actual disciples of Buddha named Upagupta, and sent her servant to him to declare her passion. Upagupta was young and of singular beauty. In a short time the servant returned with the following enigmatic reply :—

" The time has not yet arrived when the disciple Upagupta will pay a visit to the courtesan Vâsava-datta ! "

[1] Burnouf, Introd. p. 138.

Vâsavadatta was astonished at this reply. Her
class at this time was a caste, a body organized, and
indeed fostered, by the State, and she lived in great
magnificence. She was the most beautiful woman in
the king's dominions, and not accustomed to have
her love rejected. When her first moments of
petulance had passed, she reflected that the young
man was poor. Again she sent her servant to Upagupta. "Tell him that Vâsavadatta desires love,
not gold and pearls." By-and-by the servant returned
with the same enigmatic answer, "The time has not
yet arrived when the disciple Upagupta will visit the
courtesan Vâsavadatta!"

Some few months after this, Vâsavadatta had a
love intrigue with the head of the artisans of Maṭhurâ,
and whilst this was in progress a very wealthy
merchant arrived at the city with five hundred horses
that he desired to sell. Hearing of the beauty of
Vâsavadatta, he contrived to see her and also to fall
in love with her. His pearls and suverṇas were too
much for the giddy woman. She assassinated the
head of the artisans and ordered his corpse to be
flung on a dung-heap. By-and-by his relations,
alarmed at his disappearance, caused a search to be
made, and the body was found.

Vâsavadatta was arrested and carried before the
king, who gave orders that her ears, her nose, her

hands, and her feet should at once be cut off by the common executioner and her body flung in a grave-yard. Her maid still clung to her, for she had been a kind mistress. She tried to assuage her pain, and drove away the crows from her bleeding body.

Vâsavadatta now received a third message from Upagupta : " The time *has* arrived when the disciple Upagupta will pay a visit to the courtesan Vâsava-datta ! " The poor woman, in whom an echo of the old passion still reverberated, hurriedly ordered her maid to collect and hide away under a cloth her severed feet and limbs, the poor remnants of her old beauty ; and when the young man appeared she said with some petulance—

" Once this body was fragrant like the lotus, and I offered you my love. In those days I was covered with pearls and fine muslin. Now I am mangled and covered with filth and blood. My hands, my feet, my nose, my ears have been struck off by the common executioner ! "

The young man with great gentleness comforted poor Vâsavadatta in her agony. " Sister, it is not for my pleasure and happiness that I now draw near." And he pointed out the " true nature " of the charms that she mourned. He proved to her that they had proved torments and not joys, and if immodesty, and vanity, and greed, and the murderous instinct had been lopped away, she had sustained a gain and not a loss. He then told her of the Tathâgata that he had seen walking upon this very earth, a Tathâgata who specially loves the suffering.

His speech brought calm to the soul of Vâsavadatta. She died after having professed her faith in Buddha.[1]

She was carried by spirits to the penitential heavens of the Devaloka.

Parable of the Blazing Mansion.

Once there was an old man, broken, decrepit, but very rich. He possessed much land and many gold pieces. Moreover, he possessed a large rambling mansion which also showed plain proofs of time's decay. Its rafters were worm-eaten; its pillars were rotten; its galleries were tumbling down; the thatch on its roof was dry and combustible. Inside this mansion were several hundreds of the old man's servants and retainers, so extensive was the collection of rambling old buildings.

Unfortunately this mansion possessed only one door.

The old man was also the father of many children —five, ten, twenty, let us say. One day there was a

---

[1] Burnouf, Introd., pp. 131, 132.

smell of burning, and he ran out by the solitary door. To his horror he saw the thatch in a mass of flame, the rotten old pillars were catching fire one by one, the rafters were blazing like tinder.   Inside, his children, whom he loved most tenderly, were romping and amusing themselves with their toys.

The distracted father said to himself, " I will run in and save my children.   I will seize them in my strong arms.   I will bear them harmless through the falling rafters and the blazing beams!"   Then the sad thought seized him that his children were romping and ignorant.   "If I tell them that the house is on fire they will not understand me.   If I try to seize them they will romp about and try to escape.   Alas! not a moment is to be lost!"

Suddenly a bright thought flashed across the old man's mind.   "My children are ignorant," he mentally said, "but they love toys and glittering playthings. I will promise them some playthings of unheard-of beauty.   Then they will listen to me!"

So the old man shouted out with a loud voice, "Children, children, come out of the house and see these beautiful toys.   Chariots with white oxen, all gold and tinsel.   See these exquisite little antelopes! Whoever saw such goats as these!   Children, children, come quickly or they will all be gone!"

Forth from the blazing ruin came the children in

hot haste. The word "playthings" was almost the only word that they could understand. Then the fond father, in his great joy at seeing his offspring freed from peril, procured for them some of the most beautiful chariots ever seen. Each chariot had a canopy like a pagoda. It had tiny rails and balustrades and rows of jingling bells. It was formed of the seven precious substances. Chaplets of glittering pearls were hung aloft upon it; standards and wreaths of the most lovely flowers. Milk-white oxen drew these chariots. The children were astonished when they were placed inside.

The meaning of this parable is thus rendered in the White Lotus of Dharma. The old man is Tathâgata, and his children the blind, suffering children of sin and passion. Tathâgata fondly loves them, and would save them from their unhappiness. The old rambling mansion, unsightly, rotten, perilous, is the domain of Kâma, the domain of appetite, the three great worlds of the visible kosmos. This old mansion is ablaze with the fire of mortal passions and hates and lusts. Tathâgata in his "immense compassion" would lead all his beloved children away from this great peril, but they do not understand his language. Their only thought is of tinsel toys and childish pastimes. If he speaks to them of the great inner quickening which makes man conquer human pain, they cannot understand him. If he talks to them of wondrous supernatural gifts accorded to mortals, they turn a deaf ear to him. The tinsel chariots provided for the children of Tathâgata are the "Greater" and "Lesser" Vehicles of the Buddhist teaching.

THE SERMON TO RÂHULA RESPECTING FALSEHOOD.

Of the seven sacred books recognized in the days of Aśoka, one mentioned in the Bhabra edict has lately come to light ; and this has been found, not in the vaunted ancient canon of Ceylon, but in China. I give this short work *in extenso* as translated by the invaluable Professor Beal.[1]

"In days of old, before Râhula had attained to supreme wisdom, his natural disposition being somewhat low and disorderly, his words were not always marked by love of truth. On one occasion Buddha had ordered him to go to the Kien-tai [Ghanda or Ghanta ?] Vihâra, and there remain guarding his mouth [tongue] and governing his thoughts, at the same time diligently studying [or observing] the rules of conduct laid down in the Scriptures. Râhula, having heard the command, made his obeisance and went. For ninety days he remained in deep shame and penitence. At length Buddha repaired to the place

[1] Dhammapada, p. 142.

and showed himself. On seeing him, Râhula was
filled with joy, and reverently bowed down and worshipped him. After this, Buddha having taken the
seat provided for him, he desired Râhula to fill a
water-basin with water and bring it to him and wash
his feet. Having done so, and the washing being
over, Buddha asked Râhula if the water so used was
now fit for any purpose of domestic use [drinking,
etc.]; and on Râhula replying in the negative because
the water was defiled with dust and dirt, Buddha
added, 'And such is your case; for although you are
my son and the grandchild of the king, although you
have voluntarily given up everything to become a
Shaman, nevertheless you are unable to guard your
tongue from untruth and the defilement of loose con-
versation, and so you are like this defiled water—
useful for no further purpose.' And again he asked
him, after the water had been thrown away, whether
the vessel was now fit for holding water to drink; to
which Râhula replied, 'No, for the vessel is still
defiled, and is known as an unclean thing, and therefore not used for any purpose such as that indicated.'
To which Buddha again replied, 'And such is your
case. By not guarding your tongue, etc., you are
known and recognized as unfit for any high purpose,
although you profess to be a Shaman.' And then
once more lifting the empty basin on to his foot, and

whirling it round and round, he asked Râhula if he were not afraid lest it should fall and be broken; to which Râhula replied that he had no such fear, for the vessel was but a cheap and common one, and therefore its loss would be a matter of small moment. 'And such is your case,' again said Buddha; 'for though you are a Shaman, yet being unable to guard your mouth or your tongue, you are destined, as a small and insignificant thing, to be whirled in the endless eddies of transmigration, an object of contempt to all the wise.' Râhula being filled with shame, Buddha addressed him once more. 'Listen, and I will speak to you a parable. There was in old time the king of a certain country, who had a large and very powerful elephant, able to overpower by its own strength five hundred smaller elephants. This king, being about to go to war with some rebellious dependency, brought forth the iron armour belonging to the elephant, and directed the master of the animal to put it on him, to wit, two sharp-pointed swords on his tusks, two iron hooks [scythes] on his ears, a crooked spear on each foot, an iron club [or ball] attached to his tail, and to accompany him were appointed nine soldiers as escort. Then the elephant-master rejoiced to see the creature thus equipped, and trained him above all things to keep his trunk well coiled up, knowing that an arrow piercing *that* in the midst must be fatal. But lo! in the middle of the battle the elephant, uncoiling his trunk, sought to seize a sword with it. On which the master was affrighted, and, in consultation with the king and his ministers, it was agreed that he should no more be brought into the battlefield.' In continuation Buddha said: 'Râhula! if men, committing the nine faults, only guard their tongue as this elephant was trained to guard his trunk, all would be well. Let them guard against the arrow that strikes in the middle! let them keep their mouth, lest they die, and fall into the misery of future births in the three evil paths!' And then he added these stanzas :—

"'I am like the fighting elephant without any fear of the middle arrow [the arrow wounding the middle part]. By sincerity and truth I escape the un-principled man [lawless man]. Like the elephant, well subdued and quiet, permits the king to mount on his trunk [offers his trunk for the king to ascend], thus tamed is the reverend man; he also endures truthfully and in faith.'

"Râhula, hearing these words, was filled with sorrow for his careless disregard of his words, and gave himself up to renewed exertion, and so became a Rahat."

Against Buddha's teaching two main objections have been urged :—

1. That his Bodhi, viewed from a spiritual point of view, is mere selfishness. The individual isolates himself from his race for his own advantage.

2. The monkish system that he spread abroad has, in point of fact, produced many grave evils—idleness, immorality, depravity, etc.—and is, in fact, pure pessimism. One answer meets both objections, that is, as far as they are unjust.

The problem before a reformer in Buddha's day was essentially practical. To enfranchise the world what possible apparatus was available? The oratory of the uninspired demagogue would not have been listened to by the masses, and would have been quickly silenced by the dominant caste. Books, printing presses, even the letters of the alphabet, were unavailable; and the victories of material force in Buddha's view meant merely the firmer riveting of chains. So Buddha, himself a king, in commencing his conflict, handed over an army of soldiers and an army of priests to his antagonists, determined that the victory should be a purely moral one. One weapon alone was within reach—the tree of the Rishi. Under that tree God spake. Such was the belief of the people, based on the teaching of the Vedic hymns, as recited at every sacrifice. With Buddha the Bodhi meant not selfishness, but the complete conquest of self; and the initiation of the Rishi under his tree was merely a means to an end. Instead of being sloth, that end was boundless activity in contributing to the happiness of others. His blameless soldiers, having given up wife and wealth, were ordered to march from tree to tree, never resting for two nights under the same one. No halt was to be allowed but the grave as long as a king oppressed his subjects, a priest tortured animals, or as long as spiritual ignorance tortured priests and kings.

Viewed from the historical side, the following originalities may be accredited to Buddhism :—

1. Enforced vegetarianism for the whole nation.

2. Enforced national abstinence from wine.

3. Abolition of slavery.

4. The introduction of the principle of forgiveness of injuries in opposition to the national *lex talionis*.

5. Uncompromising antagonism to all national religious rites that were opposed to the gnosis or spiritual development of the individual.

6. Beggary, continence, and asceticism for the religious teachers.

These are the six originalities of the Buddhist movement.

CHAPTER XXIV.

THE DEATH OF BUDDHA.

SOME eighty miles due east of Buddha's birth-place, Kapilavastu, now stands a modest village called Mâthâ Kuär (the "Dead Prince"). At the date of the pilgrimage of Hwen Thsang there was a reason for this. Under a splendid temple-canopy reposed in marble a "Dead Prince," and this circumstance is still remembered by the natives. The ruins of this temple can still be traced. Exactly four hundred and seventy years before Christ, the spot was a jañgal of Śâla-trees, and beneath the shade of two of these lay calm and rigid the gentle teacher whom Indians call the "Best Friend of all the World." Buddha was journeying from Râjâgriha when he reached this resting-place. Its name was Kuśinagara. At Beluva, near Vaiśâlî, he was attacked with a severe illness. Violent pains seized him. He was very nearly dying. Ânanda was disconsolate, but Buddha comforted him.

"What need hath the body of my followers of me

now, Ânanda? I have declared the doctrine, and I
have made no distinction between within and without.
He who says, 'I will rule over the Sangha!' or, 'Let
the Sangha be subjected to me!' he, Ânanda, might
declare his will in the Church. The Tathâgata, however, does not say, 'I will rule over the Church.' . . . I
am now frail, Ânanda; I am aged, I am an old man
who has finished his pilgrimage and reached old age.
Eighty years old am I.

"Be to yourselves, Ânanda, your own light, your
own refuge. Seek no other refuge. Let Dharma be
your light and refuge. Seek no other refuge. . . .
Whosoever now, Ânanda, or after my departure shall
be his own light, his own refuge, and shall seek no
other refuge, will henceforth be my true disciple and
walk in the right path."

Buddha journeyed on until he reached a place
called Pâvâ. Then he was attacked with a grievous
sickness. Weary, the old pilgrim reached a stream,
the Kakutthâ (the modern Badhi, according to General
Cunningham). Buddha bathed and sipped some of the
water; carts were passing and they thickened it with
mud. A little further on, by the side of the river
Háranyavatî (Chota Gandak), was a grove of Śâla-
trees. Between two of these blossoming trees was
the Nirvâna that the sick and weary pilgrim was
sighing for.

Under these two famous trees, with his head lying towards the north, the old man was laid. "Weep not, sorrow not, Ânanda," he said. "From all that man loves and enjoys he must tear himself.

"My existence is ripening to its close. The end of my life is near. I go hence. Ye remain behind. The place of refuge is ready for me."[1]

Before expiring, the teacher entered into the extasia of Samâdhi; and mighty thunders and earth-rockings announced the passing away of a great Chakravartin. Buddha's last words were :—

"Hearken, O disciples, I charge you. All that comes into being passes. Seek your salvation without weariness."

[1] Oldenberg, "Buddha," p. 199.

GLOSSARY AND INDEX.

Aditî, the Vedic Universal Mother.

Âdityas, Sons of Aditî, the months deified.

Amṛita, Pâli Amata, immortality, "bread of life," the food of the sacrifice after consecration.

Arhat, one emancipated from rebirths, an Adept.

Arnold, Edwin, denies the Agnosticism of early Buddhism, xi.; "Light of Asia" cited, 34.

Arûpaloka, the heavens where form ceases.

Aśoka on "God," the future life, prayer, mysticism, etc., 278 et seq.; his attitude towards Buddhism, 278 et seq.

Avîchi, the "rayless place," hell, purgatory.

Baptism, the Buddhist rite of, 86 et seq.

Beal, Professor S., condemns the views of Dr. Rhys Davids on soul, God, a future life, etc., in Buddhism, xii.

Bhagavat, lord, God, a title applied to Buddha, Vishṇu, and Śiva.

Bhikshu, beggar, one who has adopted the religious life. He is called also Parivrâjaka (wanderer), Muni (silent one), Śramaṇa (vile one), Son of Buddha, Son of Śâkya, Son of Dharma, Man of Pure Life, Smâsânîka (dwelling amid tombs), Houseless one, etc.

Bigandet, Bishop, on the Buddhist hierarchy, 185.

Bimbisâra offers crown to Buddha, 76.

Bodhi, gnosis, knowledge of the laws of spirit, annihilation of the ego, and mystical union of the soul with the non-ego, or God.

Bodhisatwa, one about to obtain the Bodhi in his next rebirth.

Brahma, the Great Spirit, the ineffable.

Brahmâ, the anthropomorphic god.

Brahmacharins, Seekers of Brahma, name for Buddha's early disciples.

Brahmajnâni, an Adept.

Z

tree of knowledge, 72 ; on the Brahma religion, 128 ; his reform, 129 ; begins to preach, 141 ; the historical Buddha, 285 ; death of, 334.

Sîlâdilya introduces Agnostic Buddhism, 171.

Skandhas, the five (lit. "bodies"), usually applied by Buddhists to the animal nature of man.

Stambha, upright monolith, menhir.

Sunya, the void, the "Great Nowhere."

Suny a pushpa, the "Carriage that drives to the Great Nowhere," or the "Flower that blooms in the Great Nowhere," a nickname for the Agnostic or innovating school of Buddhism, the Buddhism of the "Great Vehicle."

Sûtra, discourse.

Swayaṁvara, marriage by athletic competition (lit. "her own choice").

Tapas, self-torture (swinging on hooks, etc.) to gain magical power.

Tathâgata. *See* Buddha.

Tîrthas, tanks, shrines.

Tope, a dolmen, or sepulchral mound.

Tuśita, the highest heaven to be reached by unemancipated spirits.

Vaitaranî, the Brahmin River of Death, 10.

Varshâ, the rainy season, the Buddhist Lent.

Vihâra, a monastery.

Yoga (lit. "union"), the conjoining of heaven and earth, spirit and matter, the annihilation of the ego and merging of one's will with the divine will. Magical powers were conceived to be a result of this "union." Hence Yoga also means white magic.

PRINTED BY WILLIAM CLOWES AND SONS, LIMITED, LONDON AND BECCLES.

A LIST OF

KEGAN PAUL, TRENCH & CO.'S

PUBLICATIONS.

1

1.83.

1, *Paternoster Square,*
London.

A LIST OF

KEGAN PAUL, TRENCH & CO.'S PUBLICATIONS.

CONTENTS.

GENERAL LITERATURE.

ADAMS, F. O., F.R.G.S.—The History of Japan. From the Earliest Period to the Present time. New Edition, revised. 2 vols. With Maps and Plans. Demy 8vo, 21*s.* each.

ADAMSON, H. T., B.D.—The Truth as it is in Jesus. Crown 8vo, 8*s.* 6*d.*

The Three Sevens. Crown 8vo, 5*s.* 6*d.*

The Millennium ; or, the Mystery of God Finished. Crown 8vo, cloth, 6*s.*

A. K. H. B.—From a Quiet Place. A New Volume of Sermons. Crown 8vo, 5*s.*

ALLEN, Rev. R., M.A.—Abraham : his Life, Times, and Travels, 3800 years ago. With Map. Second Edition. Post 8vo, 6*s.*

ALLEN, Grant, B.A.—Physiological Æsthetics. Large post 8vo, 9*s.*

ALLIES, T. W., M.A.—Per Crucem ad Lucem. The Result of a Life. 2 vols. Demy 8vo, 25*s.*

A Life's Decision. Crown 8vo, 7*s.* 6*d.*

ANDERDON, Rev. W. H.—Fasti Apostolici ; a Chronology of the years between the Ascension of our Lord and the Martyrdom of SS. Peter and Paul. Crown 8vo, cloth, 2*s.* 6*d.*

ANDERSON, R. C., C.E.—Tables for Facilitating the Calcula-
tion of Every Detail in connection with Earthen
and Masonry Dams. Royal 8vo, £2 2s.

ARCHER, Thomas.—About my Father's Business. Work amidst
the Sick, the Sad, and the Sorrowing. Cheaper Edition. Crown
8vo, 2s. 6d.

ARMSTRONG, Richard A., B.A.—Latter-Day Teachers. Six
Lectures. Small crown 8vo, 2s. 6d.

ARNOLD, Arthur.—Social Politics. Demy 8vo, 14s.

Free Land. Second Edition. Crown 8vo, 6s.

AUBERTIN, J. J.—A Flight to Mexico. With Seven full-page
Illustrations and a Railway Map of Mexico. Crown 8vo, 7s. 6d.

BADGER, George Percy, D.C.L.—An English-Arabic Lexicon.
In which the equivalent for English Words and Idiomatic
Sentences are rendered into literary and colloquial Arabic.
Royal 4to, £9 9s.

BAGEHOT, Walter.—The English Constitution. Third Edition.
Crown 8vo, 7s. 6d.

Lombard Street. A Description of the Money Market. Seventh
Edition. Crown 8vo, 7s. 6d.

Some Articles on the Depreciation of Silver, and Topics
connected with it. Demy 8vo, 5s.

BAGENAL, Philip H.—The American-Irish and their Influence on Irish Politics. Crown 8vo, 5s.

BAGOT, Alan, C.E.—Accidents in Mines: their Causes and
Prevention. Crown 8vo, 6s.

The Principles of Colliery Ventilation. Second Edition,
greatly enlarged. Crown 8vo, 5s.

BAKER, Sir Sherston, Bart.—Halleck's International Law; or,
Rules Regulating the Intercourse of States in Peace and War.
A New Edition, revised, with Notes and Cases. 2 vols. Demy
8vo, 38s.

The Laws relating to Quarantine. Crown 8vo, 12s. 6d.

BALDWIN, Capt. J. H.—The Large and Small Game of
Bengal and the North-Western Provinces of India.
With numerous Illustrations. Second Edition. 4to, 21s.

BALLIN, Ada S. and F. L.—A Hebrew Grammar. With
Exercises selected from the Bible. Crown 8vo, 7s. 6d.

BARCLAY, Edgar.—Mountain Life in Algeria. With numerous
Illustrations by Photogravure. Crown 4to, 16s.

BARLOW, James H.—The Ultimatum of Pessimism. An
Ethical Study. Demy 8vo, cloth, 6s.

BARNES, William.—An Outline of English Speechcraft.
Crown 8vo, 4s.

BARNES, William.—continued.

Outlines of Redecraft (Logic). With English Wording. Crown 8vo, 3*s.*

BARTLEY, G. C. T.—Domestic Economy: Thrift in Every-Day Life. Taught in Dialogues suitable for children of all ages. Small crown 8vo, 2*s.*

BAUR, Ferdinand, Dr. Ph.—A Philological Introduction to Greek and Latin for Students. Translated and adapted from the German, by C. KEGAN PAUL, M.A., and E. D. STONE, M.A. Second Edition. Crown 8vo, 6*s.*

BAYNES, Rev. Canon R. H.—At the Communion Time. A Manual for Holy Communion. With a preface by the Right Rev. the Lord Bishop of Derry and Raphoe. 1*s.* 6*d.*

BELLARS, Rev. W.—The Testimony of Conscience to the Truth and Divine Origin of the Christian Revelation. Burney Prize Essay. Small crown 8vo, 3*s.* 6*d.*

BELLINGHAM, Henry, M.P.—Social Aspects of Catholicism and Protestantism in their Civil Bearing upon Nations. Translated and adapted from the French of M. le Baron de Haulleville. With a preface by His Eminence Cardinal Manning. Second and Cheaper Edition. Crown 8vo, 3*s.* 6*d.*

BENN, Alfred W.—The Greek Philosophers. 2 vols. Demy 8vo, cloth, 28*s.*

BENT, J. Theodore.—Genoa: How the Republic Rose and Fell. With 18 Illustrations. Demy 8vo, 18*s.*

BLOOMFIELD, The Lady.—Reminiscences of Court and Diplomatic Life. With three portraits and six illustrations by the Author. Third edition. 2 vols. Demy 8vo, cloth, 28*s.*

BLUNT, The Ven. Archdeacon.—The Divine Patriot, and other Sermons. Preached in Scarborough and in Cannes. Crown 8vo, 6*s.*

BLUNT, Wilfred S.—The Future of Islam. Crown 8vo, 6*s.*

BONWICK, J., F.R.G.S.—Pyramid Facts and Fancies. Crown 8vo, 5*s.*

Egyptian Belief and Modern Thought. Large post 8vo, 10*s.* 6*d.*

BOUVERIE-PUSEY, S. E. B.—Permanence and Evolution. An Inquiry into the Supposed Mutability of Animal Types. Crown 8vo, 5*s.*

BOWEN, H. C., M.A.—Studies in English. For the use of Modern Schools. Third Edition. Small crown 8vo, 1*s.* 6*d.*

English Grammar for Beginners. Fcap. 8vo, 1*s.*

BRIDGETT, Rev. T. E.—History of the Holy Eucharist in Great Britain. 2 vols. Demy 8vo, 18*s.*

BRODRICK, the Hon. G. C.—Political Studies. Demy 8vo, 14*s.*

BROOKE, Rev. S. A.—Life and Letters of the Late Rev. F. W. Robertson, M.A. Edited by.

    I. Uniform with Robertson's Sermons. 2 vols. With Steel Portrait. 7*s.* 6*d.*
    II. Library Edition. With Portrait. 8vo, 12*s.*
    III. A Popular Edition. In 1 vol., 8vo, 6*s.*

The Spirit of the Christian Life. A New Volume of Sermons. Second Edition. Crown 8vo, 7*s.* 6*d.*

The Fight of Faith. Sermons preached on various occasions. Fifth Edition. Crown 8vo, 7*s.* 6*d.*

Theology in the English Poets.—Cowper, Coleridge, Wordsworth, and Burns. Fourth and Cheaper Edition. Post 8vo, 5*s.*

Christ in Modern Life. Sixteenth and Cheaper Edition. Crown 8vo, 5*s.*

Sermons. First Series. Twelfth and Cheaper Edition. Crown 8vo, 5*s.*

Sermons. Second Series. Fifth and Cheaper Edition. Crown 8vo, 5*s.*

BROOKE, W. G., M.A.—The Public Worship Regulation Act. With a Classified Statement of its Provisions, Notes, and Index. Third Edition, revised and corrected. Crown 8vo, 3*s.* 6*d.*

Six Privy Council Judgments.—1850-72. Annotated by. Third Edition. Crown 8vo, 9*s.*

BROWN, Rev. J. Baldwin, B.A.—The Higher Life. Its Reality, Experience, and Destiny. Fifth Edition. . Crown 8vo, 5*s.*

Doctrine of Annihilation in the Light of the Gospel of Love. Five Discourses. Third Edition. Crown 8vo, 2*s.* 6*d.*

The Christian Policy of Life. A Book for Young Men of Business. Third Edition. Crown 8vo, 3*s.* 6*d.*

BROWN, J. Croumbie, LL.D.—Reboisement in France; or, Records of the Replanting of the Alps, the Cevennes, and the Pyrenees with Trees, Herbage, and Bush. Demy 8vo, 12*s.* 6*d.*

The Hydrology of Southern Africa. Demy 8vo, 10*s.* 6*d.*

BROWN, S. Borton, B.A.—The Fire Baptism of all Flesh; or, the Coming Spiritual Crisis of the Dispensation. Crown 8vo, 6*s.*

BROWNE, W. R.—The Inspiration of the New Testament. With a Preface by the Rev. J. P. NORRIS, D.D. Fcap. 8vo, 2*s.* 6*d.*

BURCKHARDT, Jacob.—The Civilization of the Period of the Renaissance in Italy. Authorized translation, by S. G. C. Middlemore. 2 vols. Demy 8vo, 24*s.*

BURTON, Mrs. Richard.—The Inner Life of Syria, Palestine, and the Holy Land. With Maps, Photographs, and Coloured Plates. Cheaper Edition in one volume. Large post 8vo, 10s. 6d.

BUSBECQ, Ogier Ghiselin de.—His Life and Letters. By CHARLES THORNTON FORSTER, M.A., and F. H. BLACKBURNE DANIELL, M.A. 2 vols. With Frontispieces. Demy 8vo, 24s.

CARPENTER, Dr. Phillip P.—His Life and Work. Edited by his brother, Russell Lant Carpenter. With Portrait and Vignettes. Second Edition. Crown 8vo, 7s. 6d.

CARPENTER, W. B., LL.D., M.D., F.R.S., etc.—The Principles of Mental Physiology. With their Applications to the Training and Discipline of the Mind, and the Study of its Morbid Conditions. Illustrated. Sixth Edition. 8vo, 12s.

CERVANTES.—The Ingenious Knight Don Quixote de la Mancha. A New Translation from the Originals of 1605 and 1608. By A. J. DUFFIELD. With Notes. 3 vols. Demy 8vo, 42s.

CHEYNE, Rev. T. K.—The Prophecies of Isaiah. Translated with Critical Notes and Dissertations. 2 vols. Second Edition. Demy 8vo, 25s.

CLAIRAUT.—Elements of Geometry. Translated by Dr. KAINES. With 145 Figures. Crown 8vo, 4s. 6d.

CLAYDEN, P. W.—England under Lord Beaconsfield. The Political History of the Last Six Years, from the end of 1873 to the beginning of 1880. Second Edition, with Index and continuation to March, 1880. Demy 8vo, 16s.

CLODD, Edward, F.R.A.S.—The Childhood of the World : a Simple Account of Man in Early Times. Sixth Edition. Crown 8vo, 3s.
    A Special Edition for Schools. 1s.

The Childhood of Religions. Including a Simple Account of the Birth and Growth of Myths and Legends. Ninth Thousand. Crown 8vo, 5s.
    A Special Edition for Schools. 1s. 6d.

Jesus of Nazareth. With a brief sketch of Jewish History to the Time of His Birth. Small crown 8vo, 6s.

COGHLAN, J. Cole, D.D.—The Modern Pharisee and other Sermons. Edited by the Very Rev. H. H. DICKINSON, D.D., Dean of Chapel Royal, Dublin. New and Cheaper Edition. Crown 8vo, 7s. 6d.

COLERIDGE, Sara.—Phantasmion. A Fairy Tale. With an Introductory Preface, by the Right Hon. Lord Coleridge, of Ottery St. Mary. A New Edition. Illustrated. Crown 8vo, 7s. 6d.

Memoir and Letters of Sara Coleridge. Edited by her Daughter. With Index. Cheap Edition. With one Portrait. 7s. 6d.

Collects Exemplified. Being Illustrations from the Old and New Testaments of the Collects for the Sundays after Trinity. By the Author of " A Commentary on the Epistles and Gospels." Edited by the Rev. JOSEPH JACKSON. Crown 8vo, 5s.

COLLINS, Mortimer.—The Secret of Long Life. Small crown 8vo, 3s. 6d.

CONNELL, A. K.—Discontent and Danger in India. Small crown 8vo, 3s. 6d.

COOKE, Prof. J. P.—Scientific Culture. Crown 8vo, 1s.

COOPER, H. J.—The Art of Furnishing on Rational and Æsthetic Principles. New and Cheaper Edition. Fcap. 8vo, 1s. 6d.

CORFIELD, Prof., M.D.—Health. Crown 8vo, 6s.

CORY, William.—A Guide to Modern English History. Part I.—MDCCCXV.-MDCCCXXX. Demy 8vo, 9s. Part II.—MDCCCXXX.-MDCCCXXXV., 15s.

CORY, Col. Arthur.—The Eastern Menace. Crown 8vo, 7s. 6d.

COTTERILL, H. B.—An Introduction to the Study of Poetry. Crown 8vo, 7s. 6d.

COURTNEY, W. L.—The Metaphysics of John Stuart Mill. Crown 8vo, 5s. 6d.

COX, Rev. Sir George W., M.A., Bart.—A History of Greece from the Earliest Period to the end of the Persian War. New Edition. 2 vols. Demy 8vo, 36s.

The Mythology of the Aryan Nations. New Edition. Demy 8vo, 16s.

A General History of Greece from the Earliest Period to the Death of Alexander the Great, with a sketch of the subsequent History to the present time. New Edition. Crown 8vo, 7s. 6d.

Tales of Ancient Greece. New Edition. Small crown 8vo, 6s.

School History of Greece. New Edition. With Maps. Fcap. 8vo, 3s. 6d.

The Great Persian War from the History of Herodotus. New Edition. Fcap. 8vo, 3s. 6d.

A Manual of Mythology in the form of Question and Answer. New Edition. Fcap. 8vo, 3s.

An Introduction to the Science of Comparative Mythology and Folk-Lore. Crown 8vo, 9s.

COX, Rev. Sir G. W., M.A., Bart., and JONES, Eustace Hinton.—Popular Romances of the Middle Ages. Second Edition, in 1 vol. Crown 8vo, 6s.

COX, Rev. Samuel.—Salvator Mundi ; or, Is Christ the Saviour of all Men? Seventh Edition. Crown 8vo, 5s.

COX, Rev. Samuel.—continued.

The Genesis of Evil, and other Sermons, mainly expository. Second Edition. Crown 8vo, 6s.

A Commentary on the Book of Job. With a Translation. Demy 8vo, 15s.

CRAUFURD, A. H.—Seeking for Light : Sermons. Crown 8vo, 5s.

CRAVEN, Mrs.—A Year's Meditations. Crown 8vo, 6s.

CRAWFURD, Oswald.—Portugal, Old and New. With Illustrations and Maps. New and Cheaper Edition. Crown 8vo, 6s.

CROZIER, John Beattie, M.B.—The Religion of the Future. Crown 8vo, 6s.

Cyclopædia of Common things. Edited by the Rev. Sir GEORGE W. Cox, Bart., M.A. With 500 Illustrations. Third Edition. Large post 8vo, 7s. 6d.

DALTON, Rev. John Neale, M.A., R.N.—Sermons to Naval Cadets. Preached on board H.M.S. "Britannia." Second Edition. Small crown 8vo, 3s. 6d.

DAVIDSON, Rev. Samuel, D.D., LL.D.—The New Testament, translated from the Latest Greek Text of Tischendorf. A New and thoroughly revised Edition. Post 8vo, 10s. 6d.

Canon of the Bible : Its Formation, History, and Fluctuations. Third and revised Edition. Small crown 8vo, 5s.

The Doctrine of Last Things contained in the New Testament compared with the Notions of the Jews and the Statements of Church Creeds. Small crown 8vo, cloth, 3s. 6d.

DAVIDSON, Thomas.—The Parthenon Frieze, and other Essays. Crown 8vo, 6s.

DAVIES, Rev. J. L., M.A.—Theology and Morality. Essays on Questions of Belief and Practice. Crown 8vo, 7s. 6d.

DAWSON, Geo., M.A.—Prayers, with a Discourse on Prayer. Edited by his Wife. Eighth Edition. Crown 8vo, 6s.

Sermons on Disputed Points and Special Occasions. Edited by his Wife. Third Edition. Crown 8vo, 6s.

Sermons on Daily Life and Duty. Edited by his Wife. Third Edition. Crown 8vo, 6s.

The Authentic Gospel. A New Volume of Sermons. Edited by GEORGE ST. CLAIR. Second Edition. Crown 8vo, 6s.

Three Books of God : Nature, History, and Scripture. Sermons edited by George St. Clair. Crown 8vo, cloth, 6s.

DE REDCLIFFE, Viscount Stratford.—Why am I a Christian ? Fifth Edition. Crown 8vo, 3s.

DESPREZ, Phillip S., B.D.—Daniel and John ; or, the Apocalypse of the Old and that of the New Testament. Demy 8vo, 12s.

DIDON, Rev. Father. — Science without God. Conferences by. Translated from the French by ROSA CORDER. Crown 8vo, cloth, 5*s.*

DOWDEN, Edward, LL.D. — Shakspere : a Critical Study of his Mind and Art. Sixth Edition. Post 8vo, 12*s.*

Studies in Literature, 1789-1877. Second and Cheaper Edition. Large post 8vo, 6*s.*

DREWRY, G. O., M.D. — The Common-Sense Management of the Stomach. Fifth Edition. Fcap. 8vo, 2*s.* 6*d.*

DREWRY, G. O., M.D., and BARTLETT, H. C., Ph.D. — Cup and Platter ; or, Notes on Food and its Effects. New and Cheaper Edition. Small 8vo, 1*s.* 6*d.*

DUFFIELD, A. J. — Don Quixote : his Critics and Commentators. With a brief account of the minor works of MIGUEL DE CERVANTES SAAVEDRA, and a statement of the aim and end of the greatest of them all. A [handy book for general readers Crown 8vo, 3*s.* 6*d.*

DU MONCEL, Count. — The Telephone, the Microphone, and the Phonograph. With 74 Illustrations. Second Edition. Small crown 8vo, 5*s.*

EDGEWORTH, F. Y. — Mathematical Psychics. An Essay on the Application of Mathematics to Social Science. Demy 8vo, 7*s.* 6*d.*

EDIS, Robert W., F.S.A., etc. — Decoration and Furniture of Town Houses : a Series of Cantor Lectures, delivered before the Society of Arts, 1880. Amplified and Enlarged. With 29 Full-page Illustrations and numerous Sketches. Second Edition. Square 8vo, 12*s.* 6*d.*

Educational Code of the Prussian Nation, in its Present Form. In accordance with the Decisions of the Common Provincial Law, and with those of Recent Legislation. Crown 8vo, 2*s.* 6*d.*

Education Library. Edited by PHILIP MAGNUS :—

An Introduction to the History of Educational Theories. By OSCAR BROWNING, M.A. Second Edition. 3*s.* 6*d.*

John Amos Comenius : his Life and Educational Work. By Prof. S. S. LAURIE, A.M. 3*s.* 6*d.*

Old Greek Education. By the Rev. Prof. MAHAFFY, M.A. 3*s.* 6*d.*

Eighteenth Century Essays. Selected and Edited by AUSTIN DOBSON. With a Miniature Frontispiece by R. Caldecott. Parchment Library Edition, 6*s.* ; vellum, 7*s.* 6*d.*

ELSDALE, Henry. — Studies in Tennyson's Idylls. Crown 8vo, 5*s.*

ELYOT, Sir Thomas.—The Boke named the Gouernour. Edited from the First Edition of 1531 by HENRY HERBERT STEPHEN CROFT, M.A., Barrister-at-Law. With Portraits of Sir Thomas and Lady Elyot, copied by permission of her Majesty from Holbein's Original Drawings at Windsor Castle. 2 vols. Fcap. 4to, 50s.

Eranus. A Collection of Exercises in the Alcaic and Sapphic Metres. Edited by F. W. CORNISH, Assistant Master at Eton. Crown 8vo, 2s.

EVANS, Mark.—The Story of Our Father's Love, told to Children. Fifth and Cheaper Edition. With Four Illustrations. Fcap. 8vo, 1s. 6d.

A Book of Common Prayer and Worship for Household Use, compiled exclusively from the Holy Scriptures. Second Edition. Fcap. 8vo, 1s.

The Gospel of Home Life. Crown 8vo, 4s. 6d.

The King's Story-Book. In Three Parts. Fcap. 8vo, 1s. 6d. each.

*** Parts I. and II. with Eight Illustrations and Two Picture Maps, now ready.

"Fan Kwae" at Canton before Treaty Days 1825–1844. By an old Resident. With frontispiece. Crown 8vo, cloth, 5s.

FELKIN, H. M.—Technical Education in a Saxon Town. Published for the City and Guilds of London Institute for the Advancement of Technical Education. Demy 8vo, 2s.

FLOREDICE, W. H.—A Month among the Mere Irish. Small crown 8vo, 5s.

Folkestone Ritual Case : the Arguments, Proceedings, Judgment, and Report. Demy 8vo, 25s.

FORMBY, Rev. Henry.—Ancient Rome and its Connection with the Christian Religion : An Outline of the History of the City from its First Foundation down to the Erection of the Chair of St. Peter, A.D. 42–47. With numerous Illustrations of Ancient Monuments, Sculpture, and Coinage, and of the Antiquities of the Christian Catacombs. Royal 4to, cloth extra, £2 10s. ; roxburgh half-morocco, £2 12s. 6d.

FRASER, Donald.—Exchange Tables of Sterling and Indian Rupee Currency, upon a new and extended system, embracing Values from One Farthing to One Hundred Thousand Pounds, and at rates progressing, in Sixteenths of a Penny, from 1s. 9d. to 2s. 3d. per Rupee. Royal 8vo, 10s. 6d.

FRISWELL, J. Hain.—The Better Self. Essays for Home Life. Crown 8vo, 6s.

*GARDINER, Samuel R., and J. BASS MULLINGER, M.A.—*Introduction to the Study of English History. Large Crown 8vo, 9s.

*GARDNER, Dorsey.—*Quatre Bras, Ligny, and Waterloo. A Narrative of the Campaign in Belgium, 1815. With Maps and Plans. Demy 8vo, 16s.

*GARDNER, J., M.D.—*Longevity : The Means of Prolonging Life after Middle Age. Fourth Edition, revised and enlarged. Small crown 8vo, 4s.

*GEDDES, James.—*History of the Administration of John de Witt, Grand Pensionary of Holland. Vol. I. 1623–1654. With Portrait. Demy 8vo, 15s.

*GENNA, E.—*Irresponsible Philanthropists. Being some Chapters on the Employment of Gentlewomen. Small crown 8vo, 2s. 6d.

*GEORGE, Henry.—*Progress and Poverty : an Inquiry into the Causes of Industrial Depressions, and of Increase of Want with Increase of Wealth. The Remedy. Second Edition. Post 8vo, 7s. 6d. Also a cheap edition. Sewed, price 6d.

*GILBERT, Mrs.—*Autobiography and other Memorials. Edited by Josiah Gilbert. Third and Cheaper Edition With Steel Portrait and several Wood Engravings. Crown 8vo, 7s. 6d.

*GLOVER, F., M.A.—*Exempla Latina. A First Construing Book, with Short Notes, Lexicon, and an Introduction to the Analysis of Sentences. Fcap. 8vo, 2s.

*GODWIN, William.—*The Genius of Christianity Unveiled. Being Essays never before published. Edited, with a Preface, by C. Kegan Paul. Crown 8vo, 7s. 6d.

*GOLDSMID, Sir Francis Henry, Bart., Q.C., M.P.—*Memoir of. With Portrait. Second Edition, revised. Crown 8vo, 6s.

*GOODENOUGH, Commodore J. G.—*Memoir of, with Extracts from his Letters and Journals. Edited by his Widow. With Steel Engraved Portrait. Square 8vo, 5s.

  ⁎⁎⁎ Also a Library Edition with Maps, Woodcuts, and Steel Engraved Portrait. Square post 8vo, 14s.

*GOSSE, Edmund W.—*Studies in the Literature of Northern Europe. With a Frontispiece designed and etched by Alma Tadema. New and cheaper edition. Large crown 8vo, 6s.

*GOULD, Rev. S. Baring, M.A.—*The Vicar of Morwenstow : a Memoir of the Rev. R. S. Hawker. With Portrait. Third Edition, revised. Square post 8vo, 10s. 6d.

  Germany, Present and Past. New and Cheaper Edition. Large crown 8vo, 7s. 6d.

*GOWAN, Major Walter E.—*A. Ivanoff's Russian Grammar. (16th Edition.) Translated, enlarged, and arranged for use of Students of the Russian Language. Demy 8vo, 6s.

GRAHAM, William, M.A.—The Creed of Science, Religious, Moral, and Social. Demy 8vo, 12s.

GRIFFITH, Thomas, A.M.—The Gospel of the Divine Life: a Study of the Fourth Evangelist. Demy 8vo, 14s.

GRIMLEY, Rev. H. N., M.A.—Tremadoc Sermons, chiefly on the Spiritual Body, the Unseen World, and the Divine Humanity. Third Edition. Crown 8vo, 6s.

GRÜNER, M.L.—Studies of Blast Furnace Phenomena. Translated by L. D. B. GORDON, F.R.S.E., F.G.S. Demy 8vo, 7s. 6d.

GURNEY, Rev. Archer.—Words of Faith and Cheer. A Mission of Instruction and Suggestion. Crown 8vo, 6s.

HAECKEL, Prof. Ernst.—The History of Creation. Translation revised by Professor E. RAY LANKESTER, M.A., F.R.S. With Coloured Plates and Genealogical Trees of the various groups of both Plants and Animals. 2 vols. Second Edition. Post 8vo, 32s.

> The History of the Evolution of Man. With numerous Illustrations. 2 vols. Post 8vo, 32s.

> Freedom in Science and Teaching. With a Prefatory Note by T. H. HUXLEY, F.R.S. Crown 8vo, 5s.

HALF-CROWN SERIES :—

> Sister Dora : a Biography. By MARGARET LONSDALE.
> True Words for Brave Men : a Book for Soldiers and Sailors. By the late CHARLES KINGSLEY.
> An Inland Voyage. By R. L. STEVENSON.
> Travels with a Donkey. By R. L. STEVENSON.
> A Nook in the Apennines. By LEADER SCOTT.
> Notes of Travel : being Extracts from the Journals of Count VON MOLTKE.
> Letters from Russia. By Count VON MOLTKE.
> English Sonnets. Collected and Arranged by J. DENNIS.
> Lyrics of Love. From Shakespeare to Tennyson, Selected and Arranged by W. D. ADAMS.
> London Lyrics. By F. LOCKER.
> Home Songs for Quiet Hours. By the Rev. Canon R. H. BAYNES.

HALLECK'S International Law ; or, Rules Regulating the Intercourse of States in Peace and War. A New Edition, revised, with Notes and Cases by Sir SHERSTON BAKER, Bart. 2 vols. Demy 8vo, 38s.

HARTINGTON, The Right Hon. the Marquis of, M.P.—Election Speeches in 1879 and 1880. With Address to the Electors of North-East Lancashire. Crown 8vo, 3s. 6d.

HAWEIS, Rev. H. R., M.A.—Current Coin. Materialism—The Devil—Crime—Drunkenness—Pauperism—Emotion—Recreation —The Sabbath. Fourth and Cheaper Edition. Crown 8vo, 5*s.*

Arrows in the Air. Fourth and Cheaper Edition. Crown 8vo, 5*s.*

Speech in Season. Fifth and Cheaper Edition. Crown 8vo, 5*s.*

Thoughts for the Times. Twelfth and Cheaper Edition. Crown 8vo, 5*s.*

Unsectarian Family Prayers. New and Cheaper Edition. Fcap. 8vo, 1*s.* 6*d.*

HAWKINS, Edwards Comerford.—Spirit and Form. Sermons preached in the Parish Church of Leatherhead. Crown 8vo, 6*s.*

HAYES, A. H., Junr.—New Colorado, and the Santa Fé Trail. With Map and 60 Illustrations. Crown 8vo, 9*s.*

HELLWALD, Baron F. Von.—The Russians in Central Asia. A Critical Examination, down to the Present Time, of the Geography and History of Central Asia. Translated by Lieut.-Col. THEODORE WIRGMAN, LL.B. With Map. Large post 8vo, 12*s.*

HENRY, Philip.—Diaries and Letters of. Edited by Matthew Henry Lee, M.A. Large crown 8vo, cloth, 7*s.* 6*d.*

HIDE, Albert.—The Age to Come. Small crown 8vo, cloth, 2*s.* 6*d.*

HIME, Major H. W. L., R.A.—Wagnerism : A Protest. Crown 8vo, cloth, 2*s.* 6*d.*

HINTON, J.—The Place of the Physician. To which is added Essays on the Law of Human Life, and on the Relations between Organic and Inorganic Worlds. Second Edition. Crown 8vo, 3*s.* 6*d.*

Philosophy and Religion. Selections from the MSS. of the late JAMES HINTON. Edited by CAROLINE HADDON. Crown 8vo, 5*s.*

Physiology for Practical Use. By Various Writers. With 50 Illustrations. Third and Cheaper Edition. Crown 8vo, 5*s.*

An Atlas of Diseases of the Membrana Tympani. With Descriptive Text. Post 8vo, £10 10*s.*

The Questions of Aural Surgery. With Illustrations. 2 vols. Post 8vo, 12*s.* 6*d.*

Chapters on the Art of Thinking, and other Essays. With an Introduction by SHADWORTH HODGSON. Edited by C. H. HINTON. Crown 8vo, 8*s.* 6*d.*

The Mystery of Pain. New Edition. Fcap. 8vo, 1*s.*

Life and Letters. Edited by ELLICE HOPKINS, with an Introduction by Sir W. W. GULL, Bart., and Portrait engraved on Steel by C. H. JEENS. Fourth Edition. Crown 8vo, 8*s.* 6*d.*

HOOPER, Mary.—**Little Dinners: How to Serve them with Elegance and Economy.** Seventeenth Edition. Crown 8vo, 2s. 6d.

Cookery for Invalids, Persons of Delicate Digestion, and Children. Third Edition. Crown 8vo, 2s. 6d.

Every-Day Meals. Being Economical and Wholesome Recipes for Breakfast, Luncheon, and Supper. Fifth Edition. Crown 8vo, 2s. 6d.

HOPKINS, Ellice.—**Life and Letters of James Hinton,** with an Introduction by Sir W. W. GULL, Bart., and Portrait engraved on Steel by C. H. JEENS. Fourth Edition. Crown 8vo, 8s. 6d.

Work amongst Working Men. Fourth edition. Crown 8vo, cloth, 3s. 6d.

HORNER, The Misses.—**Walks in Florence.** A New and thoroughly Revised Edition. 2 vols. Crown 8vo. Limp cloth. With Illustrations.
> VOL. I.—Churches, Streets, and Palaces. 10s. 6d.
> VOL. II.—Public Galleries and Museums. 5s.

HOSPITALIER, E.—**The Modern Applications of Electricity.** Translated and Enlarged by JULIUS MAIER, Ph.D. With 170 Illustrations. Demy 8vo, 16s.

Household Readings on Prophecy. By a Layman. Small crown 8vo, 3s. 6d.

HUGHES, Henry.—**The Redemption of the World.** Crown 8vo, 3s. 6d.

HULL, Edmund C. P.—**The European in India.** With a Medical Guide for Anglo-Indians. By R. S. MAIR, M.D., F.R.C.S.E. Third Edition, Revised and Corrected. Post 8vo, 6s.

HUNTINGFORD, Rev. E., D.C.L.—**The Apocalypse.** With a Commentary and Introductory Essay. Demy 8vo, 9s.

HUTTON, Arthur, M.A.—**The Anglican Ministry:** Its Nature and Value in relation to the Catholic Priesthood. With a Preface by His Eminence Cardinal Newman. Demy 8vo, 14s.

HUTTON, Rev. C. F.—**Unconscious Testimony;** or, the Silent Witness of the Hebrew to the Truth of the Historical Scriptures. Crown 8vo, cloth, 2s. 6d.

JENKINS, E., and RAYMOND, J.—**The Architect's Legal Handbook.** Third Edition, Revised. Crown 8vo, 6s.

JENKINS, Rev. R. C., M.A.—**The Privilege of Peter,** and the Claims of the Roman Church confronted with the Scriptures, the Councils, and the Testimony of the Popes themselves. Fcap. 8vo, 3s. 6d.

JERVIS, Rev. W. Henley.—**The Gallican Church and the Revolution.** A Sequel to the History of the Church of France, from the Concordat of Bologna to the Revolution. Demy 8vo, 18s.

JOEL, L.—A Consul's Manual and Shipowner's and Ship-master's Practical Guide in their Transactions Abroad. With Definitions of Nautical, Mercantile, and Legal Terms; a Glossary of Mercantile Terms in English, French, German, Italian, and Spanish; Tables of the Money, Weights, and Measures of the Principal Commercial Nations and their Equivalents in British Standards; and Forms of Consular and Notarial Acts. Demy 8vo, 12s.

JOHNSTONE, C. F., M.A.—Historical Abstracts: being Outlines of the History of some of the less known States of Europe. Crown 8vo, 7s. 6d.

JOLLY, William, F.R.S.E., etc.—The Life of John Duncan, Scotch Weaver and Botanist. With Sketches of his Friends and Notices of his Times. Large crown 8vo, with etched portrait, cloth, 9s.

JONCOURT, Madame Marie de.—Wholesome Cookery. Crown 8vo, 3s. 6d.

JONES, C. A.—The Foreign Freaks of Five Friends. With 30 Illustrations. Crown 8vo, 6s.

JONES, Lucy.—Puddings and Sweets: being Three Hundred and Sixty-five Receipts approved by experience. Crown 8vo, 2s. 6d.

JOYCE, P. W., LL.D., etc.—Old Celtic Romances. Translated from the Gaelic. Crown 8vo, 7s. 6d.

JOYNES, J. L.—The Adventures of a Tourist in Ireland. Second edition. Small crown 8vo, cloth, 2s. 6d.

KAUFMANN, Rev. M., B.A.—Socialism: its Nature, its Dangers, and its Remedies considered. Crown 8vo, 7s. 6d.

Utopias; or, Schemes of Social Improvement, from Sir Thomas More to Karl Marx. Crown 8vo, 5s.

KAY, Joseph.—Free Trade in Land. Edited by his Widow. With Preface by the Right Hon. JOHN BRIGHT, M.P. Sixth Edition. Crown 8vo, 5s.

KEMPIS, Thomas à.—Of the Imitation of Christ. Parchment Library Edition, 6s.; or vellum, 7s. 6d. The Red Line Edition, fcap. 8vo, red edges, 2s. 6d. The Cabinet Edition, small 8vo, cloth limp, 1s.; cloth boards, red edges, 1s. 6d. The Miniature Edition, red edges, 32mo, 1s.

*** All the above Editions may be had in various extra bindings.

KENT, C.—Corona Catholica ad Petri successoris Pedes Oblata. De Summi Pontificis Leonis XIII. Assumptione Epigramma. In Quinquaginta Linguis. Fcap. 4to, 15s.

KERNER, Dr. A.—Flowers and their Unbidden Guests. Translation edited by W. OGLE, M.A., M.D. With Illustrations. Square 8vo, 9s.

KETTLEWELL, Rev. S.—Thomas à Kempis and the Brothers of Common Life. 2 vols. With Frontispieces. Demy 8vo, 30*s.*

KIDD, Joseph, M.D.—The Laws of Therapeutics ; or, the Science and Art of Medicine. Second Edition. Crown 8vo, 6*s.*

KINAHAN, G. Henry, M.R.I.A.—The Geology of Ireland, with numerous Illustrations and a Geological Map of Ireland. Square 8vo, 15*s.*

KINGSFORD, Anna, M.D.—The Perfect Way in Diet. A Treatise advocating a Return to the Natural and Ancient Food of our Race. Small crown 8vo, 2*s.*

KINGSLEY, Charles, M.A.—Letters and Memories of his Life. Edited by his Wife. With two Steel Engraved Portraits, and Vignettes on Wood. Eleventh Cabinet Edition. 2 vols. Crown 8vo, 12*s.*

All Saints' Day, and other Sermons. Edited by the Rev. W. HARRISON. Third Edition. Crown 8vo, 7*s.* 6*d.*

True Words for Brave Men. A Book for Soldiers' and Sailors' Libraries. Eighth Edition. Crown 8vo, 2*s.* 6*d.*

KNIGHT, Professor W.—Studies in Philosophy and Literature. Large Post 8vo, 7*s.* 6*d.*

KNOX, Alexander A.—The New Playground ; or, Wanderings in Algeria. New and cheaper edition. Large crown 8vo, 6*s.*

LAURIE, S. S.—The Training of Teachers, and other Educational Papers. Crown 8vo, 7*s.* 6*d.*

LEE, Rev. F. G., D.C.L.—The Other World ; or, Glimpses of the Supernatural. 2 vols. A New Edition. Crown 8vo, 15*s.*

LEWIS, Edward Dillon.—A Draft Code of Criminal Law and Procedure. Demy 8vo, 21*s.*

LINDSAY, W. Lauder, M.D.—Mind in the Lower Animals in Health and Disease. 2 vols. Demy 8vo, 32*s.*
Vol. I.—Mind in Health. Vol. II.—Mind in Disease.

LLOYD, Walter.—The Hope of the World : An Essay on Universal Redemption. Crown 8vo, 5*s.*

LONSDALE, Margaret.—Sister Dora : a Biography. With Portrait. Twenty-fifth Edition. Crown 8vo, 2*s.* 6*d.*

LORIMER, Peter, D.D.—John Knox and the Church of England. His Work in her Pulpit, and his Influence upon her Liturgy, Articles, and Parties. Demy 8vo, 12*s.*

John Wiclif and his English Precursors. By GERHARD VICTOR LECHLER. Translated from the German, with additional Notes. New and Cheaper Edition. Demy 8vo, 10*s.* 6*d.*

LOWDER, Charles.—**A Biography.** By the Author of "St. Teresa." New and Cheaper Edition. Crown 8vo. With Portrait. 3s. 6d.

MACHIAVELLI, Niccoli. **The Prince.** Translated from the Italian by N. H. T. Small crown 8vo, printed on hand-made paper, bevelled boards, 6s.

MACKENZIE, Alexander.—**How India is Governed.** Being an Account of England's work in India. Small crown 8vo, 2s.

MACNAUGHT, Rev. John.—**Cœna Domini :** An Essay on the Lord's Supper, its Primitive Institution, Apostolic Uses, and Subsequent History. Demy 8vo, 14s.

MAGNUS, Mrs.—**About the Jews since Bible Times.** From the Babylonian Exile till the English Exodus. Small crown 8vo, 6s.

MAIR, R. S., M.D., F.R.C.S.E.—**The Medical Guide for Anglo-Indians.** Being a Compendium of Advice to Europeans in India, relating to the Preservation and Regulation of Health. With a Supplement on the Management of Children in India. Second Edition. Crown 8vo, limp cloth, 3s. 6d.

MANNING, His Eminence Cardinal.—**The True Story of the Vatican Council.** Crown 8vo, 5s.

Many Voices. Crown 8vo, cloth extra, red edges, 6s.

MARKHAM, Capt. Albert Hastings, R.N.—**The Great Frozen Sea :** A Personal Narrative of the Voyage of the *Alert* during the Arctic Expedition of 1875-6. With 6 Full-page Illustrations, 2 Maps, and 27 Woodcuts. Fifth and Cheaper Edition. Crown 8vo, 6s.

A Polar Reconnaissance : being the Voyage of the *Isbjörn* to Novaya Zemlya in 1879. With 10 Illustrations. Demy 8vo, 16s.

Marriage and Maternity ; or, Scripture Wives and Mothers. Small crown 8vo, 4s. 6d.

MARTINEAU, Gertrude.—**Outline Lessons on Morals.** Small crown 8vo, 3s. 6d.

McGRATH, Terence.—**Pictures from Ireland.** New and Cheaper Edition. Crown 8vo, 2s.

MEREDITH, M.A.—**Theotokos, the Example for Woman.** Dedicated, by permission, to Lady AGNES WOOD. Revised by the Venerable Archdeacon DENISON. 32mo, limp cloth, 1s. 6d.

MILLER, Edward.—**The History and Doctrines of Irvingism ;** or, the so-called Catholic and Apostolic Church. 2 vols. Large post 8vo, 25s.

The Church in Relation to the State. Large crown 8vo, 7s. 6d.

MILNE, James.—**Tables of Exchange** for the Conversion of Sterling Money into Indian and Ceylon Currency, at Rates from 1s. 8d. to 2s. 3d. per Rupee. Second Edition. Demy 8vo, £2 2s.

MINCHIN, J. G.—**Bulgaria since the War :** Notes of a Tour in the Autumn of 1879. Small crown 8vo, 3s. 6d.

c

MIVART, St. George.—**Nature and Thought :** An Introduction to a Natural Philosophy. Demy 8vo, cloth, 10s. 6d.

MOCKLER, E.—**A Grammar of the Baloochee Language,** as it is spoken in Makran (Ancient Gedrosia), in the Persia-Arabic and Roman characters. Fcap. 8vo, 5s.

MOLESWORTH, Rev. W. Nassau, M.A.—**History of the Church of England from 1660.** Large crown 8vo, 7s. 6d.

MORELL, J. R.—**Euclid Simplified in Method and Language.** Being a Manual of Geometry. Compiled from the most important French Works, approved by the University of Paris and the Minister of Public Instruction. Fcap. 8vo, 2s. 6d.

MORSE, E. S., Ph.D.—**First Book of Zoology.** With numerous Illustrations. New and Cheaper Edition. Crown 8vo, 2s. 6d.

MURPHY, John Nicholas.—**The Chair of Peter ;** or, the Papacy considered in its Institution, Development, and Organization, and in the Benefits which for over Eighteen Centuries it has conferred on Mankind. Demy 8vo, cloth, 18s.

MUNRO, Major-Gen. Sir Thomas, Bart., K.C.B., Governor of Madras. —SELECTIONS FROM HIS MINUTES AND OTHER OFFICIAL WRITINGS. Edited, with an Introductory Memoir, by Sir ALEX-ANDER ARBUTHNOT, K.C.S.I., C.I.E. 2 vols. Demy 8vo, 30s.

NELSON, J. H., M.A.—**A Prospectus of the Scientific Study of the Hindû Law.** Demy 8vo, 9s.

NEWMAN, J. H., D.D.—**Characteristics from the Writings of.** Being Selections from his various Works. Arranged with the Author's personal Approval. Sixth Edition. With Portrait. Crown 8vo, 6s.
⁎⁎⁎ A Portrait of Cardinal Newman, mounted for framing, can be had, 2s. 6d.

New Werther. By LOKI. Small crown 8vo, 2s. 6d.

NICHOLSON, Edward Byron.—**The Gospel according to the Hebrews.** Its Fragments Translated and Annotated with a Critical Analysis of the External and Internal Evidence relating to it. Demy 8vo, 9s. 6d.

A New Commentary on the Gospel according to Matthew. Demy 8vo, 12s.

The Rights of an Animal. Crown 8vo, 3s. 6d.

NICOLS, Arthur, F.G.S., F.R.G.S.—**Chapters from the Physical History of the Earth :** an Introduction to Geology and Palæontology. With numerous Illustrations. Crown 8vo, 5s.

NOPS, Marianne.—**Class Lessons on Euclid.** Part I. containing the First two Books of the Elements. Crown 8vo, cloth, 2s. 6d.

Notes on St. Paul's Epistle to the Galatians. For Readers of the Authorised Version or the Original Greek. Demy 8vo, 2s. 6d.

Nuces: EXERCISES ON THE SYNTAX OF THE PUBLIC SCHOOL LATIN PRIMER. New Edition in Three Parts. Crown 8vo, each 1s.
* * * The Three Parts can also be had bound together, 3s.

OATES, Frank, F.R.G.S.—Matabele Land and the Victoria Falls. A Naturalist's Wanderings in the Interior of South Africa. Edited by C. G. OATES, B.A. With numerous Illustrations and 4 Maps. Demy 8vo, 21s.

OGLE, W., M.D., F.R.C.P.—Aristotle on the Parts of Animals. Translated, with Introduction and Notes. Royal 8vo, 12s. 6d.

O'MEARA, Kathleen.—Frederic Ozanam, Professor of the Sorbonne: His Life and Work. Second Edition. Crown 8vo, 7s. 6d.

Henri Perreyve and his Counsels to the Sick. Small crown 8vo, 5s.

OSBORNE, Rev. W. A.—The Revised Version of the New Testament. A Critical Commentary, with Notes upon the Text. Crown 8vo, cloth, 5s.

OTTLEY, H. Bickersteth.—The Great Dilemma. Christ His Own Witness or His Own Accuser. Six Lectures. Second Edition. Crown 8vo, cloth, 3s. 6d.

Our Public Schools—Eton, Harrow, Winchester, Rugby, Westminster, Marlborough, The Charterhouse. Crown 8vo, 6s.

OWEN, F. M.—John Keats: a Study. Crown 8vo, 6s.

OWEN, Rev. Robert, B.D.—Sanctorale Catholicum; or, Book of Saints. With Notes, Critical, Exegetical, and Historical. Demy 8vo, 18s.

An Essay on the Communion of Saints. Including an Examination of the Cultus Sanctorum. 2s.

OXENHAM, Rev. F. Nutcombe.—What is the Truth as to Everlasting Punishment. Part II. Being an Historical Inquiry into the Witness and Weight of certain Anti-Origenist Councils. Crown 8vo, 2s. 6d.
* * * Parts I. and II. complete in one volume, 7s.

OXONIENSES.—Romanism, Protestantism, Anglicanism. Being a Layman's View of some questions of the Day. Together with Remarks on Dr. Littledale's "Plain Reasons against joining the Church of Rome." Crown 8vo, cloth, 3s. 6d.

PALMER, the late William.—Notes of a Visit to Russia in 1840-1841. Selected and arranged by JOHN H. CARDINAL NEWMAN, with portrait. Crown 8vo, cloth, 8s. 6d.

Parchment Library. Choicely Printed on hand-made paper, limp parchment antique, 6s.; vellum, 7s. 6d. each volume.

French Lyrics. Selected and Annotated by GEORGE SAINTSBURY. With a minature frontispiece designed and etched by H. G. Glindoni.

Parchment Library.—*continued.*

> The Fables of Mr. John Gay. With Memoir by AUSTIN
> DOBSON, and an etched portrait from an unfinished Oil Sketch
> by Sir Godfrey Kneller.
>
> Select Letters of Percy Bysshe Shelley. Edited, with an
> Introduction, by RICHARD GARNETT.
>
> The Christian Year. Thoughts in Verse for the Sundays and
> Holy Days throughout the Year. With Miniature Portrait of the
> Rev. J. Keble, after a Drawing by G. Richmond, R.A.
>
> Shakspere's Works. Now publishing in Twelve Monthly
> Volumes.
>
> Eighteenth Century Essays. Selected and Edited by AUSTIN
> DOBSON. With a Miniature Frontispiece by R. Caldecott.
>
> Q. Horati Flacci Opera. Edited by F. A. CORNISH, Assistant
> Master at Eton. With a Frontispiece after a design by L. ALMA
> TADEMA, etched by Leopold Lowenstam.
>
> Edgar Allan Poe's Poems. With an Essay on his Poetry by
> ANDREW LANG, and a Frontispiece by Linley Sambourne.
>
> Shakspere's Sonnets. Edited by EDWARD DOWDEN. With a
> Frontispiece etched by Leopold Lowenstam, after the Death Mask.
>
> English Odes. Selected by EDMUND W. GOSSE. With Frontis-
> piece on India paper by Hamo Thornycroft, A.R.A.
>
> Of the Imitation of Christ. By THOMAS λ KEMPIS. A
> revised Translation. With Frontispiece on India paper, from a
> Design by W. B. Richmond.
>
> Tennyson's The Princess: a Medley. With a Miniature
> Frontispiece by H. M. Paget, and a Tailpiece in Outline by
> Gordon Browne.
>
> Poems: Selected from PERCY BYSSHE SHELLEY. Dedicated to
> Lady Shelley. With a Preface by RICHARD GARNETT and a
> Miniature Frontispiece.
>
> Tennyson's "In Memoriam." With a Miniature Portrait
> in *eau-forte* by Le Rat, after a Photograph by the late Mrs.
> Cameron.

PARKER, Joseph, D.D.—The Paraclete: An Essay on the Personality
and Ministry of the Holy Ghost, with some reference to current
discussions. Second Edition. Demy 8vo, 12s.

PARR, Capt. H. Hallam, C.M.G.—A Sketch of the Kafir and
Zulu Wars: Guadana to Isandhlwana. With Maps. Small
crown 8vo, 5s.

PARSLOE, Joseph.—Our Railways. Sketches, Historical and
Descriptive. With Practical Information as to Fares and Rates,
etc., and a Chapter on Railway Reform. Crown 8vo, 6s.

PATTISON, Mrs. Mark.—**The Renaissance of Art in France.** With Nineteen Steel Engravings. 2 vols. Demy 8vo, 32*s.*

PEARSON, Rev. S.—**Week-day Living.** A Book for Young Men and Women. Second Edition. Crown 8vo, 5*s.*

PENRICE, Maj. J., B.A.—**A Dictionary and Glossary of the Ko-ran.** With Copious Grammatical References and Explanations of the Text. 4to, 21*s.*

PESCHEL, Dr. Oscar.—**The Races of Man and their Geographical Distribution.** Large crown 8vo, 9*s.*

PETERS, F. H.—**The Nicomachean Ethics of Aristotle.** Translated by. Crown 8vo, 6*s.*

PIDGEON, D.—**An Engineer's Holiday ;** or, Notes of a Round Trip from Long. 0° to 0°. New and cheaper edition. Large crown 8vo, 7*s.* 6*d.*

PLAYFAIR, Lieut.-Col.—**Travels in the Footsteps of Bruce in Algeria and Tunis.** Illustrated by facsimiles of Bruce's original Drawings, Photographs, Maps, etc. Royal 4to cloth, bevelled boards, gilt leaves, £3 3*s.*

POLLOCK, Frederick.—**Spinoza, his Life and Philosophy.** Demy 8vo, 16*s.*

POLLOCK, W. H.—**Lectures on French Poets.** Delivered at the Royal Institution. Small crown 8vo, 5*s.*

POOR, Laura E.—**Sanskrit and its Kindred Literatures.** Studies in Comparative Mythology. Small crown 8vo, 5*s.*

PRICE, Prof. Bonamy.—**Currency and Banking.** Crown 8vo, 6*s.*

Chapters on Practical Political Economy. Being the Substance of Lectures delivered before the University of Oxford. New and Cheaper Edition. Large post 8vo, 5*s.*

Proteus and Amadeus. A Correspondence. Edited by AUBREY DE VERE. Crown 8vo, 5*s.*

Pulpit Commentary, The. (Old Testament Series.) Edited by the Rev. J. S. EXELL and the Rev. Canon H. D. M. SPENCE.

Genesis. By the Rev. T. WHITELAW, M.A. ; with Homilies by the Very Rev. J. F. MONTGOMERY, D.D., Rev. Prof. R. A. REDFORD, M.A., LL.B., Rev. F. HASTINGS, Rev. W. ROBERTS, M.A. An Introduction to the Study of the Old Testament by the Rev. Canon FARRAR, D.D., F.R.S. ; and Introductions to the Pentateuch by the Right Rev. H. COTTERILL, D.D., and Rev. T. WHITELAW, M.A. Seventh Edition. 1 vol., 15*s.*

Exodus. By the Rev. Canon RAWLINSON. With Homilies by Rev. J. ORR, Rev. D. YOUNG, Rev. C. A. GOODHART, Rev. J. URQUHART, and the Rev. H. T. ROBJOHNS. Third Edition. 16*s.*

Pulpit Commentary, The.—*continued.*

> **Leviticus.** By the Rev. Prebendary MEYRICK, M.A. With Introductions by the Rev. R. COLLINS, Rev. Professor A. CAVE, and Homilies by Rev. Prof. REDFORD, LL.B., Rev. J. A. MACDONALD, Rev. W. CLARKSON, Rev. S. R. ALDRIDGE, LL.B., and Rev. McCHEYNE EDGAR. Third Edition. 15*s.*

> **Numbers.** By the Rev. R. WINTERBOTHAM, LL.B.; with Homilies by the Rev. Professor W. BINNIE, D.D., Rev. E. S. PROUT, M.A., Rev. D. YOUNG, Rev. J. WAITE, and an Introduction by the Rev. THOMAS WHITELAW, M.A. Fourth Edition. 15*s.*

> **Deuteronomy.** By the Rev. W. L. ALEXANDER, D.D. With Homilies by Rev. C. Clemance, D.D., Rev. J. Orr, B.D., Rev. R. M. Edgar, M.A., Rev. D. Davies, M.A. Second edition. 15*s.*

> **Joshua.** By Rev. J. J. LIAS, M.A.; with Homilies by Rev. S. R. ALDRIDGE, LL.B., Rev. R. GLOVER, REV. E. DE PRESSENSÉ, D.D., Rev. J. WAITE, B.A., Rev. F. W. ADENEY, M.A.; and an Introduction by the Rev. A. PLUMMER, M.A., D.D. Fourth Edition. 12*s.* 6*d.*

> **Judges and Ruth.** By the Right Rev. Lord A. C. HERVEY, D.D., and Rev. J. MORRISON, D.D.; with Homilies by Rev. A. F. MUIR, M.A., Rev. W. F. ADENEY, M.A., Rev. W. M. STATHAM, and Rev. Professor J. THOMSON, M.A. Fourth Edition. 10*s.* 6*d.*

> **1 Samuel.** By the Very Rev. R. P. SMITH, D.D.; with Homilies by Rev. DONALD FRASER, D.D., Rev. Prof. CHAPMAN, and Rev. B. DALE. Fifth Edition. 15*s.*

> **1 Kings.** By the Rev. JOSEPH HAMMOND, LL.B. With Homilies by the Rev. E. DE PRESSENSÉ, D.D., Rev. J. WAITE, B.A., Rev. A ROWLAND, LL.B., Rev. J. A. MACDONALD, and Rev. J. URQUHART. Third Edition. 15*s.*

> **Ezra, Nehemiah, and Esther.** By Rev. Canon G. RAWLINSON, M.A.; with Homilies by Rev. Prof. J. R. THOMSON, M.A., Rev. Prof. R. A. REDFORD, LL.B., M.A., Rev. W. S. LEWIS, M.A., Rev. J. A. MACDONALD, Rev. A. MACKENNAL, B.A., Rev. W. CLARKSON, B.A., Rev. F. HASTINGS, Rev. W. DINWIDDIE, LL.B., Rev. Prof. ROWLANDS, B.A., Rev. G. WOOD, B.A., Rev. Prof. P. C. BARKER, LL.B., M.A., and the Rev. J. S. EXELL. Fifth Edition. 1 vol., 12*s.* 6*d.*

Pulpit Commentary, The. (New Testament Series.)

> **St. Mark.** By Very Dean BICKERSTETH, D.D.; with Homilies by Rev. Prof. THOMSON, M.A,, Rev. Prof. GIVEN, M.A., Rev. Prof. Johnson, M.A., Rev. A. ROWLAND, B.A., LL.B., Rev. A. MUIR, and Rev. R. GREEN. 2 vols. Second Edition. 21*s,*

Punjaub, The, and North-Western Frontier of India. By an Old Punjaubee. Crown 8vo, 5*s.*

Rabbi Jeshua. An Eastern Story. Crown 8vo, 3*s.* 6*d.*

RADCLIFFE, Frank R. Y.—The New Politicus. Small crown 8vo, 2*s.* 6*d.*

RAVENSHAW, John Henry, B.C.S.—Gaur: Its Ruins and Inscriptions. Edited by his Widow. With 44 Photographic Illustrations, and 25 facsimiles of Inscriptions. Royal 4to, £3 13*s.* 6*d.*

READ, Carveth.—On the Theory of Logic: An Essay. Crown 8vo, 6*s.*

Realities of the Future Life. Small crown 8vo, 1*s.* 6*d.*

RENDELL, J. M.—Concise Handbook of the Island of Madeira. With Plan of Funchal and Map of the Island. Fcap. 8vo, 1*s.* 6*d.*

REYNOLDS, Rev. J. W.—The Supernatural in Nature. A Verification by Free Use of Science. Second Edition, revised and enlarged. Demy 8vo, 14*s.*

The Mystery of Miracles. New and Enlarged Edition. Crown 8vo, 6*s.*

RIBOT, Prof. Th.—English Psychology. Second Edition. A Revised and Corrected Translation from the latest French Edition. Large post 8vo, 9*s.*

Heredity: A Psychological Study on its Phenomena, its Laws, its Causes, and its Consequences. Large crown 8vo, 9*s.*

ROBERTSON, The late Rev. F. W., M.A.—Life and Letters of. Edited by the Rev. Stopford Brooke, M.A.
I. Two vols., uniform with the Sermons. With Steel Portrait. Crown 8vo, 7*s.* 6*d.*
II. Library Edition, in Demy 8vo, with Portrait. 12*s.*
III. A Popular Edition, in 1 vol. Crown 8vo, 6*s.*

Sermons. Four Series. Small crown 8vo, 3*s.* 6*d.* each.

The Human Race, and other Sermons. Preached at Cheltenham, Oxford, and Brighton. Large post 8vo, 7*s.* 6*d.*

Notes on Genesis. New and Cheaper Edition. Crown 8vo, 3*s.* 6*d.*

Expository Lectures on St. Paul's Epistles to the Corinthians. A New Edition. Small crown 8vo, 5*s.*

Lectures and Addresses, with other Literary Remains. A New Edition. Crown 8vo, 5*s.*

An Analysis of Mr. Tennyson's "In Memoriam." (Dedicated by Permission to the Poet-Laureate.) Fcap. 8vo, 2*s.*

The Education of the Human Race. Translated from the German of Gotthold Ephraim Lessing. Fcap. 8vo, 2*s.* 6*d.*
The above Works can also be had, bound in half morocco.

⁂ A Portrait of the late Rev. F. W. Robertson, mounted for framing, can be had, 2*s.* 6*d.*

RODWELL, G. F., F.R.A.S., F.C.S.—**Etna : A History of the Mountain and its Eruptions.** With Maps and Illustrations. Square 8vo, 9s.

ROLLESTON, T. W. H., B.A.—**The Encheiridion of Epictetus.** Translated from the Greek, with a Preface and Notes. Small crown 8vo, 3s. 6d.

Rosmini's Origin of Ideas. Translated from the Fifth Italian Edition of the Nuovo Saggio *Sull' origine delle idee.* 3 vols. Demy 8vo, cloth. Vol. I. now ready, price 16s.

Rosmini's Philosophical System. Translated, with a Sketch of the Author's Life, Bibliography, Introduction, and Notes by THOMAS DAVIDSON. Demy 8vo, 16s.

RULE, Martin, M.A.—**The Life and Times of St. Anselm, Archbishop of Canterbury and Primate of the Britains.** 2 vols. Demy 8vo, cloth, 21s.

SALTS, Rev. Alfred, LL.D.—**Godparents at Confirmation.** With a Preface by the Bishop of Manchester. Small crown 8vo, limp cloth, 2s.

SALVATOR, Archduke Ludwig.—**Levkosia, the Capital of Cyprus.** Crown 4to, 10s. 6d.

SAMUEL, Sydney M.—**Jewish Life in the East.** Small crown 8vo, 3s. 6d.

SAYCE, Rev. Archibald Henry.—**Introduction to the Science of Language.** 2 vols. Large post 8vo, 25s.

Scientific Layman. The New Truth and the Old Faith : are they Incompatible ? Demy 8vo, 10s. 6d.

SCOONES, W. Baptiste.—**Four Centuries of English Letters :** A Selection of 350 Letters by 150 Writers, from the Period of the Paston Letters to the Present Time. Second Edition. Large crown 8vo, 9s.

SCOTT, Robert H.—**Weather Charts and Storm Warnings.** Second Edition. Illustrated. Crown 8vo, 3s. 6d.

SHAKSPEARE, Charles.—**Saint Paul at Athens.** Spiritual Christianity in relation to some aspects of Modern Thought. Five Sermons preached at St. Stephen's Church, Westbourne Park. With a Preface by the Rev. Canon FARRAR. Crown 8vo, 5s.

SHELLEY, Lady.—**Shelley Memorials from Authentic Sources.** With (now first printed) an Essay on Christianity by Percy Bysshe Shelley. With Portrait. Third Edition. Crown 8vo, 5s.

SHILLITO, Rev. Joseph.—**Womanhood :** its Duties, Temptations, and Privileges. A Book for Young Women. Third Edition. Crown 8vo, 3s. 6d.

SHIPLEY, Rev. Orby, M.A.—**Church Tracts : or, Studies in Modern Problems.** By various Writers. 2 vols. Crown 8vo, 5s. each.

SHIPLEY, Rev. Orby, M.A.—continued.

Principles of the Faith in Relation to Sin. Topics for Thought in Times of Retreat. Eleven Addresses delivered during a Retreat of Three Days to Persons living in the World. Demy 8vo, 12s.

SKINNER, the late James.—**A Synopsis of Moral and Ascetical Theology.** With a Catalogue of Ancient and Modern Authorities. Arranged according to Centuries. With a prefatory Note by Rev. T. T. CARTER. Demy 4to, cloth, 10s. 6d.

Sister Augustine, Superior of the Sisters of Charity at the St. Johannis Hospital at Bonn. Authorised Translation by HANS THARAU, from the German "Memorials of AMALIE VON LASAULX." Second Edition. Large crown 8vo, 7s. 6d.

SMITH, Edward, M.D., LL.B., F.R.S.—**Health and Disease,** as Influenced by the Daily, Seasonal, and other Cyclical Changes in the Human System. A New Edition. Post 8vo, 7s. 6d.

Tubercular Consumption in its Early and Remediable Stages. Second Edition. Crown 8vo, 6s.

SPEDDING, James.—**Reviews and Discussions, Literary, Political, and Historical not relating to Bacon.** Demy 8vo, 12s. 6d.

Evenings with a Reviewer; or, Bacon and Macaulay. With a Prefatory Notice by G. S. VENABLES, Q.C. 2 vols. Demy 8vo, 18s.

STAPFER, Paul.—**Shakspeare and Classical Antiquity:** Greek and Latin Antiquity as presented in Shakspeare's Plays. Translated by EMILY J. CAREY. Large post 8vo, 12s.

ST. BERNARD.—**A Little Book on the Love of God.** Translated by MARIANNE CAROLINE and COVENTRY PATMORE. Extra, gilt top, 4s. 6d.

STEPHENS, Archibald John, LL.D.—**The Folkestone Ritual Case.** The Substance of the Argument delivered before the Judicial Committee of the Privy Council on behalf of the Respondents. Demy 8vo, 6s.

STEVENSON, Rev. W. F.—**Hymns for the Church and Home.** Selected and Edited by the Rev. W. Fleming Stevenson.

The Hymn Book consists of Three Parts :—I. For Public Worship.—II. For Family and Private Worship.—III. For Children.

*** Published in various forms and prices, the latter ranging from 8d. to 6s.

Lists and full particulars will be furnished on application to the Publishers.

STEVENSON, Robert Louis.—**Travels with a Donkey in the Cevennes.** With Frontispiece by Walter Crane. Small crown 8vo, 2s. 6d.

STEVENSON, Robert Louis.—continued.

An Inland Voyage. With Frontispiece by Walter Crane. Small Crown 8vo, 2s. 6d.

Virginibus Puerisque, and other Papers. Crown 8vo, 6s.

STRACHEY, Sir John, G.C.S.I., and *Lieut.-Gen. Richard STRACHEY, R.E., F.R.S.*—The Finances and Public Works of India, from 1869 to 1881. Demy 8vo, 18s.

STRECKER-WISLICENUS.—Organic Chemistry. Translated and Edited, with Extensive Additions, by W. R. Hodgkinson, Ph.D., and A. J. Greenaway, F.I.C. Demy 8vo, 21s.

SULLY, James, M.A.—Sensation and Intuition. Demy 8vo, 10s. 6d.

Pessimism : a History and a Criticism. Second Edition. Demy 8vo, 14s.

SYME, David.—Outlines of an Industrial Science. Second Edition. Crown 8vo, 6s.

Representative Government in England. Its Faults and Failures. Second Edition. Large crown 8vo, 6s.

TAYLOR, Algernon.—Guienne. Notes of an Autumn Tour. Crown 8vo, 4s. 6d.

THOM, J. Hamilton.—Laws of Life after the Mind of Christ. Crown 8vo, cloth, 7s. 6d.

THOMSON, J. Turnbull.—Social Problems; or, An Inquiry into the Laws of Influence. With Diagrams. Demy 8vo, 10s. 6d.

TIDMAN, Paul F.—Gold and Silver Money. Part I.—A Plain Statement. Part II.—Objections Answered. Third Edition. Crown 8vo, 1s.

TIPPLE, Rev. S. A.—Sunday Mornings at Norwood. Prayers and Sermons. Crown 8vo, cloth, 6s.

TODHUNTER, Dr. J.—A Study of Shelley. Crown 8vo, 7s.

TREMENHEERE, Hugh Seymour, C.B.—A Manual of the Principles of Government, as set forth by the Authorities of Ancient and Modern Times. New and enlarged Edition. Crown 8vo, 5s.

TUKE, Daniel Hack, M.D., F.R.C.P.—Chapters in the History of the Insane in the British Isles. With 4 Illustrations. Large crown 8vo, 12s.

TWINING, Louisa.—Workhouse Visiting and Management during Twenty-Five Years. Small crown 8vo, 3s. 6d.

UPTON, Major R. D.—Gleanings from the Desert of Arabia. Large post 8vo, 10s. 6d.

VACUUS, Viator.—**Flying South.** Recollections of France and its Littoral. Small crown 8vo, 3*s.* 6*d.*

VAUGHAN, H. Halford.—**New Readings and Renderings of Shakespeare's Tragedies.** 2 vols. Demy 8vo, 25*s.*

VILLARI, Professor.—**Niccolò Machiavelli and his Times.** Translated by Linda Villari. 2 vols. Large post 8vo, 24*s.*

VOLCKXSOM, E. W. V.—**Catechism of Elementary Modern Chemistry.** Small crown 8vo, 3*s.*

VYNER, Lady Mary.—**Every Day a Portion.** Adapted from the Bible and the Prayer Book, for the Private Devotion of those living in Widowhood. Collected and Edited by Lady Mary Vyner. Square crown 8vo, 5*s.*

WALDSTEIN, Charles, Ph.D.—**The Balance of Emotion and Intellect**; an Introductory Essay to the Study of Philosophy. Crown 8vo, 6*s.*

WALLER, Rev. C. B.—**The Apocalypse,** reviewed under the Light of the Doctrine of the Unfolding Ages, and the Restitution of All Things. Demy 8vo, 12*s.*

WALPOLE, Chas. George.—**History of Ireland from the Earliest Times to the Union with Great Britain.** With 5 Maps and Appendices. Crown 8vo, 10*s.* 6*d.*

WALSHE, Walter Hayle, M.D.—**Dramatic Singing Physiologically Estimated.** Crown 8vo, 3*s.* 6*d.*

WATSON, Sir Thomas, Bart., M.D.—**The Abolition of Zymotic Diseases,** and of other similar Enemies of Mankind. Small crown 8vo, 3*s.* 6*d.*

WEDMORE, Frederick.—**The Masters of Genre Painting.** With Sixteen Illustrations. Crown 8vo, 7*s.* 6*d.*

WHEWELL, William, D.D.—**His Life and Selections from his Correspondence.** By Mrs. STAIR DOUGLAS. With a Portrait from a Painting by SAMUEL LAURENCE. Demy 8vo, 21*s.*

WHITE, A. D., LL.D.—**Warfare of Science.** With Prefatory Note by Professor Tyndall. Second Edition. Crown 8vo, 3*s.* 6*d.*

WHITE, F. A.—**English Grammar.** Small crown 8vo, cloth, 2*s.*

WHITNEY, Prof. William Dwight.—**Essentials of English Grammar,** for the Use of Schools. Crown 8vo, 3*s.* 6*d.*

WICKSTEED, P. H.—**Dante : Six Sermons.** Crown 8vo, 5*s.*

WILLIAMS, Rowland, D.D.—**Psalms, Litanies, Counsels, and Collects for Devout Persons.** Edited by his Widow. New and Popular Edition. Crown 8vo, 3*s.* 6*d.*

WILLIAMS, Rowland D.D.—continued.

Stray Thoughts Collected from the Writings of the late Rowland Williams, D.D. Edited by his Widow. Crown 8vo, 3s. 6d.

*WILLIS, R., M.D.—***Servetus and Calvin :** a Study of an Important Epoch in the Early History of the Reformation. 8vo, 16s.

William Harvey. A History of the Discovery of the Circulation of the Blood : with a Portrait of Harvey after Faithorne. Demy 8vo, 14s.

*WILSON, Sir Erasmus.—***Egypt of the Past.** With Chromo-lithograph and numerous Illustrations in the text. Second Edition, Revised. Crown 8vo, 12s.

*WILSON, H. Schütz.—***The Tower and Scaffold.** A Miniature Monograph. Large fcap. 8vo, 1s.

*WOLLSTONECRAFT, Mary.—***Letters to Imlay.** New Edition, with a Prefatory Memoir by C. KEGAN PAUL. Two Portraits in *eau-forte* by Anna Lea Merritt. Crown 8vo, 6s.

*WOLTMANN, Dr. Alfred, and WOERMANN, Dr. Karl.—***History of Painting.** Edited by Sidney Colvin. Vol. I. Painting in Antiquity and the Middle Ages. With numerous Illustrations. Medium 8vo, 28s. ; bevelled boards, gilt leaves, 30s.

*WOOD, Major-General J. Creighton.—***Doubling the Consonant.** Small crown 8vo, 1s. 6d.

Word was Made Flesh. Short Family Readings on the Epistles for each Sunday of the Christian Year. Demy 8vo, 10s. 6d.

*WREN, Sir Christopher.—***His Family and His Times.** With Original Letters, and a Discourse on Architecture hitherto unpublished. By LUCY PHILLIMORE. With Portrait. Demy 8vo, 14s.

*WRIGHT, Rev. David, M.A.—***Waiting for the Light,** and other Sermons. Crown 8vo, 6s.

*YORKE, J. F.—***Notes on Evolution and Christianity.** Crown 8vo, cloth, 6s.

*YOUMANS, Eliza A.—***An Essay on the Culture of the Observing Powers of Children,** especially in connection with the Study of Botany. Edited, with Notes and a Supplement, by Joseph Payne, F.C.P., Author of "Lectures on the Science and Art of Education," etc. Crown 8vo, 2s. 6d.

First Book of Botany. Designed to Cultivate the Observing Powers of Children. With 300 Engravings. New and Cheaper Edition. Crown 8vo, 2s. 6d.

*YOUMANS, Edward L., M.D.—***A Class Book of Chemistry,** on the Basis of the New System. With 200 Illustrations. Crown 8vo, 5s.

THE INTERNATIONAL SCIENTIFIC SERIES.

I. **Forms of Water:** a Familiar Exposition of the Origin and Phenomena of Glaciers. By J. Tyndall, LL.D., F.R.S. With 25 Illustrations. Eighth Edition. Crown 8vo, 5*s*.

II. **Physics and Politics;** or, Thoughts on the Application of the Principles of "Natural Selection" and "Inheritance" to Political Society. By Walter Bagehot. Sixth Edition. Crown 8vo, 4*s*.

III. **Foods.** By Edward Smith, M.D., LL.B., F.R.S. With numerous Illustrations. Seventh Edition. Crown 8vo, 5*s*.

IV. **Mind and Body:** the Theories of their Relation. By Alexander Bain, LL.D. With Four Illustrations. Seventh Edition. Crown 8vo, 4*s*.

V. **The Study of Sociology.** By Herbert Spencer. Tenth Edition. Crown 8vo, 5*s*.

VI. **On the Conservation of Energy.** By Balfour Stewart, M.A., LL.D., F.R.S. With 14 Illustrations. Sixth Edition. Crown 8vo, 5*s*.

VII. **Animal Locomotion;** or Walking, Swimming, and Flying. By J. B. Pettigrew, M.D., F.R.S., etc. With 130 Illustrations. Second Edition. Crown 8vo, 5*s*.

VIII. **Responsibility in Mental Disease.** By Henry Maudsley, M.D. Fourth Edition. Crown 8vo, 5*s*.

IX. **The New Chemistry.** By Professor J. P. Cooke. With 31 Illustrations. Sixth Edition. Crown 8vo, 5*s*.

X. **The Science of Law.** By Professor Sheldon Amos. Fifth Edition. Crown 8vo, 5*s*.

XI. **Animal Mechanism:** a Treatise on Terrestrial and Aerial Locomotion. By Professor E. J. Marey. With 117 Illustrations. Second Edition. Crown 8vo, 5*s*.

XII. **The Doctrine of Descent and Darwinism.** By Professor Oscar Schmidt. With 26 Illustrations. Fifth Edition. Crown 8vo, 5*s*.

XIII. **The History of the Conflict between Religion and Science.** By J. W. Draper, M.D., LL.D. Seventeenth Edition. Crown 8vo, 5*s*.

XIV. **Fungi:** their Nature, Influences, Uses, etc. By M. C. Cooke, M.D., LL.D. Edited by the Rev. M. J. Berkeley, M.A., F.L.S. With numerous Illustrations. Third Edition. Crown 8vo, 5*s*.

XV. **The Chemical Effects of Light and Photography.** By Dr. Hermann Vogel. Translation thoroughly revised. With 100 Illustrations. Third Edition. Crown 8vo, 5*s*.

XVI. **The Life and Growth of Language.** By Professor William Dwight Whitney. Third Edition. Crown 8vo, 5*s*.

XVII. **Money and the Mechanism of Exchange.** By W. Stanley Jevons, M.A., F.R.S. Fifth Edition. Crown 8vo, 5*s.*

XVIII. **The Nature of Light.** With a General Account of Physical Optics. By Dr. Eugene Lommel. With 188 Illustrations and a Table of Spectra in Chromo-lithography. Third Edition. Crown 8vo, 5*s.*

XIX. **Animal Parasites and Messmates.** By Monsieur Van Beneden. With 83 Illustrations. Second Edition. Crown 8vo, 5*s.*

XX. **Fermentation.** By Professor Schützenberger. With 28 Illustrations. Third Edition. Crown 8vo, 5*s.*

XXI. **The Five Senses of Man.** By Professor Bernstein. With 91 Illustrations. Third Edition. Crown 8vo, 5*s.*

XXII. **The Theory of Sound in its Relation to Music.** By Professor Pietro Blaserna. With numerous Illustrations. Second Edition. Crown 8vo, 5*s.*

XXIII. **Studies in Spectrum Analysis.** By J. Norman Lockyer, F.R.S. With six photographic Illustrations of Spectra, and numerous engravings on Wood. Crown 8vo. Second Edition. 6*s.* 6*d.*

XXIV. **A History of the Growth of the Steam Engine.** By Professor R. H. Thurston. With numerous Illustrations. Second Edition. Crown 8vo, 6*s.* 6*d.*

XXV. **Education as a Science.** By Alexander Bain, LL.D. Fourth Edition. Crown 8vo, 5*s.*

XXVI. **The Human Species.** By Professor A. de Quatrefages. Third Edition. Crown 8vo, 5*s.*

XXVII. **Modern Chromatics.** With Applications to Art and Industry. By Ogden N. Rood. With 130 original Illustrations. Second Edition. Crown 8vo, 5*s.*

XXVIII. **The Crayfish :** an Introduction to the Study of Zoology. By Professor T. H. Huxley. With 82 Illustrations. Third Edition. Crown 8vo, 5*s.*

XXIX. **The Brain as an Organ of Mind.** By H. Charlton Bastian, M.D. With numerous Illustrations. Third Edition. Crown 8vo, 5*s.*

XXX. **The Atomic Theory.** By Prof. Wurtz. Translated by G. Cleminshaw, F.C.S. Third Edition. Crown 8vo, 5*s.*

XXXI. **The Natural Conditions of Existence as they affect Animal Life.** By Karl Semper. With 2 Maps and 106 Woodcuts. Second Edition. Crown 8vo, 5*s.*

XXXII. **General Physiology of Muscles and Nerves.** By Prof. J. Rosenthal. Second Edition. With Illustrations. Crown 8vo, 5*s.*

XXXIII. **Sight:** an Exposition of the Principles of Monocular and Binocular Vision. By Joseph le Conte, LL.D. With 132 Illustrations. Crown 8vo, 5*s.*

XXXIV. **Illusions:** a Psychological Study. By James Sully. Second Edition. Crown 8vo, 5*s.*

XXXV. **Volcanoes: what they are and what they teach.** By Professor J. W. Judd, F.R.S. With 92 Illustrations on Wood. Second Edition. Crown 8vo, 5*s.*

XXXVI. **Suicide:** an Essay in Comparative Moral Statistics. By Prof. E. Morselli. With Diagrams. Crown 8vo, 5*s.*

XXXVII. **The Brain and its Functions.** By J. Luys. With Illustrations. Second Edition. Crown 8vo, 5*s.*

XXXVIII. **Myth and Science:** an Essay. By Tito Vignoli. Crown 8vo, 5*s.*

XXXIX. **The Sun.** By Professor Young. With Illustrations. Second Edition. Crown 8vo, 5*s.*

XL. **Ants, Bees, and Wasps:** a Record of Observations on the Habits of the Social Hymenoptera. By Sir John Lubbock, Bart., M.P. With 5 Chromo-lithographic Illustrations. Fifth Edition. Crown 8vo, 5*s.*

XLI. **Animal Intelligence.** By G. J. ROMANES, LL.D., F.R.S. Second Edition. Crown 8vo, 5*s.*

XLII. **The Concepts and Theories of Modern Physics.** By J. B. STALLO. Second Edition. Crown 8vo, 5*s.*

XLIII. **Diseases of the Memory;** An Essay in the Positive Psychology. By Prof. Th. RIBOT. Second Edition. Crown 8vo, cloth, 5*s.*

XLIV. **Man before Metals.** By N. JOLY, with 148 Illustrations. Second Edition. Crown 8vo, 5*s.*

XLV. **The Science of Politics.** By Prof. SHELDON AMOS. Crown 8vo, cloth, 5*s.*

MILITARY WORKS.

Army of the North German Confederation: a Brief Description of its Organisation, of the Different Branches of the Service and their *rôle* in War, of its Mode of Fighting, etc. Translated from the Corrected Edition, by permission of the Author, by Colonel Edward Newdigate. Demy 8vo, 5*s.*

BARRINGTON, Capt. J. T.—**England on the Defensive;** or, the Problem of Invasion Critically Examined. Large crown 8vo, with Map, 7*s. 6d.*

BLUME, Major W.—The Operations of the German Armies in France, from Sedan to the end of the War of 1870–71. With Map. From the Journals of the Head-quarters Staff. Translated by the late E. M. Jones, Maj. 20th Foot, Prof. of Mil. Hist., Sandhurst. Demy 8vo, 9s.

BOGUSLAWSKI, Capt. A. von.—Tactical Deductions from the War of 1870-1. Translated by Colonel Sir Lumley Graham, Bart., late 18th (Royal Irish) Regiment. Third Edition, Revised and Corrected. Demy 8vo, 7s.

BRACKENBURY, Col. C. B., R.A., C.B.—Military Handbooks for Regimental Officers. I. Military Sketching and Reconnaissance, by Col. F. J. Hutchison, and Major H. G. Mac-Gregor. Fourth Edition. With 15 Plates. Small 8vo, 6s. II. The Elements of Modern Tactics Practically applied to English Formations, by Lieut-Col. Wilkinson Shaw. Fourth Edition. With 25 Plates and Maps. Small crown 8vo, 9s.

BRIALMONT, Col. A.—Hasty Intrenchments. Translated by Lieut. Charles A. Empson, R.A. With Nine Plates. Demy 8vo, 6s.

CLERY, C., Lieut.-Col.—Minor Tactics. With 26 Maps and Plans. Fifth and revised Edition. Demy 8vo, 16s.

DU VERNOIS, Col. von Verdy.—Studies in Leading Troops. An authorised and accurate Translation by Lieutenant H. J. T. Hildyard, 71st Foot. Parts I. and II. Demy 8vo, 7s.

GOETZE, Capt. A. von.—Operations of the German Engineers during the War of 1870-1. Published by Authority, and in accordance with Official Documents. Translated from the German by Colonel G. Graham, V.C., C.B., R.E. With 6 large Maps. Demy 8vo, 21s.

HARRISON, Lieut.-Col. R.—The Officer's Memorandum Book for Peace and War. Third Edition. Oblong 32mo, roan, with pencil, 3s. 6d.

HELVIG, Capt. H.—The Operations of the Bavarian Army Corps. Translated by Captain G. S. Schwabe. With 5 large Maps. In 2 vols. Demy 8vo, 24s.

    Tactical Examples : Vol. I. The Battalion, 15s. Vol. II. The Regiment and Brigade, 10s. 6d. Translated from the German by Col. Sir Lumley Graham. With nearly 300 Diagrams. Demy 8vo.

HOFFBAUER, Capt.—The German Artillery in the Battles near Metz. Based on the Official Reports of the German Artillery. Translated by Captain E. O. Hollist. With Map and Plans. Demy 8vo, 21s.

LAYMANN, Capt.—The Frontal Attack of Infantry. Translated by Colonel Edward Newdigate. Crown 8vo, 2s. 6d.

Notes on Cavalry Tactics, Organisation, etc. By a Cavalry Officer. With Diagrams. Demy 8vo, 12s.

PARR, Capt. H. Hallam, C.M.G.—The Dress, Horses, and Equipment of Infantry and Staff Officers. Crown 8vo, 1s.

SCHAW, Col. H.—The Defence and Attack of Positions and Localities. Second Edition, revised and corrected. Crown 8vo, 3s. 6d.

SCHELL, Maj. von.—The Operations of the First Army under Gen. von Goeben. Translated by Col. C. H. von Wright. Four Maps. Demy 8vo, 9s.

The Operations of the First Army under Gen. von Steinmetz. Translated by Captain E. O. Hollist. Demy 8vo, 10s. 6d.

SCHELLENDORF, Major-Gen. B. von.—The Duties of the General Staff. Translated from the German by Lieutenant Hare. Vol. I. Demy 8vo, 10s. 6d.

SCHERFF, Maj. W. von.—Studies in the New Infantry Tactics. Parts I. and II. Translated from the German by Colonel Lumley Graham. Demy 8vo, 7s. 6d.

SHADWELL, Maj.-Gen., C.B.—Mountain Warfare. Illustrated by the Campaign of 1799 in Switzerland. Being a Translation of the Swiss Narrative compiled from the Works of the Archduke Charles, Jomini, and others. Also of Notes by General H. Dufour on the Campaign of the Valtelline in 1635. With Appendix, Maps, and Introductory Remarks. Demy 8vo, 16s.

SHERMAN, Gen. W. T.—Memoirs of General W. T. Sherman, Commander of the Federal Forces in the American Civil War. By Himself. 2 vols. With Map. Demy 8vo, 24s. *Copyright English Edition.*

STUBBS, Lieut.-Col. F. W.—The Regiment of Bengal Artillery. The History of its Organisation, Equipment, and War Services. Compiled from Published Works, Official Records, and various Private Sources. With numerous Maps and Illustrations. 2 vols. Demy 8vo, 32s.

STUMM, Lieut. Hugo.—Russia's Advance Eastward. Based on Official Reports. Translated by Capt. C. E. H. VINCENT. With Map. Crown 8vo, 6s.

VINCENT, Capt. C. E. H.—Elementary Military Geography, Reconnoitring, and Sketching. Compiled for Non-commissioned Officers and Soldiers of all Arms. Square crown 8vo, 2s. 6d.

Volunteer, the Militiaman, and the Regular Soldier. By a Public Schoolboy. Crown 8vo, 5s.

WARTENSLEBEN, Count H. von.—The Operations of the South Army in January and February, 1871. Compiled from the Official War Documents of the Head-quarters of the Southern Army. Translated by Colonel C. H. von Wright. With Maps. Demy 8vo, 6s.

D

WARTENSLEBEN, Count H. von.—continued.
> The Operations of the First Army under Gen. von Manteufel. Translated by Col. C. H. von Wright. Uniform with the above. Demy 8vo, 9s.

*WICKHAM, Capt. E. H., R.A.—*Influence of Firearms upon Tactics: Historical and Critical Investigations. By an OFFICER OF SUPERIOR RANK (in the German Army). Translated by Captain E. H. Wickham, R.A. Demy 8vo, 7s. 6d.

*WOINOVITS, Capt. I.—*Austrian Cavalry Exercise. Translated by Captain W. S. Cooke. Crown 8vo, 7s.

POETRY.

*ADAMS, W. D.—*Lyrics of Love, from Shakspeare to Tennyson. Selected and arranged by. Fcap. 8vo, extra, gilt edges, 3s. 6d.

*ADAM OF ST. VICTOR.—*The Liturgical Poetry of Adam of St. Victor. From the text of Gautier. With Translations into English in the Original Metres, and Short Explanatory Notes, by Digby S. Wrangham, M.A. 3 vols. Crown 8vo, printed on hand-made paper, boards, 21s.

Antiope: a Tragedy. Large crown 8vo, 6s.

*AUBERTIN, J. J.—*Camoens' Lusiads. Portuguese Text, with Translation. Map and Portraits. 2 vols. Demy 8vo, 30s.

> Seventy Sonnets of Camoens. Portuguese Text and Translation, with some original Poems. Dedicated to Capt. Richard F. Burton. Printed on hand-made paper, bevelled boards, gilt top, 7s. 6d.

*AUCHMUTY, A. C.—*Poems of English Heroism: From Brunanburh to Lucknow; from Athelstan to Albert. Small crown 8vo, 1s. 6d.

*AVIA.—*The Odyssey of Homer. Done into English Verse by. Fcap. 4to, 15s.

*BANKS, Mrs. G. L.—*Ripples and Breakers: Poems. Square 8vo, 5s.

*BARNES, William.—*Poems of Rural Life, in the Dorset Dialect. New Edition, complete in one vol. Crown 8vo, 8s. 6d.

*BAYNES, Rev. Canon H. R.—*Home Songs for Quiet Hours. Fourth and cheaper Edition. Fcap. 8vo, cloth, 2s. 6d.
> *₊* This may also be had handsomely bound in morocco with gilt edges.

*BENNETT, Dr. W. C.—*Narrative Poems and Ballads. Fcap. 8vo, sewed in coloured wrapper, 1s.

BENNETT, Dr. W. C.—continued.

Songs for Sailors. Dedicated by Special Request to H.R.H. the Duke of Edinburgh. With Steel Portrait and Illustrations. Crown 8vo, 3s. 6d.
An Edition in Illustrated Paper Covers, 1s.

Songs of a Song Writer. Crown 8vo, 6s.

*BEVINGTON, L. S.—*Key Notes. Small crown 8vo, 5s.

*BILLSON, C. J.—*The Acharnians of Aristophanes. Crown 8vo, 3s. 6d.

*BOWEN, H. C., M.A.—*Simple English Poems. English Literature for Junior Classes. In Four Parts. Parts I., II., and III., 6d. each, and Part IV., 1s.

*BRYANT, W. C.—*Poems. Red-line Edition. With 24 Illustrations and Portrait of the Author. Crown 8vo, extra, 7s. 6d.
A Cheap Edition, with Frontispiece. Small crown 8vo, 3s. 6d.

*BYRNNE, E. Fairfax.—*Milicent : a Poem. Small crown 8vo, 6s.

Calderon's Dramas : the Wonder-Working Magician — Life is a Dream—the Purgatory of St. Patrick. Translated by Denis Florence MacCarthy. Post 8vo, 10s.

Chronicles of Christopher Columbus. A Poem in 12 Cantos. By M. D. C. Small crown 8vo.

*CLARKE, Mary Cowden.—*Honey from the Weed. Verses. Crown 8vo, 7s.

*COLOMB, Colonel.—*The Cardinal Archbishop : a Spanish Legend. In 29 Cancions. Small crown 8vo, 5s.

*CONWAY, Hugh.—*A Life's Idylls. Small crown 8vo, 3s. 6d.

*COPPÉE, Francois.—*L'Exilée. Done into English Verse, with the sanction of the Author, by I. O. L. Crown 8vo, vellum, 5s.

David Rizzio, Bothwell, and the Witch Lady. Three Tragedies by the author of " Ginevra," etc. Crown 8vo, cloth, 6s.

*DAVIE, G. S., M.D.—*The Garden of Fragrance. Being a complete translation of the ⌊Bostán of Sádi from the original Persian into English Verse. Crown 8vo, cloth, 7s. 6d.

*DAVIES, T. Hart.—*Catullus. Translated into English Verse. Crown 8vo, 6s.

*DE VERE, Aubrey.—*The Foray of Queen Meave, and other Legends of Ireland's Heroic Age. Small crown 8vo, 5s.

Alexander the Great : a Dramatic Poem. Small crown 8vo, 5s.

The Legends of St. Patrick, and other Poems. Small crown 8vo, 5s.

DE VERE, Aubrey.—continued.

St. Thomas of Canterbury : a Dramatic Poem. Large fcap. 8vo, 5s.

Legends of the Saxon Saints. Small crown 8vo, 6s.

Antar and Zara : an Eastern Romance. Inisfail, and other Poems, Meditative and Lyrical. Fcap. 8vo, 6s.

The Fall of Rora, The Search after Proserpine, and other Poems, Meditative and Lyrical. Fcap. 8vo, 6s.

The Infant Bridal, and other Poems. A New and Enlarged Edition. Fcap. 8vo, 7s. 6d.

DILLON, Arthur.—River Songs and other Poems. With 13 autotype Illustrations from designs by Margery May. Fcap. 4to, cloth extra, gilt leaves, 10s. 6d.

DOBELL, Mrs. Horace.—Ethelstone, Eveline, and other Poems. Crown 8vo, 6s.

DOBSON, Austin.—Vignettes in Rhyme, and Vers de Société. Third Edition. Fcap. 8vo, 5s.

Proverbs in Porcelain. By the Author of "Vignettes in Rhyme." Second Edition. Crown 8vo, 6s.

Dorothy : a Country Story in Elegiac Verse. With Preface. Demy 8vo, 5s.

DOWDEN, Edward, LL.D.—Poems. Second Edition. Fcap. 8vo, 5s.

Shakspere's Sonnets. With Introduction. Large post 8vo, 7s. 6d.

DOWNTON, Rev. H., M.A.—Hymns and Verses. Original and Translated. Small crown 8vo, 3s. 6d.

DUGMORE, Rev. Ernest Edward.—From the Mountains of the East : A Quasi-Dramatic Poem on the Story of the Prophet-Soothsayer Balaam. Crown 8vo, cloth, 3s. 6d.

DUTT, Toru.—A Sheaf Gleaned in French Fields. New Edition, with Portrait. Demy 8vo, 10s. 6d.

Ancient Ballads and Legends of Hindustan. With an Introductory Memoir by Edmund W. Gosse. Small crown 8vo, printed on hand-made paper, 5s.

EDWARDS, Rev. Basil.—Minor Chords ; or, Songs for the Suffering : a Volume of Verse. Fcap. 8vo, 3s. 6d. ; paper, 2s. 6d.

ELDRYTH, Maud.—Margaret, and other Poems. Small crown 8vo, 3s. 6d.

ELLIOTT, Ebenezer, The Corn Law Rhymer.—Poems. Edited by his son, the Rev. Edwin Elliott, of St. John's, Antigua. 2 vols. Crown 8vo, 18s.

English Odes. Selected, with a Critical Introduction by EDMUND W. GOSSE, and a miniature frontispiece by Hamo Thornycroft, A.R.A. Elzevir 8vo, limp parchment antique, 6*s.* ; vellum, 7*s.* 6*d.*

Epic of Hades, The. By the Author of "Songs of Two Worlds." Thirteenth Edition. Fcap. 8vo, 7*s.* 6*d.*

** Also an Illustrated Edition, with 17 full-page designs in photo-mezzotint by George R. Chapman. 4to, extra, gilt leaves, 25*s.* ; and a Large Paper Edition, with Portrait, 10*s.* 6*d.*

EVANS, Anne.—**Poems and Music.** With Memorial Preface by ANN THACKERAY RITCHIE. Large crown 8vo, 7*s.*

GOSSE, Edmund W.—**New Poems.** Crown 8vo, 7*s.* 6*d.*

GROTE, A. R.—**Rip van Winkle** : a Sun Myth ; and other Poems. Small crown 8vo, printed on hand-made paper, limp parchment antique, 5*s.*

GURNEY, Rev. Alfred.—**The Vision of the Eucharist,** and other Poems. Crown 8vo, 5*s.*

Gwen : a Drama in Monologue. By the Author of the "Epic of Hades." Third Edition. Fcap. 8vo, 5*s.*

HAWKER, Robt. Stephen.—**The Poetical Works of.** Now first collected and arranged. With a Prefatory Notice by J. G. Godwin. With Portrait. Crown 8vo, 12*s.*

HELLON, H. G.—**Daphnis** : a Pastoral Poem. Small crown 8vo, 3*s.* 6*d.*

HICKEY, E. H.—**A Sculptor,** and other Poems. Small crown 8vo, 5*s.*

HOLMES, E. G. A.—**Poems.** First and Second Series. Fcap. 8vo, 5*s.* each.

Horati Opera. Edited by F. A. CORNISH, Assistant Master at Eton. With a Frontispiece after a design by L. Alma Tadema, etched by Leopold Lowenstam. Parchment Library Edition, 6*s.*; vellum, 7*s.* 6*d.*

INGHAM, Sarson, C. J.—**Cædmon's Vision,** and other Poems. Small crown 8vo, 5*s.*

JENKINS, Rev. Canon.—**The Girdle Legend of Prato.** Small crown 8vo, 2*s.*

Alfonso Petrucci, Cardinal and Conspirator : an Historical Tragedy in Five Acts. Small crown 8vo, 3*s.* 6*d.*

KING, Mrs. Hamilton.—**The Disciples.** Fourth Edition, with Portrait and Notes. Crown 8vo, 7*s.* 6*d.*

Aspromonte, and other Poems. Second Edition. Fcap. 8vo, 4*s.* 6*d.*

LANG, A.—XXXII Ballades in Blue China. Elzevir 8vo, parchment, 5*s.*

LEIGH, Arran and Isla.—Bellerophon. Small crown 8vo, 5*s.*

LEIGHTON, Robert.—Records, and other Poems. With Portrait. Small crown 8vo, 7*s.* 6*d.*

Living English Poets MDCCCLXXXII. With Frontispiece by Walter Crane. Second Edition. Large crown 8vo. Printed on hand-made paper. Parchment, 12*s.*, vellum, 15*s.*

LOCKER, F.—London Lyrics. A New and Revised Edition, with Additions and a Portrait of the Author. Crown 8vo, 6*s.*

　** Also a New and Cheaper Edition. Small crown 8vo, 2*s.* 6*d.*

Love Sonnets of Proteus. With Frontispiece by the Author. Elzevir 8vo, 5*s.*

LOWNDES, Henry.—Poems and Translations. Crown 8vo, 6*s.*

LUMSDEN, Lieut.-Col. H. W.—Beowulf: an Old English Poem. Translated into Modern Rhymes. Small crown 8vo, 5*s.*

MACLEAN, Charles Donald.—Latin and Greek Verse Translations. Small crown 8vo, 2*s.*

MAGNUSSON, Eirikr, M.A., and PALMER, E. H., M.A.—Johan Ludvig Runeberg's Lyrical Songs, Idylls, and Epigrams. Fcap. 8vo, 5*s.*

M.D.C.—Chronicles of Christopher Columbus. A Poem in Twelve Cantos. Small Crown 8vo, cloth, 7*s.* 6*d.*

MEREDITH, Owen, The Earl of Lytton.—Lucile. With 160 Illustrations. Crown 4to, extra, gilt leaves, 21*s.*

MIDDLETON, The Lady.—Ballads. Square 16mo, 3*s.* 6*d.*

MOORE, Mrs. Bloomfield.—Gondaline's Lesson : The Warden's Tale, Stories for Children, and other Poems. Crown 8vo, 5*s.*

MORICE, Rev. F. D., M.A.—The Olympian and Pythian Odes of Pindar. A New Translation in English Verse. Crown 8vo, 7*s.* 6*d.*

MORRIS, Lewis.—Poetical Works of. New and cheaper Edition, with Portrait. Complete in 3 vols., 5*s.* each.

　Vol. I. contains "Songs of Two Worlds." Vol. II. contains "The Epic of Hades." Vol. III. contains "Gwen" and "The Ode of Life."

MORSHEAD, E. D. A.— The House of Atreus. Being the Agamemnon, Libation-Bearers, and Furies of Æschylus. Translated into English Verse. Crown 8vo, 7*s.*

NADEN, Constance W.—Songs and Sonnets of Spring Time. Small crown 8vo, 5*s.*

NEWELL, E. J.—The Sorrows of Simona and Lyrical Verses. Small crown 8vo, cloth, 3*s.* 6*d.*

NICHOLSON, Edward B.—The Christ Child, and other Poems. Crown 8vo, 4*s.* 6*d.*

NOAKE, Major R. Compton.—The Bivouac ; or, Martial Lyrist. With an Appendix : Advice to the Soldier. Fcap. 8vo, 5*s.* 6*d.*

NOEL, The Hon. Roden.—A Little Child's Monument. Second Edition. Small crown 8vo, 3*s.* 6*d.*

NORRIS, Rev. Alfred.—The Inner and Outer Life Poems. Fcap. 8vo, 6*s.*

Ode of Life, The. By the Author of "The Epic of Hades," etc. Fourth Edition. Crown 8vo, 5*s.*

O'HAGAN, John.—The Song of Roland. Translated into English Verse. Large post 8vo, parchment antique, 10*s.* 6*d.*

PAUL, C. Kegan.—Goethe's Faust. A New Translation in Rhyme. Crown 8vo, 6*s.*

PAYNE, John.—Songs of Life and Death. Crown 8vo, 5*s.*

PENNELL, H. Cholmondeley.—Pegasus Resaddled. By the Author of " Puck on Pegasus," etc., etc. With 10 Full-page Illustrations by George Du Maurier. Second Edition. Fcap. 4to, elegant, 12*s.* 6*d.*

PFEIFFER, Emily.—Glan Alarch : His Silence and Song : a Poem. Second Edition. Crown 8vo, 6*s.*

Gerard's Monument, and other Poems. Second Edition. Crown 8vo, 6*s.*

Quarterman's Grace, and other Poems. Crown 8vo, 5*s.*

Poems. Second Edition. Crown 8vo, 6*s.*

Sonnets and Songs. New Edition. 16mo, handsomely printed and bound in cloth, gilt edges, 4*s.*

Under the Aspens ; Lyrical and Dramatic. With Portrait. Crown 8vo, 6*s.*

PIKE, Warburton.—The Inferno of Dante Allighieri. Demy 8vo, 5*s.*

POE, Edgar Allan.—Poems. With an Essay on his Poetry by ANDREW LANG, and a Frontispiece by Linley Sambourne. Parchment Library Edition, 6*s.* ; vellum, 7*s.* 6*d.*

RHOADES, James.—The Georgics of Virgil. Translated into English Verse. Small crown 8vo, 5*s.*

ROBINSON, A. Mary F.—A Handful of Honeysuckle. Fcap. 8vo, 3*s.* 6*d.*

The Crowned Hippolytus. Translated from Euripides. With New Poems. Small crown 8vo, 5*s.*

SAUNDERS, John.—Love's Martyrdom. A Play and Poem. Small crown 8vo, cloth, 5*s.*

Schiller's Mary Stuart. German Text, with English Translation on opposite page by LEEDHAM WHITE. Crown 8vo, 6*s.*

Shakspere's Sonnets. Edited by EDWARD DOWDEN. With a Frontispiece etched by Leopold Lowenstam, after the Death Mask. Parchment Library Edition, 6*s.* ; vellum, 7*s.* 6*d.*

Shakspere's Works. In 12 Monthly Volumes. Parchment Library Edition, 6*s.* each ; vellum, 7*s.* 6*d.* each.

SHAW, W. F., M.A.—Juvenal, Persius, Martial, and Catullus. An Experiment in Translation. Crown 8vo, cloth, 5*s.*

SHELLEY, Percy Bysshe.—Poems Selected from. Dedicated to Lady Shelley. With Preface by Richard Garnett. Parchment Library Edition, 6*s.* ; vellum, 7*s.* 6*d.*

Six Ballads about King Arthur. Crown 8vo, extra, gilt edges, 3*s.* 6*d.*

SKINNER, James.—Cœlestia. The Manual of St. Augustine. The Latin Text side by side with an English Interpretation in Thirty-six Odes with Notes, *and* a plea *for the* study *of* Mystical Theology. Large crown 8vo, 6*s.*

SLADEN, Douglas B.—Frithjof and Ingebjorg, and other Poems. Small crown 8vo, cloth, 5*s.*

Songs of Two Worlds. By the Author of " The Epic of Hades." Seventh Edition. Complete in One Volume, with Portrait. Fcap. 8vo, 7*s.* 6*d.*

Songs for Music. By Four Friends. Containing Songs by Reginald A. Gatty, Stephen H. Gatty, Greville J. Chester, and Juliana Ewing. Square crown 8vo, 5*s.*

STEDMAN, Edmund Clarence.—Lyrics and Idylls, with other Poems. Crown 8vo, 7*s.* 6*d.*

STEVENS, William.—The Truce of God, and other Poems. Small crown 8vo, 3*s.* 6*d.*

TAYLOR, Sir H.—Works Complete in Five Volumes. Crown 8vo, 30*s.*

TENNYSON, Alfred.—Works Complete :—

The Imperial Library Edition. Complete in 7 vols. Demy 8vo, 10*s.* 6*d.* each ; in Roxburgh binding, 12*s.* 6*d.* each.

Author's Edition. In 7 vols. Post 8vo, gilt 43*s.* 6*d.* ; or half-morocco, Roxburgh style, 52*s.* 6*d.*

Cabinet Edition. 13 vols. Each with Frontispiece. Fcap. 8vo, 2*s.* 6*d.* each.

Cabinet Edition. 13 vols. Complete in handsome Ornamental Case. 35*s.*

TENNYSON, Alfred.—continued.

The Royal Edition. In 1 vol. With 26 Illustrations and Portrait. Extra, bevelled boards, gilt leaves, 21s.

The Guinea Edition. Complete in 13 vols. neatly bound and enclosed in box, 21s. ; French morocco or parchment, 31s. 6d.

Shilling Edition. In 13 vols. pocket size, 1s. each, sewed.

The Crown Edition. Complete in 1 vol. strongly bound, 6s. ; extra gilt leaves, 7s. 6d. ; Roxburgh, half-morocco, 8s. 6d.

** Can also be had in a variety of other bindings.

In Memoriam. With a Miniature Portrait in *eau-forte* by Le Rat, after a Photograph by the late Mrs. Cameron. Parchment Library Edition, 6s. ; vellum, 7s. 6d.

The Princess. A Medley. With a Miniature Frontispiece by H. M. Paget, and a Tailpiece in Outline by Gordon Browne. Parchment Library Edition, 6s. ; vellum, 7s. 6d.

Songs Set to Music by various Composers. Edited by W. J. Cusins. Dedicated, by express permission, to Her Majesty the Queen. Royal 4to, extra, gilt leaves, 21s. ; or in half-morocco, 25s.

Original Editions :—

Ballads, and other Poems. Small 8vo, 5s.

Poems. Small 8vo, 6s.

Maud, and other Poems. Small 8vo, 3s. 6d. ;

The Princess. Small 8vo, 3s. 6d.

Idylls of the King. Small 8vo, 5s.

Idylls of the King. Complete. Small 8vo, 6s.

The Holy Grail, and other Poems. Small 8vo, 4s. 6d.

Gareth and Lynette. Small 8vo, 3s.

Enoch Arden, etc. Small 8vo, 3s. 6d.

In Memoriam. Small 8vo, 4s.

Harold : a Drama. New Edition. Crown 8vo, 6s.

Queen Mary : a Drama. New Edition. Crown 8vo, 6s.

The Lover's Tale. Fcap. 8vo, 3s. 6d.

Selections from the above Works. Super royal 16mo, 3s. 6d. ; gilt extra, 4s.

Songs from the above Works. 16mo, 2s. 6d. ; extra, 3s. 6d.

Idylls of the King, and other Poems. Illustrated by Julia Margaret Cameron. 2 vols. folio, half-bound morocco, £6 6s. each.

Tennyson for the Young and for Recitation. Specially arranged. Fcap. 8vo, 1s. 6d.

The Tennyson Birthday Book. Edited by Emily Shakespear. 32mo, limp, 2s. ; extra, 3s.

⁎⁎⁎ A superior Edition, printed in red and black, on antique paper, specially prepared. Small crown 8vo, extra, gilt leaves, 5s. ; and in various calf and morocco bindings.

Horæ Tennysonianæ sive Eclogæ e Tennysono Latine Redditæ Cura A. J. Church, A.M. Small crown 8vo, 6s.

THOMPSON, Alice C.—**Preludes :** a Volume of Poems. Illustrated by Elizabeth Thompson (Painter of "The Roll Call "). 8vo, 7s. 6d.

TODHUNTER, Dr. J.—**Laurella,** and other Poems. Crown 8vo, 6s. 6d.

    Forest Songs. Small crown 8vo, 3s. 6d.

    The True Tragedy of Rienzi : a Drama. 3s. 6d.

    Alcestis : a Dramatic Poem. Extra fcap. 8vo, 5s.

    A Study of Shelley. Crown 8vo, 7s.

Translations from Dante, Petrarch, Michael Angelo, and Vittoria Colonna. Fcap. 8vo, 7s. 6d.

TURNER, Rev. C. Tennyson.—**Sonnets, Lyrics, and Translations.** Crown 8vo, 4s. 6d.

    Collected Sonnets, Old and New. With Prefatory Poem by ALFRED TENNYSON ; also some Marginal Notes by S. T. COLERIDGE, and a Critical Essay by JAMES SPEDDING. Fcap. 8vo, 7s. 6d.

WALTERS, Sophia Lydia.—**The Brook :** a Poem. Small crown 8vo, 3s. 6d.

    A Dreamer's Sketch Book. With 21 Illustrations by Percival Skelton, R. P. Leitch, W. H. J. BOOT, and T. R. PRITCHETT. Engraved by J. D. Cooper. Fcap. 4to, 12s. 6d.

WATERFIELD, W.—**Hymns for Holy Days and Seasons.** 32mo, 1s. 6d.

WAY, A., M.A.—**The Odes of Horace Literally Translated in Metre.** Fcap. 8vo, 2s.

WEBSTER, Augusta.—**Disguises :** a Drama. Small crown 8vo, 5s.

    In a Day : a Drama. Small crown 8vo, cloth, 2s. 6d.

Wet Days. By a Farmer. Small crown 8vo, 6s.

WILKINS, William.—**Songs of Study.** Crown 8vo, 6s.

WILLOUGHBY, The Hon. Mrs.—**On the North Wind—Thistledown :** a Volume of Poems. Elegantly bound, small crown 8vo, 7s. 6d.

WOODS, James Chapman.—A Child of the People, and other Poems. Small crown 8vo, 5s.

YOUNG, Wm.—Gottlob, etcetera. Small crown 8vo, 3s. 6d.

YOUNGS, Ella Sharpe.—Paphus, and other Poems. Small crown 8vo, 3s. 6d.

WORKS OF FICTION IN ONE VOLUME.

BANKS, Mrs. G. L.—God's Providence House. New Edition. Crown 8vo, 3s. 6d.

BETHAM-EDWARDS, Miss M.—Kitty. With a Frontispiece. Crown 8vo, 6s.

Blue Roses; or, Helen Malinofska's Marriage. By the Author of "Véra." New and Cheaper Edition. With Frontispiece. Crown 8vo, 6s.

FRISWELL, J. Hain.—One of Two; or, The Left-Handed Bride. Crown 8vo, 3s. 6d.

GARRETT, E.—By Still Waters : a Story for Quiet Hours. With 7 Illustrations. Crown 8vo, 6s.

HARDY, Thomas.—A Pair of Blue Eyes. Author of "Far from the Madding Crowd." New Edition. Crown 8vo, 6s.

The Return of the Native. New Edition. With Frontispiece. Crown 8vo, 6s.

HOOPER, Mrs. G.—The House of Raby. Crown 8vo, 3s. 6d.

INGELOW, Jean.—Off the Skelligs : a Novel. With Frontispiece. Second Edition. Crown 8vo, 6s.

MACDONALD, G.—Malcolm. With Portrait of the Author engraved on Steel. Sixth Edition. Crown 8vo, 6s.

The Marquis of Lossie. Fourth Edition. With Frontispiece. Crown 8vo, 6s.

St. George and St. Michael. Third Edition. With Frontispiece. Crown 8vo, 6s.

MASTERMAN, J.—Half-a-Dozen Daughters. Crown 8vo, 3s. 6d.

MEREDITH, George.—Ordeal of Richard Feverel. New Edition. Crown 8vo, 6s.

The Egoist : A Comedy in Narrative. New and Cheaper Edition, with Frontispiece. Crown 8vo, 6s.

PALGRAVE, W. Gifford.—Hermann Agha : an Eastern Narrative. Third Edition. Crown 8vo, 6s.

Pandurang Hari ; or, Memoirs of a Hindoo. With an Introductory Preface by Sir H. Bartle E. Frere, G.C.S.I., C.B. Crown 8vo, 6*s*.

PAUL, Margaret Agnes.—**Gentle and Simple** ; a Story. New and Cheaper Edition, with Frontispiece. Crown 8vo, 6*s*.

SHAW, Flora L.—**Castle Blair** ; a Story of Youthful Lives. New and Cheaper Edition. Crown 8vo, 3*s*. 6*d*.

STRETTON, Hesba.—**Through a Needle's Eye** : a Story. New and Cheaper Edition, with Frontispiece. Crown 8vo, 6*s*.

TAYLOR, Col. Meadows, C.S.I., M.R.I.A.—**Seeta** : a Novel. New and Cheaper Edition. With Frontispiece. Crown 8vo, 6*s*.

Tippoo Sultaun : a Tale of the Mysore War. New Edition, with Frontispiece. Crown 8vo, 6*s*.

Ralph Darnell. New and Cheaper Edition. With Frontispiece. Crown 8vo, 6*s*.

A Noble Queen. New and Cheaper Edition. With Frontispiece. Crown 8vo, 6*s*.

The Confessions of a Thug. Crown 8vo, 6*s*.

Tara : a Mahratta Tale. Crown 8vo, 6*s*.

THOMAS, Moy.—**A Fight for Life.** Crown 8vo, 3*s*. 6*d*.

Within Sound of the Sea. New and Cheaper Edition, with Frontispiece. Crown 8vo, 6*s*.

BOOKS FOR THE YOUNG.

Aunt Mary's Bran Pie. By the Author of "St. Olave's." Illustrated. 3*s*. 6*d*.

BARLEE, Ellen.—**Locked Out** : a Tale of the Strike. With a Frontispiece. Royal 16mo, 1*s*. 6*d*.

BONWICK, J., F.R.G.S.—**The Tasmanian Lily.** With Frontispiece. Crown 8vo, 5*s*.

Mike Howe, the Bushranger of Van Diemen's Land. New and Cheaper Edition. With Frontispiece. Crown 8vo, 3*s*. 6*d*.

Brave Men's Footsteps. A Book of Example and Anecdote for Young People. By the Editor of "Men who have Risen." With 4 Illustrations by C. Doyle. Seventh Edition. Crown 8vo, 3*s*. 6*d*.

Children's Toys, and some Elementary Lessons in General Knowledge which they teach. Illustrated. Crown 8vo, 5*s*.

COLERIDGE, Sara. — **Pretty Lessons in Verse for Good Children,** with some Lessons in Latin, in Easy Rhyme. A New Edition. Illustrated. Fcap. 8vo, 3*s*. 6*d*.

COXHEAD, *Ethel.*—**Birds and Babies.** Imp. 16mo. With 33 Illustrations. Cloth gilt, 2*s. 6d.*

D'ANVERS, *N. R.*—**Little Minnie's Troubles : an** Every-day Chronicle. With 4 Illustrations by W. H. Hughes. Fcap. 8vo, 3*s. 6d.*

    Parted : a Tale of Clouds and Sunshine. With 4 Illustrations. Extra fcap. 8vo, 3*s. 6d.*

    Pixie's Adventures ; or, the Tale of a Terrier. With 21 Illustrations. 16mo, 4*s. 6d.*

    Nanny's Adventures : or, the Tale of a Goat. With 12 Illustrations. 16mo, 4*s. 6d.*

DAVIES, *G. Christopher.*—**Rambles and Adventures of our** School Field Club. With 4 Illustrations. New and Cheaper Edition. Crown 8vo, 3*s. 6d.*

DRUMMOND, *Miss.*—**Tripp's Buildings.** A Study from Life, with Frontispiece. Small crown 8vo, 3*s. 6d.*

EDMONDS, *Herbert.*—**Well Spent Lives :** a Series of Modern Biographies. New and Cheaper Edition. Crown 8vo, 3*s. 6d.*

EVANS, *Mark.*—**The Story of our Father's Love,** told to Children. Fourth and Cheaper Edition of Theology for Children. With 4 Illustrations. Fcap. 8vo, 1*s. 6d.*

FARQUHARSON, *M.*

    I. **Elsie Dinsmore.** Crown 8vo, 3*s. 6d.*

    II. **Elsie's Girlhood.** Crown 8vo, 3*s. 6d.*

    III. **Elsie's Holidays at Roselands.** Crown 8vo, 3*s. 6d.*

HERFORD, *Brooke.*—**The Story of Religion in England :** a Book for Young Folk. Crown 8vo, 5*s.*

INGELOW, *Jean.*—**The Little Wonder-horn.** With 15 Illustrations. Small 8vo, 2*s. 6d.*

JOHNSON, *Virginia W.*—**The Catskill Fairies.** Illustrated by ALFRED FREDERICKS. 5*s.*

KER, *David.*—**The Boy Slave in Bokhara :** a Tale of Central Asia. With Illustrations. New and Cheaper Edition. Crown 8vo, 3*s. 6d.*

    The Wild Horseman of the Pampas. Illustrated. New and Cheaper Edition. Crown 8vo, 3*s. 6d.*

LAMONT, *Martha MacDonald.*—**The Gladiator :** a Life under the Roman Empire in the beginning of the Third Century. With 4 Illustrations by H. M. Paget. Extra fcap. 8vo, 3*s. 6d.*

LEANDER, *Richard.*—**Fantastic Stories.** Translated from the German by Paulina B. Granville. With 8 Full-page Illustrations by M. E. Fraser-Tytler. Crown 8vo, 5*s.*

LEE, Holme.—Her Title of Honour. A Book for Girls. New Edition. With a Frontispiece. Crown 8vo, 5*s.*

LEWIS, Mary A.—A Rat with Three Tales. New and Cheaper Edition. With 4 Illustrations by Catherine F. Frere. 3*s.* 6*d.*

MAC KENNA, S. J.—Plucky Fellows. A Book for Boys. With 6 Illustrations. Fifth Edition. Crown 8vo, 3*s.* 6*d.*

At School with an Old Dragoon. With 6 Illustrations. New and Cheaper Edition. Crown 8vo, 3*s.* 6*d.*

Mc CLINTOCK, L.—Sir Spangle and the Dingy Hen. Illustrated. Square crown 8vo, 2*s.* 6*d.*

MALDEN, H. E.—Princes and Princesses: Two Fairy Tales. Illustrated. Small crown 8vo, 2*s.* 6*d.*

Master Bobby. By the Author of "Christina North." With 6 Illustrations. Fcap. 8vo, 3*s.* 6*d.*

NAAKE, J. T.—Slavonic Fairy Tales. From Russian, Servian, Polish, and Bohemian Sources. With 4 Illustrations. Crown 8vo, 5*s.*

PELLETAN, E.—The Desert Pastor, Jean Jarousseau. Translated from the French. By Colonel E. P. De L'Hoste. With a Frontispiece. New Edition. Fcap. 8vo, 3*s.* 6*d.*

REANEY, Mrs. G. S.—Waking and Working; or, From Girlhood to Womanhood. New and Cheaper Edition. With a Frontispiece. Crown 8vo, 3*s.* 6*d.*

Blessing and Blessed: a Sketch of Girl Life. New and Cheaper Edition. Crown 8vo, 3*s.* 6*d.*

Rose Gurney's Discovery. A Book for Girls. Dedicated to their Mothers. Crown 8vo, 3*s.* 6*d.*

English Girls: Their Place and Power. With Preface by the Rev. R. W. Dale. Third Edition. Fcap. 8vo, 2*s.* 6*d.*

Just Anyone, and other Stories. Three Illustrations. Royal 16mo, 1*s.* 6*d.*

Sunbeam Willie, and other Stories. Three Illustrations. Royal 16mo, 1*s.* 6*d.*

Sunshine Jenny, and other Stories. Three Illustrations. Royal 16mo, 1*s.* 6*d.*

ROSS, Mrs. E. ("Nelsie Brook")—Daddy's Pet. A Sketch from Humble Life. With 6 Illustrations. Royal 16mo, 1*s.*

SADLER, S. W., R.N.—The African Cruiser: a Midshipman's Adventures on the West Coast. With 3 Illustrations. New and Cheaper Edition. Crown 8vo, 2*s.* 6*d.*

Seeking his Fortune, and other Stories. With 4 Illustrations. New and Cheaper Edition. Crown 8vo, 2s. 6d.

Seven Autumn Leaves from Fairy Land. Illustrated with 9 Etchings. Square crown 8vo, 3s. 6d.

STOCKTON, Frank R.—**A Jolly Fellowship.** With 20 Illustrations. Crown 8vo, 5s.

STORR, Francis, and TURNER, Hawes.—**Canterbury Chimes;** or, Chaucer Tales retold to Children. With 6 Illustrations from the Ellesmere MS. Second Edition. Fcap. 8vo, 3s. 6d.

STRETTON, Hesba.—**David Lloyd's Last Will.** With 4 Illustrations. New Edition. Royal 16mo, 2s. 6d.

    The Wonderful Life. Sixteenth Thousand. Fcap. 8vo, 2s. 6d.

Sunnyland Stories. By the Author of "Aunt Mary's Bran Pie." Illustrated. Second Edition. Small 8vo, 3s. 6d.

Tales from Ariosto Re-told for Children. By a Lady. With 3 Illustrations. Crown 8vo, 4s. 6d.

WHITAKER, Florence.—**Christy's Inheritance.** A London Story. Illustrated. Royal 16mo, 1s. 6d.

ZIMMERN, H.—**Stories in Precious Stones.** With 6 Illustrations. Third Edition. Crown 8vo, 5s.

PRINTED BY WILLIAM CLOWES AND SONS, LIMITED, LONDON AND BECCLES.

www.ingramcontent.com/pod-product-compliance
Lightning Source LLC
Chambersburg PA
CBHW051510100726
47898CB00005B/1403